THE GENDERED SCORE

To my parents
Doris and Bill Laing

The Gendered Score

Music in 1940s Melodrama and the Woman's Film

HEATHER LAING

ASHGATE

Published by

Ashgate Publishing Limited
Gower House
Croft Road
Aldershot
Hampshire GU11 3HR
England

Ashgate Publishing Company
Suite 420
101 Cherry Street
Burlington, VT 05401-4405
USA

Ashgate website: http://www.ashgate.com

British Library Cataloguing in Publication Data

Laing, Heather

The Gendered Score: Music in 1940s Melodrama and the Woman's Film – (Ashgate popular and folk music series) 1. Motion picture music – History and criticism 2. Women in motion pictures 3. Sex role in motion pictures 4. Music – 20th century – History and criticism 5. Melodrama in motion pictures

I. Title

781.5'42'082

Library of Congress Cataloging-in-Publication Data

Laing, Heather.

The Gendered Score: Music in 1940s Melodrama and the Woman's Film / by Heather Laing.

p. cm – (Ashgate popular and folk music series)

Includes bibliographical references (p.) and filmography (p). ISBN 978-0-7546-5100-0 (alk. paper)

1. Motion picture music – History and criticism. 2. Gender identity in motion pictures. 3. Gender identity in music. I. Title

ML2075.L33 2007
781.5'42082–dc22

2006032406

ISBN 978 0 7546 5100 0

Printed and bound in Great Britain by MPG Books Ltd. Bodmin, Cornwall.

Contents

List of figures

The Publisher acknowledges that the quality of certain figures (where the images have been captured from video stills) are not perfect quality, but this was the best that could be achieved considering the age and rarity of the recordings

List of music examples

General Editor's Preface

The upheaval that occurred in musicology during the last two decades of the twentieth century has created a new urgency for the study of popular music alongside the development of new critical and theoretical models. A relativistic outlook has replaced the universal perspective of modernism (the international ambitions of the 12-note style); the grand narrative of the evolution and dissolution of tonality has been challenged, and emphasis has shifted to cultural context, reception and subject position. Together, these have conspired to eat away at the status of canonical composers and categories of high and low in music. A need has arisen, also, to recognize and address the emergence of crossovers, mixed and new genres, to engage in debates concerning the vexed problem of what constitutes authenticity in music and to offer a critique of musical practice as the product of free, individual expression.

Popular musicology is now a vital and exciting area of scholarship, and the *Ashgate Popular and Folk Music Series* aims to present the best research in the field. Authors will be concerned with locating musical practices, values and meanings in cultural context, and may draw upon methodologies and theories developed in cultural studies, semiotics, poststructuralism, psychology and sociology. The series will focus on popular musics of the twentieth and twenty-first centuries. It is designed to embrace the world's popular musics from Acid Jazz to Zydeco, whether high tech or low tech, commercial or non-commercial, contemporary or traditional.

Professor Derek B. Scott
Chair of Music
University of Salford

Acknowledgements

This book began life as a doctoral thesis at the University of Warwick, and my first thanks must therefore go to Richard Dyer—firstly for his intellectual support and guidance as my supervisor and secondly for his encouragement to develop the thesis into this book. Thanks also go to the many others who have offered advice and support, be it intellectual or practical, at various stages, including Victor Perkins, Ed Gallafent, José Arroyo, Phil Ellis, Valerie Orpen, Susan Bowles, Rachel Moseley, David Wordsworth, Robynn Stilwell, Kate Daubney, Ian Garwood, Sarah Moore and Peter Krämer. My parents gave me practical and emotional support for which I am very grateful and my brother Keith Laing offered technical computing support. I also express my gratitude to the AHRB for funding this period of study.

For their help in establishing copyright information and obtaining permission for the use of copyright material in the book, I would like to thank Ralph Holmes at BBC Television; Matt Smith at International Music Publications/Faber Music; Sheree Bevins and Zaid Ahmad at Faber Music; Keith Wakefield at Stainer & Bell; Sally Goodliffe and Ray Jenkins at Granada International; Jill Little at London Features International; Liddy Barrow, Sarah Holcroft and Catherine Walker at Music Sales; Shari Wied at Hal Leonard; and Cari Ginell at Alfred Music Ltd.

At Ashgate, I wish to thank Derek Scott for his enthusiasm, encouragement and guidance, and Heidi May for her patience and invaluable advice on all sorts of matters. Finally, as ever, my thanks go to my husband Tim Ayling for supporting me through every aspect of the whole process.

Gratitude is also expressed for the following permissions to use copyright material:

Introduction

> A film of the forties is airing on television. Even though you're in the next room, you are likely to find that a certain kind of music will cue you in correctly to the presence of Woman on screen. It is as if the emotional excess of this presence must find its outlet in the euphony of a string orchestra.[1]

In the academic study of both film music and gender representation in film, the intimate relationship between female characters and non-diegetic music has been largely accepted as a given. The effect of this association is usually interpreted as Claudia Gorbman describes it, linking women to the emotional and even irrational aspects of the narrative and distancing them from the rational world of male characters and its attendant emphasis on the power of vision. It seems that female characters are burdened with a mode of musical–emotional representation that, as Gorbman suggests, serves less to characterize them as 'ordinarily' emotional than to distinguish them through an association with the 'excessively' emotional. As a result, when female emotions become a particular focus of the melodrama and woman's film of the 1940s, the lush symphonic scores that seem to define cinema at that time are bound to follow.

The sheer force of this representational convention, however, means that we are in danger of being blinded to the fact that it is just that—a convention. Academic study tends to focus more commonly on *how* female film characters are represented through music—that is to say, the various compositional styles and conventions that tend to accompany and characterize them. When it comes to the question of *why* they are so surrounded by music in the first place, recourse is often made to psychoanalytical explanations, which conceptualize non-diegetic music and its predominant link with female characters and emotional subject matter through ideas of the maternal voice and nostalgia for that voice. This explanation suggests, by definition, that both the appeal and the affect of music in this context are deeply rooted in subconscious responses, and thus that music enables the triggering of a 'universal' affect. While not wishing to dispute the possibility of this explanation, it is inevitably more concerned with questions of emotional engagement with female characters and their narratives. What it does not address is the question of the very real effect that such a predominant association with music must surely have on the actual characterization of the woman. As a result, several important questions have been left unanswered. What, first of all, is the effect on the female characters themselves of constant emotional determination through their association with music? And by extension, what role does music actually play in the construction of emotional and/or gendered characterization?

---

1 Claudia Gorbman (1987), *Unheard Melodies: Narrative Film Music*, Bloomington: Indiana University Press, London: BFI, p. 80.

These questions cannot be answered without being tied in to the very specific style of music that is most commonly used in this respect. It may be particularly important to psychoanalytical theories that music is essentially abstract in its nature. The fact remains, however, that the music chosen to codify emotion in 1940s cinema is composed predominantly in the late-nineteenth-century symphonic style. There have been many explanations offered for the dominant adoption of this style in 1940s film music composition, and the nineteenth-century belief in its capacity for emotional signification and communication is generally accepted as its primary role in relation to characterization—a capacity that also, of course, chimes with psychoanalytical accounts of its role. However, can one element of contemporaneous thinking around this music be adopted without also bringing with it an equal inheritance of associated beliefs? The nineteenth-century ideas that contextualized this capacity for emotional expression and representation must surely also be taken into account, or at the very least held up for question, in any discussion of its role in or effect on characterization. An examination of the musical–emotional representation of women in 1940s melodrama and women's films cannot, therefore, ask only: 'Why women and music?' It must also ask: 'Why women and nineteenth-century music?'

In all these respects, it is necessary to return to a basic interrogation of the very assumption of the 'given' nature of the relationship of women and music. This involves examining, from a cultural–historical point of view, why female characters are so commonly associated with music, why this does indeed seem to make sense to audiences, composers and filmmakers alike, and what, most importantly of all, the real cost is to female characters in terms of their characterization and place within the narrative. In short, we need to determine what is at stake in investing female characters with this very particular style of emotional representation and what burden of meaning it places upon them. This book approaches these questions by examining the underlying related conventions of music, emotion and gender that inform this association, and considering how they impact on both female and male characterization in film. Its aim is to replace a fundamental assumption—in terms of the study of both film music and gender representation in film—with a more nuanced understanding of the place of music in gendered characterization.

The search for such conventions must begin with the music itself. Music shares a long and complex historical relationship with cultural concepts of women, men, 'femininity', 'masculinity', human emotionality and self-expression. In order to understand the way in which music works in association with women in film, it is therefore necessary to look outside of cinema itself and recontextualize this relationship within its own cultural–historical trajectory. Considering the broader history of configurations of music and gender allows models and patterns to emerge against which female characterization, or indeed cultural attitudes to real women, may be assessed at any period of time, be it in 1940s film or any time or context before or after. Following the lead of film itself, therefore, the primary focus of Chapter 1 is on the cultural tenets of Romanticism and how they relate to women. These are in turn contextualized within broader historical conceptions of gender that return to the most ancient archetypes of female musicality, emotionality and sexuality.

This consideration of historical 'models' and ideas indicates the various codes and assumptions that may be at work both in film's general association of women and music and in its representation of their involvement with actual musical activity. It also clarifies the parameters of the study. It should be clear by now that it is not the intention of this book to maintain any inherent, ahistorical connection between women and music, any 'natural' musical mode of expression for either femaleness or femininity, or indeed any 'inescapable' psychological reason why film music affects audiences as it does. Rather, the emphasis is on how culture has positioned women—and men—in relation to both music and emotion, as a result of music's conceptualization according to prevalent related definitions of femininity and masculinity. The more refined definition of music and emotion as related to cultural constructions of masculinity and femininity—rather than the biological distinctions of male and female—that this initial survey reveals, re-opens questions of both gender and genre. In order to relate such definitions to film melodrama, the generic and musical precedents of theatrical melodrama and ideas of the melodramatic mode are considered, as well as the representation of female characters in opera. This, together with consideration of theories of musical–emotional expression and characterization in film melodrama, allow me to theorize the broad position occupied by the female protagonist of film melodrama in relation to self-expression and narrative agency.

The following three chapters then move progressively closer to the heart of the issue that informs the musical–emotional representation of women in film—the presumed 'proximity' of women and emotion, implied within both cultural thinking on music and gender and the formal representations of film. This involves the systematic removal of the protecting degrees of distance between the female character and the music that represents her, thus gradually revealing the truth behind the association. This gradual revelation, however, proves to be fraught with increasing difficulty for the female characters themselves, the depth of which is incontrovertibly revealed as the investigation culminates with the actual characterization of the female musician. Chapter 2 begins by focusing on the woman's film and ascertaining its particular mode of female musical–emotional characterization in relation to the broader melodramatic codes explored in Chapter 1. Its closer examination of the particular dynamic of narrative and social agency, access to self-expression and musical emotionality that characterizes the melodramatic female, establishes the broad generic parameters on which the following chapters build. The woman's film is scrutinized in terms of its claim to represent female subjectivity, through an exploration of the dynamic between the representation of the female character's emotions and subjective experience, and her actual personal and/or social ability to express herself. Since non-diegetic music is one of the key means through which unexpressed or inexpressible emotions are conveyed, the nature of its interaction with diegetic speech and behaviour is a crucial means of ascertaining the woman's film's construction of femaleness. This concerns not only the level of expression allowed to 'feminine' emotion, but also the degree to which femininity and femaleness are conflated.

This brings into play a further key element of the study, which is concerned with the potential range and balance of emotional functions that music can fulfil in film. In particular, the balance must be addressed between the possibility of music representing a particular character's subjectivity, and its capacity for a more independent interpretation of events or characters. Women in melodrama and the woman's film, for example, are often placed in weak or vulnerable social positions. If the music appears to represent or reflect their emotions as singular characters, however, the implications of such a contradictory strong and privileged *narrative* position must be investigated. This raises the question of how close musical representation functions in relation to emotional 'ownership', self-expression and agency. Close examination is therefore necessary of not only the meaning that the music appears to carry, but also its relationship to the actions of female characters and their narrative, filmic and generic context. Chapter 2's case study film, *Now, Voyager* (1942), is notable for the eloquence of its dialogue.[2] It also combines various sub-genres of the woman's film in a particularly fluid way. Both factors render it eminently productive as an introductory case study. The detail with which the characters express themselves verbally is matched by the eloquence and intricacy of the music, which gives voice to both their silences and the real thoughts, memories and emotions that lie behind their words. At the same time, the importance of the gendered relationship of music to the voice and modes of behaviour indicates the necessity of maintaining a study of music as part of both overall soundtrack analysis and a wider textual and narrative analysis.

Music is, of course, a defining element of the very term 'melodrama'. It therefore goes without saying—in terms of both generic parameters and gender focus—that non-diegetic music will be prevalent in both the melodrama itself and the woman's film as its female-centred variant. The importance of music is, in fact, frequently reflected in its actual thematicization. Through the involvement of a character who is a professional or amateur musician, the interaction of all the characters with diegetic, and by extension non-diegetic, music becomes foregrounded as part of the wider narrative operation of the film. Since it is likely that such interaction will reflect broader conceptions of music in relation to emotion and gender, these films offer an obvious route through which to progress the investigation and reduce the distance between the female character and her representative music still further. Chapter 3 therefore considers the first of three narrative configurations of musicians and diegetic listeners/audiences as subject matter. It deals with the female character reacting to both diegetic music and its male creator or performer, and considers her positioning as both listener and potential muse. This not only develops the ideas of the woman's relationship to her own emotions, voice and mainly non-diegetic music suggested in Chapter 2, but also considers the importance of broader musical and narrative issues to an understanding of this very specific scenario. Before the musician and listener can be closely examined, this chapter therefore considers the possible purposes and effects of situating a musician within a narrative and the wider nature of the performer–audience/listener relationship.

Chapter 3's case study of *Letter from an Unknown Woman* (1948) then centres primarily on its representation of the female listener. It focuses on the gendered

---

2 Christine Gledhill attributes the verbal articulacy of *Now, Voyager* to the source novel of the same name. Christine Gledhill (1987), 'The Melodramatic Field: An Investigation', in *Home Is Where the Heart Is: Studies in Melodrama and the Woman's Film*, London: BFI, p. 36.

tension between respected ideas of Romanticism pertinent to nineteenth-century music and the related—and often denigrated—concept of 'romance'. This tension is expressed in this film through a particular and perhaps unique twist on the pattern of interaction between muse/listener and creator/performer that appears to be conventional to male musician–female listener narratives. It suggests the woman's—notably youthful/immature—capacity for romantic elaboration as being entirely responsible for a lifetime of seemingly 'errant' perception and action. At the same time as taking a partially critical stance on her point of view, however, it also sympathizes with her and actually accords a certain degree of truth to her romantic interpretation of events. It admires the veracity and strength of her emotional vision and mocks the blandness and pomposity of the 'realistic' life alternatives that the film offers her. This apparently paradoxical approach is made possible by the creation of a distinct place for 'emotional truth' within the film's schema. Such a complex representation successfully exposes and questions attitudes towards the woman and her own 'feminine' musical–emotional imagination.

Despite the very careful construction and interrogation of the female listener's relationship to diegetic music, however, the male musician–female listener film does not generally challenge the distance between the woman's voice and her underlying emotions. Instead, its starker exposure of this distance, and the injustice in terms of its frustration of the female protagonist, remains an emotionally raw spectacle. It therefore begs but also bodes ill for the final stage of the investigation, which considers the results of allowing the woman a more active diegetic relationship to music, either through the secondary means of playing records and/or making requests for music to be played, or even as a composer and/or performer herself. Chapter 4 takes up this challenge and examines the various consequences of removing the distance between the woman and musical agency or production. What might be presumed to be an antidote to the male musician–female listener relationship, however, in fact turns out to confirm the worst fears attending previous chapters. Their implication of the impossibility of collapsing the all-important 'chasm' of non-expression that Chapter 1 found in relation to the restricted woman of the melodramatic mode is finally realized. Chapter 4 therefore considers how 1940s cinema conceptualizes the continuing problem of a female relationship to active creativity, and questions whether Romantic ideas of the necessary constitution of the artist are still in evidence. It also balances Chapter 3's consideration of the female as musical or non-musical muse with an assessment of the extent to which the Siren survives as a 'model' for active female musicality and related behaviour. As a result, it confronts the still evidently highly problematic nature of identifying a positive characterization for a musically and creatively active female character.

Together with Chapter 5, Chapter 4 also provides a contrast through nationality—both case study films are British—and through the type of musician that they represent, as both feature performers who also compose their own music. The subject matter of Chapter 4's *Love Story* (1944) and Chapter 5's *Dangerous Moonlight* (1941) concerns the relationship of the home front to combat in the Second World War. The social codification of melodrama and gendered characterization is therefore targeted towards very particular propagandist ends. The extremity of the situations into which characters are placed in this context, however, actually highlights the processes of constructing and testing ideas of gender and emotion. At a time when emotions are placed under extraordinary pressure both in reality and fictitious representation, the respective roles of non-diegetic music's 'mute' signification and diegetic music's non-denotative but highly self-conscious communication become particularly fascinating. In the case of *Love Story*, the test concerns the very attempt to envision an active but safe female musicality. The fact that the need for this test, and indeed for this female musician, springs from the wartime context of the film, however, also allows for the establishment of clearly mitigating circumstances for such a representation. Paradoxically, therefore, *Love Story*'s apparently ambitious and well-meaning attempt to represent a female musician becomes a prime example of the impossibility of its own project. This is made clearest through the relationship of the female protagonist to her own diegetic processes of musical composition and the subsequent performances of her music—constituting as they do the moments at which the distance between the woman and her own musical–emotional representation is finally completely collapsed. It is also manifested, however, in her formally and emotionally problematic relationship with her male listener, and her consequent association with music at the non-diegetic level.

Having reached the end of the line, as it were, with regard to the musical–emotional representation of female characters, it becomes clear that a further stage of investigation is in fact necessary. Throughout Chapters 1 to 4, it emerges that the musical–emotional representation of women or female characters is dependent upon its balance with male relationships to music—be it the relationship conceptualized between real men and music or the role of music in the emotional representation of male characters in film. Not only does this suggest that a full understanding of the place of music in the emotional characterization of women cannot be complete without undertaking a matching investigation of music and male characters, but also that the musical–emotional, or indeed the explicitly *non*-musical–emotional, representation of these male characters is by no means as straightforward as it first appears. This book therefore ends with a chapter that offers the beginnings of this matching investigation. Despite the apparently less prevalent relationship of male characters and music, and their seemingly greater distance from the excesses of emotions signified by that music, it would be overly dismissive to suggest that the subject of male musical–emotional characterization is any less complex than that of its female counterpart. I will not pretend, therefore, that a single chapter can fully do it justice. This said, Chapter 5 does build on the groundwork offered by men and male characters in earlier chapters: the Romantic creators and apparently unromantic film viewers of Chapter 1; the overtly non-musical Elliot of *Now, Voyager*; the seemingly cool-hearted male musicians of Chapter 3; and the complex characterization of Kit, the male listener, muse and sometime musician figure of *Love Story*.

Leading on from all these men, Chapter 5 considers what happens across a range of genres when film represents male characters through a more conventionally 'female' style of music, so raising the question of femininity as a necessary element to the construction of masculinity. What is most striking about this survey is the revelation of the degree to which male characters are also restricted by this mode of representation. Because of its association with the feminine, their emotional representation through music is prohibited in all but the most extreme of moments—

resulting in specifically and carefully contextualized 'glimpses' of what lies beneath their otherwise controlled and socially acceptable exteriors. The musical revelation of femininity thus becomes proof of the constructed nature of masculinity and the behavioural demands that it makes on men, while simultaneously providing assurance of the continuation of that construct and upholding it as painfully heroic. It also emerges as a more fluid aspect of characterization than is at first evident.

A focus on the personality of the male musician himself, placed within the wider context of masculinity and music, then examines how the balance of masculinity and femininity is maintained when a display of emotion is necessary, but excessive outburst is not a viable option. The case study of *Dangerous Moonlight* examines both male and female characters in their balanced relationship to music. The account of the female listener in this case offers a more explicit critique of the female musical–emotional characteristics examined in Chapters 2 and 3. The most important focus, however, is on the characterization of the male musician in a film that foregrounds his own relationship to music as much as, if not more so than, that of his female listener. Through this focus, his more conventionally elusive relationship to his own creativity and the different types of emotion that his composition and performance involve is itself thematicized. Even though, like the female musician of Chapter 4, it emerges that such a potentially compromising representation must be couched in clearly mitigating circumstances—to the different end of protecting his masculinity against the threat of feminine emotionality and vulnerability—this does evidence the much greater fluidity of music's role in emotional, and therefore gendered, characterization.

This allows me finally to arrive at a definition of gendered characterization based on the interaction of cultural assumptions and cinematic–musical representation—the underlying principle of which is that cultural codes of gender 'allow' and 'disallow' certain musical–emotional implications. This definition confirms that the representation of gender in melodrama and the woman's film is still informed in the 1940s by a combination of Romantic conceptions of emotion, music and gender, and more ancient archetypes of musical, emotional, sexual and (anti-)social behaviour. Following the investigation of Chapter 5, however, a broad model for gendered characterization that extends beyond the generic boundaries of the original case study texts becomes possible. This reconfigures the representation of gender according to a balance of emotion and control, which is formed through a combination of cultural expectation and filmic evidence. As a result, music takes on a crucial role less as merely a signifier of emotion and more as a central element of the way in which we actually understand emotion within the construction of gender.

Chapter 1

The Siren and the Muse: Ideas of gender, emotion and subjectivity in music and film

> [M]usical performance provides an excellent context for observing and understanding any society's gender structure because similar notions of power and control often lie at the heart of both gender and musical/social dynamics.[1]

The association of music and emotion—and by extension gender—was by no means an invention of sound cinema. On the contrary, it is an association that extends back through the history of Western society and its dramatic self-representations as far as the earliest records of musical activity. The use of music in 1940s film to evoke emotion, particularly in relation to gendered characterization, cannot therefore be considered in isolation, and must be seen as part of a continuing history in its own right. The dominant style through which such musical–emotional meaning was evoked in film at this time was the nineteenth-century Romantic style of composition, which indeed became little short of ubiquitous as a scoring style. It is perhaps, however, the very acceptance of this musical style as standard that has prevented important questions from being asked about the specificity of its potential inheritance of meaning. The nineteenth-century style has effectively become an 'ahistorical' signifier of emotion in film. Whereas different historical periods can be evoked through the use of appropriate musical styles, the nineteenth-century style has achieved a unique historical neutrality, and can thus be used to represent emotion in narratives set in any time period before or after its own actual historical development. Such an assumption of neutrality threatens to mask, however, the cultural–historical specificity of this music. The cultural thought on emotion that underpinned it in its own time was, in fact, highly problematic in its perceived signification in relation to gender—or rather, more specifically, in relation to women. It follows, therefore, that as it was adopted into film scoring, it brought an inheritance of cultural meaning that was of obvious potential significance to gendered characterization. By examining films through the filter of nineteenth-century musical conventions and conceptions, it is possible to see the extent to which Romantic ideas of gender and emotion

---

[1] Linda Phyllis Austern, after Ellen Koskoff, in Austern (1994), '"No women are indeed": The boy actor as vocal seductress in late sixteenth- and early seventeenth-century English drama', in Leslie C. Dunn, and Nancy A. Jones (eds), *Embodied Voices: Representing Female Vocality in Western Culture*, Cambridge: Cambridge University Press, p. 83.

continued to inform the representation of both femaleness and maleness well into the twentieth century.

In order to explore and reveal this inheritance, this chapter begins by surveying the historical relationship of music, gender and emotion, particularly as it relates to women. While this necessarily centres on the cultural concepts and musical–dramatic conventions of the nineteenth century, this is itself framed—however briefly—in just enough of a broader historical context to demonstrate its own corresponding inheritance from earlier models of representation. In the light of this survey, I then consider the generic position of women in film melodrama and their emotional representation through music. As a result, I argue that the film scoring style of the 1940s in fact *burdens* female characters with a Romantic relationship to music that carries with it both psychological and physical implications. The prevalence and frequent diegetic foregrounding of music in those genres centred on the emotional and psychological trajectories of women suggest a degree of conflation of Romantic ideas of the 'feminine' and the 'female', and the apparent adoption of this gendered musical inheritance results in a frustratingly restrictive position for female characters. The musical representation of their emotions suggests the transcendent nature of women's interiority. At the same time, however, it also demonstrates the inevitable frustration or destructive power of this interiority in the context of contemporaneous—or historical—social mores and/or nineteenth-century ideas of the female constitution.

Historical Concepts of Female Creativity and Performance in Music

The relationship of women and music has always proved problematic to patriarchal society. Charles Segal traces this difficulty back to ancient Greek mythology, where female characters are divided according to archetypal polarities of physicality, sexuality, the voice, music, social positioning and agency within such a society.[2] His suggestion that this division is informed by a fear of female sexuality, or perhaps the male fear of his own sexuality and a resultant desire to exercise control over women, is crystallized in the female musical archetypes that he invokes—and that have indeed rung down through the ages in this capacity—of the Siren and the Muse. Each of these certainly bears out Segal's theory. The terrifyingly strong and irresistible sexuality and musicality of the Siren exist solely for the purpose of seducing and destroying men. The physically subdued but nevertheless ethereally beautiful Muse dedicates her voice and music to the glory and inspiration of men. It is not difficult, however restricted these models of characterization are and however clear their ideological purpose may be, to see how they continue to inform representations of female behaviour to the present day. Indeed, the terms 'siren' and 'muse' have passed into common parlance as a means of describing the sexual demeanour and social significance of women even without any musical reference. The specificity of their mythological origins, however, emphasizes their construction according to

---

2 Charles Segal (1994), 'The Gorgon and the Nightingale: The Voice of Female Lament and Pindar's twelfth *Pythian Ode*', in Dunn and Jones (op. cit.), pp. 17–21.

the idea of the indivisibility of vocality and musicality from such behaviour, which distinguishes them in both the style and purpose of their self-expression from such comparable non-musical figures as the 'virgin' and the 'whore'. Considering the quotation with which I opened this chapter, the question therefore arises of whether musical forms and narratives have the potential to perpetuate the otherness of women in patriarchal society through the circulation of such female types.

During the Renaissance, for example, women's social and sexual conception in relation to music was clearly dependent upon their use of that music in accordance with prevailing patriarchal codes. According to Linda Phyllis Austern, the socially acceptable and desirable woman should not threaten the apparently vulnerable self-control of masculinity. She was therefore required to exercise a demure and 'proper' use of music. The most pertinent edict in this respect was that her musicality should be physically hidden from men. While performing music before men could be seen in a positive light—as a means of becoming more attractive to potential husbands—the female musician's embodiment of the most powerful sensual partnership of femaleness and music may also be too physically exciting, seducing the man into corrupt thoughts and conduct. Tellingly, of course, the choice between these options lay firmly with the women, so that any effect on men was considered entirely the result of conscious female intent.[3] Such apparently mythical musical–sexual power, however, was not only controlled by the socially drawn boundaries of decency. On the contrary, physiological theory was also mobilized to prove that women were both mentally and physically incompatible with the processes of higher artistic creativity. As Christine Battersby points out, women at this time were condemned by a conception of the female constitution that precluded the possibility of intellectual superiority, dependent as this was upon the allegedly exclusively male possession of rational 'ingenium'. Women were conceived as subject to the biologically dictated 'hysteria' rather than the more masculine and potentially inspirational 'melancholy'.[4] As a result of this, Battersby concludes that:

> In our terms, women were thought of as *too* creative, *too* original, with much *too* much subjectivity. In Renaissance terms, none of these were artistic virtues, and women lacked the fires of male physiology that could burn out an image of the truth. They were trapped in the cloud of unknowing [emphasis in original].[5]

With Romanticism, however, came a reconceptualization of creativity that re-valued these very qualities, making paramount the artist's subjective, emotional and therefore 'feminine' experience of the world. While this should have deified women as natural artists, the male prerogative of cultural superiority actually dictated otherwise. As a result of significant reconceptualizations of gender construction, the place of the female was 're-denigrated' in terms of musical and artistic understanding and creativity.

---

[3] Linda Phyllis Austern (1989), '"Sing Againe Syren": The Female Musician and Sexual Enchantment in Elizabethan Life and Literature', *Renaissance Quarterly*, **42**: 420–48.

[4] Christine Battersby (1989), *Gender and Genius: Towards a Feminist Aesthetics*, London: The Women's Press, pp. 46–7.

[5] Ibid., p. 48.

The elevation of a feminine sensibility arose from Romanticism's concern with encapsulating the verbally indescribable inner 'essence' of things, rather than merely their external appearance. Music was perceived as able to appeal directly and immediately to the senses, and so to bypass more concrete and denotative forms of representation. Instrumental music in particular was seen to epitomize this in the 'absolute' music which, '"dissolved" from verbal and functional constraints "sublimates" or "exhalts" itself above the boundedness of the finite to an intimation of the infinite'.[6] Since a feminine sensibility rendered the artist almost 'at one' with the most basic and powerful forces of nature, however, nothing short of the most masculine strength and virility could allow the individual to withstand its dramatic impact. There is, of course, nothing inherent in such an androgynous model to preclude women from creativity, but cultural and physiological constructions of femininity and femaleness conspired once again to promote a male monopoly of the arts. The elevation of intuition, emotion and imagination may have feminized the artist's soul, but his body—providing his essential supporting strength—remained necessarily male.[7] Masculine strength allowed the male artist to experience the most extreme perceptions of a feminine soul. He was therefore seen to transcend and sublimate the denigrated biology that still bound women inextricably to 'procreative and domestic duties which would take up all their (limited) energy'.[8] The female body, still being conceptualized according to long-outdated medical ideas of the debilitating effect of 'the vapours', was considered too physically fragile to withstand the rigours of sublime contemplation. As Battersby states, women who aspired to the higher reaches of creativity at this time,

> All found themselves confronted by fathers and doctors—and even by mothers and sisters—anxious for their welfare: eager to tell them that Nature had provided women with a physique that would punish them with madness and disease if they attempted to rival the males.[9]

The male artist's perceived originality allowed him to write music 'for an imaginary public, for the future, and if possible for "eternity"',[10] with the apotheosis of such creativity lying in the mysterious deity that was the virtuoso, personified in the mythical physical and sexual potency of figures such as Paganini and Liszt.[11] Perhaps unsurprisingly, however, given the nature of these examples, such

---

[6] Carl Dahlhaus (1989), *The Idea of Absolute Music*, trans. R. Lustig, Chicago and London: The University of Chicago Press, p. 60.

[7] Battersby, p. 10.

[8] Ibid., pp. 5 and 8.

[9] Ibid., p. 130.

[10] Alfred Einstein (1947), *Music in the Romantic Era*, New York: W. W. Norton & Company Inc., p. 16.

[11] See for example Heinrich Heine's description of Paganini in Arnold Whittall (1987), *Romantic Music: A Concise History from Schubert to Sibelius*, London: Thames and Hudson Ltd, p. 45, and Arthur Loesser's wry account of Paganini and Liszt—particularly the latter's affect on female admirers—in Loesser (1955), *Men, Women and Pianos: A Social History*, New York: Simon and Schuster, pp. 366–71.

powerful personal imagery and charisma was not available as a model to aspiring female artists. Apart from any perceived physical constraints, their relationship to creativity remained mediated, as in the Renaissance, by contemporaneous ideas of female propriety. The continuing social perception of the danger and aberration of active female sexuality meant that '[f]or women, the loss of identity involved in a passionate experience of the sublime threatened the boundaries of the proper femininity essential for their reputation.'[12] It was, in other words, too dangerous an activity for a respectable and 'feminine' woman. Even just to perform—particularly, as Sarah Webster Goodwin suggests, as a singer—could draw an unseemly amount of attention to the body, and this was naturally interpreted in an entirely different way to the overtly physical display of the male virtuoso.[13] Instead, women were idealized as partially educated 'companions' and muse-like inspirers of their superior husbands[14]—a model supported by the contemporaneous 'reallocation', described by Reina Lewis, of active and destructive sexuality to working-class and colonial women and a resultant respectable lack of middle-class female sexuality.[15] Within this model, only restrained self-expression was possible through the delicacy and triviality of those 'occupations superficially related to the fine arts ... known as "accomplishments"'.[16] The chief value of these lay in their enhancement of women as marriageable prospects for the more socially and economically eligible bachelors.

Women, Femininity and Emotion in Musical and Dramatic Representation

If we accept that musical and social dynamics are related, we must consider by extension the possibility of the gendering of musical semiotics. Semiotic codes which adhere to contemporaneous cultural constructions of gender have been traced in music as early as the sixteenth century. At this time, according to Leo Treitler, music was coded as masculine according to qualities such as '[c]larity, system, understandability, strength, vigor, power, reason, [and] manliness'. Femininity, on the other hand, was perceived in qualities of 'softness, roundedness, elegance, charm, [and] grace' and those features that Linda Phyllis Austern identifies such as ornamentation, elaboration, improvisation, variation and chromaticism[17]—a

---

12 Reina Lewis (1996), *Gendering Orientalism: Race, Femininity and Representation*, London: Routledge, p. 179.

13 Sarah Webster Goodwin (1994), 'Wordsworth and Romantic voice: The poet's song and the prostitute's cry', in Dunn and Jones (op. cit.), p. 68.

14 Battersby, p. 121.

15 Lewis, p. 54. This shift in thought is also described in a different context by Goodwin, p. 68.

16 Loesser, p. 267–8. Loesser points to moderate musical ability as only one area of 'accomplishment' deemed desirable in young ladies at this time. Other areas that he lists may give some indication of the level of engagement expected in these pastimes, including as they do various small-scale decorative arts and crafts and a basic ability in French.

17 Leo Treitler (1993), 'Gender and Other Dualities of Music History', in Ruth A. Solie (ed.), *Musicology and Difference: Gender and Sexuality in Music Scholarship*, Berkeley and London: California University Press, p. 27; Austern (1993), 'Alluring the Auditorie to Effeminacie: Music and the Idea of the Feminine in Early Modern England', *Music and*

codification that also, of course, allowed for the demonstration of a respectable and socially acceptable state of femininity through an appropriately controlled style of music.[18] Whatever the rigidity or universality of such a methodology for the representation of femininity and femaleness, its influence is apparent all the way through to twentieth-century ideas of 'proper' and 'improper' femininity in relation to music. 'Musical simplicity', tunefulness and modesty of scale, for example, are suggested by Marcia Citron as characteristic preferences of nineteenth-century female composers and listeners,[19] and these qualities are reflected in the musical style accorded to socially acceptable and respectable female operatic characters.[20] The elaboration and chromaticism connotative of dangerously 'excessive' femininity, on the other hand, is epitomized in Susan McClary's identification of the '"powerful"' female operatic character.[21] This fictitious woman is often so sexually and/or emotionally overdetermined as to warrant the label of 'madwoman'.[22]

The real power of such semiotic coding is realized through the unique role of music within the melodramatic text—be it melodrama itself or opera. This role hangs on two aspects of its independence: firstly, from the diegetic space of the text; and secondly, from spoken language. In the dynamic melodramatic relationship between expression and repression, music occupies a potentially quasi-independent position. It constitutes at once a narrative–thematic element, a non-denotative but highly meaningful language in itself and a stylistic means of inflecting almost every other mode of visual and verbal representation. It has the ability to support and deepen, comment upon with irony, or even completely contradict the surface appearance, words or actions of the drama. This distance from the apparent realities of the diegetic world combines with an attendant removal to the level of the connotative, free from the concrete meaning of spoken language. The melodramatic mode suspects the inadequacy of spoken language as a carrier of complete and genuine meaning and looks to music—conceptualized in the nineteenth century as the purest communication of emotion or 'essence'—as an antidote to the potential superficiality of mere words. In the dual-layered melodramatic text, therefore, music becomes a key to revealing the emotional or moral 'truth' of its characters. Such a space of integrity is crucial to a genre that typically subjects its protagonists to the cruelties, pressures and expectations of unsympathetic social contexts and requires their practical compliance whatever their actual feelings.

Letters, **74**(3): 351–4. See also Chapter 2 of Susan McClary (1991), *Feminine Endings: Music, Gender and Sexuality*, Minneapolis and London: University of Minnesota Press, on the gendering of the *stile rappresentativo* of early opera.

[18] Austern (1994), p. 91.

[19] Marcia J. Citron (1993), *Gender and the Musical Canon*, Cambridge, New York and Melbourne: Cambridge University Press, p. 132.

[20] See for example, Citron, p. 74, and McClary, p. 57.

[21] McClary notes this tendency in female characterization as early as the seventeenth century; see p. 86.

[22] Ibid., Chapter 4.

Female Characterization in Opera

Within the broad melodramatic context, opera's use of music to allow more telling representations of character interiority than words alone could achieve offers a particularly compelling model for later cinematic configurations of gender, emotion and music. Representations of women in opera frequently reveal what McClary terms a 'double frame'. This allows texts not only to present contemporaneous related artistic and social definitions of femininity and madness, but also to internalize and thematicize their patriarchal interpretation, translation and containment.[23] This structure is dependent upon music's melodramatic capacity secretly to reveal more of the woman than she may care or be able to tell, as well as the ability of the musical–dramatic narrative to present 'private' moments of female musical–emotional self-expression that would normally be considered inappropriate for public display.[24]

McClary describes how changes in the social and cultural importance accorded to rhetoric gradually positioned female characters in opera, from the seventeenth century onwards, as emotionally weak and unstable. 'First,' she states, 'the range of behaviors considered appropriate to men began to alter considerably in the seventeenth century. From this moment on in Western history, men are encouraged to stifle their feelings, while women are expected to indulge in emotional expression.'[25] The resultant operatic transfer of rhetoric to female characters leads, she suggests, to a supposed 'revelation' of female interiority that simultaneously questions the authority or self-control of the emoting subject. Giving such a musical voice to women 'purport[s] to reveal without mediation *what women are really like*: not docile … but insubordinate or threatening unless they can be reconciled … with a strong male authority [emphasis in original]'.[26] The paradox of the rhetorical outpourings of the female character—whether driven by grief or madness—was therefore the sheer, and perhaps unforeseen, power of her emotions. This offered excessive feminine emotions, in a female body, as a frightening prospect in need of control—hence the connections that McClary makes with a contemporaneous social context of a 'paranoid world, in which women were often selected as scapegoats for the crumbling social order, [wherein] such "powerful" constructions could also serve to justify patriarchal backlash'.[27] The operatic text presented the excesses of women in order to demonstrate, in turn, the desirability and necessity of their containment, control and even destruction in death.[28] The musical devices employed to represent such outbursts drew on those elements of music that were simultaneously conceptualized as weak and yet powerfully subversive within musical structures. These included

---

23 Ibid., p. 85.

24 See for example Austern (1994), p. 84, and McClary, p. 50.

25 McClary, p. 50.

26 Ibid.

27 Ibid.

28 McClary makes reference to this tendency, p. 50, but Catherine Clément (1989), *Opera, or the Undoing of Women*, trans. B. Wing, London: Virago, is wholly dedicated to an account of the systematic destruction of female characters in opera.

the florid style of McClary's 'rhetoric of seduction',[29] minor tonalities and the excessive ornamentation and elaboration already discussed as characteristic of ideas of 'dangerous' femininity.[30]

In this context, therefore, the feminine musical expressions of the overtly emotional or sexual woman place her as other to the masculine codes of rational clarity. According to Jacques Attali's ideas of the relationship of music and society, patriarchy must take control of subversive elements of femininity in order to define its own superior power. In a similar way, a musical structure exhibits its own 'noise' in order to demonstrate the return and eventual dominance of its own 'patriarchal' masculine codes.[31] McClary suggests that this parallel is intensified by the strong structural drive towards tonal closure characteristic of tonal music. The desire for musical resolution underlines the already salutary social necessity of neutralizing the disruptive female/feminine presence.[32] The coincidence of such 'masculine' musical framing of female characters with dramatic representations of patriarchal systems of control means that women's emotional and sexual containment becomes as much the prerogative of male operatic characters as of the (usually male) composers. It is through male musical codes that the excessively emotional or sexual woman is constructed by, and made other to, masculinity. Male musical and narrative systems then demonstrate her eventual containment within stronger rational forces. The male artists and characters representative of patriarchal control can therefore segment and reconfigure women's excessive expressivity in order to reduce its horrific social implications.[33] The musical codes of excessive femininity thus enable the creation of a protective distance between the represented woman and the audience, as well as the creator himself—thus removing the fear of what McClary terms the possible 'contagion' of her madness.[34]

Opera thus marks music as both expressive and repressive of female characters in an extremely complex way. In the first place, as McClary points out, it replaces the usual silence of the 'madwoman' with an actual—and generically necessary—musical voice.[35] The greater access to subjectivity that this offers for female characterization gives the mark of authenticity to women's emotions and a greater

---

29 McClary, pp. 39–42; Citron, p. 39. McClary goes on to discuss this specifically in relation to sixteenth- and early seventeenth-century opera, and Monteverdi's *L'Orfeo* in particular, mapping the shift of the style from male to female characters.

30 See, for example, Citron, p. 73, for a consideration of how the elaborate lines of Donna Elvira's first aria in *Don Giovanni* 'have been interpreted in a misogynistic manner', and Gretchen A. Wheelock, (1993), '*Schwarze Gredel* and the Engendered Minor Mode in Mozart's Operas', in Solie (op. cit.), pp. 201–21, on the gendered use of the minor mode.

31 Jacques Attali (1985), *Noise: The Political Economy of Music*, trans. B. Massumi, Minneapolis: University of Minnesota Press.

32 McClary, pp. 14–16.

33 Ibid., pp. 85–6. This patriarchal capability is also discussed in relation to the operations of song within drama and Romantic poetry respectively in Leslie C. Dunn (1994), 'Ophelia's Songs in *Hamlet*: Music, Madness and the Feminine', in Dunn and Jones (op. cit.), pp. 50–64, and Goodwin, 'Wordsworth and Romantic Voice'.

34 McClary, pp. 85–6.

35 Ibid., p. 85.

depth to their spoken words. It also suggests a crucial potential to surpass their eventual narrative defeat with the powerfully resonant memory of their 'dissonant' voices.[36] The independence of musical codes from those of the words and visual elements of the drama, however, nevertheless allow the potential mobilization of 'weak' and 'feminine' musical devices to undermine the validity of even the most apparently strong and sincere characterizations and self-professions.[37] Although given a voice for their perceived excesses, such women are therefore represented according to masculine codes and are subject to validation or undermining at the will of a male composer. As they freely express their emotions, their private suffering becomes a public spectacle. At the same time, they are distanced from the audience by compositional and narrative devices for the purpose of the audience's own 'safety' in contemplation. Finally, these women are seen to require both narrative and musical 'silencing'—a necessity that is often categorically achieved by their actual death.

Female Characterization in Melodrama

While Christine Gledhill suggests that nineteenth-century melodrama was not seen as a specifically female genre, she does acknowledge the particular role that an association of female characters with emotion may play in its retrospective categorization as such. She highlights the paradox of the value placed on 'emotional sensibility'[38] and the vulnerability associated with emotional self-expression that dictated that, in nineteenth-century melodrama, 'the realm of "feeling" was assigned to women'.[39] Thus, she states:

> The heroine, idealised as 'Angel in the House' … was often of more significance to the drama than the hero in her capacity to evoke and legitimate emotion. The obverse side of idealisation was fascinated horror at the prospect of the heroine's fall and subsequent degradation. Victorian patriarchs could weep publicly over the female victim, in demonstration of renewed feeling and virtue.[40]

As in the development of opera, therefore, female emotionality was offered as a spectacle for male consumption—with, in this case, the appealing vulnerability of the woman being determined by her position in relation to social and domestic protection, control and propriety.

---

[36] This use of the term 'dissonant' aligns ideas of musical, social and narrative dissonance, and follows the accounts of the operation of the female voice in Wheelock, p. 221, and Carolyn Abbate (1991), *Unsung Voices: Opera and Musical Narrative in the Nineteenth Century*, Princeton and Oxford: Princeton University Press.

[37] See, for example, Citron's analysis of the musical treatment of Fiordiligi and Dorabella in Mozart's *Così fan tutte*, in *Gender and the Musical Canon*, p. 72.

[38] David Grimstead, in Christine Gledhill (1987), 'The Melodramatic Field: An Investigation', in *Home is Where the Heart is: Studies in Melodrama and the Woman's Film*, London: BFI, p. 34.

[39] Gledhill in ibid.

[40] Ibid.

Concurrent with the development of melodrama in cinema, however, and particularly with the move into sound cinema, cultural attitudes shifted once again to the cost of the representation of female characters and their emotions. As Gledhill says, 'while early cinema produced melodrama by default, the power of speech instituted a critical break between a cinema destined for realism and its melodramatic origins. At the same time genre divisions were consolidated, allowing melodrama a separate identity (Bourget, 1985) which facilitated critical boundary lines drawn by gender.'[41] Sound cinema's consolidation of the distinction between such nostalgic forms and the new 'realist' conception of cinema, furthermore, coincided with the degrading of the previously valued mode of emotional sensibility as mere 'sentimentality'[42]—a reconfiguration that was to haunt the female characters so central to the genre. Against the '"classic" genres … constructed by recourse to masculine cultural values espousing male cultural values … "melodrama" was acknowledged only in those denigrated reaches of the juvenile and the popular, the feminised spheres of the women's weepie, the romance or family melodrama'.[43]

In this light, it is interesting to note the effective reconfiguration of the term 'romantic' as it becomes associated with the female/feminine realm. Rather than the sublime contemplation and grandiose originality of the nineteenth century, it tends to suggest a concern with love. As an all-consuming interest in love becomes attributed primarily to women, their capacity or compulsion to 'romanticize' becomes attached to their vision of men and relationships. While this may harness the imaginative potential of the female, it also places her in a difficult position regarding denigrated ideas of emotional sensibility. The degree of love that she experiences and the importance that she accords her relationship become redolent of a kind of misguidedly *errant* and *excessive* level of idealization and expectation. Even outside of the love story as a specific type of narrative, the melodramatic woman's motivation according to the truth and depth of her emotions may mark her, her story and her sympathetic female audience as overly emotional, even stupidly sentimental, and certainly 'unrealistic' in contemporaneous terms. By the same token, this may also imply a related slippage between the nineteenth-century ideas of transcendence and universalism and the use of the term 'transcendent' to describe female emotions in certain filmic and film-musical contexts. As the emotional becomes degraded and more specifically associated with perceived female realms such as love and motherhood, so the idea of female emotions as transcendent adopts a more specific meaning. Rather than transcending human, i.e. male, experience, the representation of female emotions allows women to transcend the more specific restrictions and propriety of the social/emotional role allowed them within patriarchy. Their emotions therefore transcend everyday 'normality' and become universal in representing an idea of the 'pure', unsullied, innate emotionality of the female sex in the form of, for example, 'the woman in love' or 'the mother'. While this offers an incredibly liberating potential to re-emphasize the real power and virtue of emotion, twentieth-century attitudes to the limitations of femaleness and femininity mean that moments

[41] Ibid.

[42] Ibid.

[43] Ibid.

of such transcendence are still often reframed as the most 'melodramatic', overblown and misguided extremes of fantastical emotional excess.

In an investigation that deals with the potential influence of nineteenth-century ideas of the feminine on twentieth-century female musical–emotional characterization, such a basic shift in thinking is crucial. As the subsequent chapters in fact demonstrate, the distinction between the 'pure' ideas of Romanticism and the denigratory representation of the emotionally confused and overdetermined woman can even be mobilized as a central narrative device in melodrama and the woman's film.[44] Despite cinema's concern with more contemporary manifestations of morality and personal responsibility, the 'highly ambivalent field' that nineteenth-century theatrical melodrama had produced for women therefore remains intact.[45] Film melodrama's ultimate valuation of moral and emotional virtue over social standing, and its gendered dynamic of sensibility and control, converge to position the feminine, music and emotion as primarily appropriate to the female realm. At the same time, however, non-diegetic music's quasi-independent position in relation to other narrative elements highlights an essential paradox in the generic desire for the victimized female characters' resonating moral and emotional superiority.

Such unfortunate protagonists are offered a very particular kind of victory. This is defined by their steadfastness in the face of an insoluble or intolerable situation, their ability to rise above a normal and even forgivable level of human selfishness, or even their destruction at the hands of vicious and unjust social structures and their human proponents. This kind of superiority is evidenced, however, through the more essential terms of non-representational gesture—most notably, in this context, their non-diegetic musical representation. The oppressed character may therefore emerge as morally victorious even if they never gain the right to actual power—or to speech or full verbal self-expression—or indeed even if they appear to fail in the face of the immediate social context. In much the same way as Carolyn Abbate and Gretchen A. Wheelock suggest can happen in opera, the musical–emotional 'voice' of the victimized woman in film melodrama may therefore remain resonant and disturbingly memorable, despite her verbal silence and/or ultimate subjugation to patriarchal social structures.

The reconfiguration of the expressive space of gesture as a kind of textual gap, however, emphasizes the fact that the presence of non-diegetic music can, by definition, also signal crucial and decisive failures of communication or misalignments

---

[44] In such cases, the frequent difficulty in determining the exact distinction between a '*R*omantic' and a '*r*omantic' sensibility can make the use of terminology problematic. In order to make my use of these terms as clear as possible, I follow the lead of the reconfiguration itself. I use the term 'Romantic' only where a clear appeal to the original tenets of nineteenth-century cultural thought or concepts of the artist or musician are suggested. The term 'romantic' is then used in connection with those emotions relating to love, relationships or fantasizing about the love object, which are most commonly represented in 1940s melodrama and women's films as being experienced by female characters towards male characters. Any areas of overlap or confusion between the two terms thus become easier to identify and examine.

[45] Gledhill (1987), p. 35.

of character recognition.[46] While the musical–emotional voice may be powerful, it nevertheless exists in a space conventionally marked by a sense of power*less*ness in the 'real' terms of the diegetic world. The film audience is therefore placed in a position of frustratingly impotent omniscience. They share the protagonist's perception of their own restricted situation, while simultaneously realizing wider truths to which crucial characters, at least initially, may have no access.[47] The female character who is caught, as it were, in this chasm of non-expression, experiencing emotions that are not or cannot be shared or realized by those around her, is therefore marked by a peculiar narrative circularity. Her emotional expression may be strong, resonant and perhaps ultimately victorious in terms of both its ability to engender audience sympathy and its memorability long after the film itself has ended. Her actual person, however, is frequently restricted, subdued and domesticated. As her music evidences the presence of the most extreme levels of sensibility in Romantic terms, her social context restricts and devalues its expression in the real world. The frustration and indeed the very subjectivity of the woman may therefore be seen as contained in the dynamic between her position, vocality and agency within the diegetic world, and her emotional representation on the non-diegetic soundtrack.

Ideas of Emotional Affect, the Feminine and Women in Film Music Theory

Most theories attempting to explain the emotional affects of music both as part of film narrative and in terms of spectatorial engagement concern themselves with interpretations of the particular significance of music's abstract mode of expression. Whatever the specific terms of these explanations, many are based on a similar perception—that music offers a connection to something that comes from *within the individual* but which at the same time extends *beyond the individual* in his or her immediate physical or spiritual context.[48] This clearly ties in with nineteenth-century

46 Such misalignments and their emotional affect are described in Thomas Elsaesser (1987), 'Tales of Sound and Fury: Observations on the Family Melodrama', in Gledhill (ed.), *Home is Where the Heart Is*, and Steve Neale (1986), 'Melodrama and Tears', *Screen*, **27**(6): 6–22.

47 Elsaesser, pp. 66–7.

48 This is conceptualized in a variety of ways. Theodor Adorno and Hans Eisler believe that music returns the listening subject to an imaginary state of collectivism; see Adorno and Eisler (1994), *Composing for the Films*, New York: Oxford University Press, London: Athlone Press, p. 21. Caryl Flinn suggests that it evokes a sense of Romantic nostalgia and universalism; see Flinn (1992), *Strains of Utopia: Gender, Nostalgia and Hollywood Film Music*, Oxford and Princeton: Princeton University Press. Drawing on psychoanalytic theory, both Claudia Gorbman and Flinn suggest that it may operate by recalling the earliest states of human perception; see Flinn, pp. 56–64, and Gorbman (1987), *Unheard Melodies: Narrative Film Music*, Bloomington: Indiana University Press, London: BFI, pp. 61–4. Royal S. Brown finds that music bestows the story with mythical resonance; see Brown (1994), *Overtones and Undertones: Reading Film Music*, California and London: California University Press, pp. 9–10. Finally, Roy M. Prendergast refers to its influence by Wagnerian operatic ideals of the evocation of psychological depth; see Prendergast. (1992), *Film Music: A Neglected Art*, New York and London: Norton, p. 40.

ideas of the expansion and universalizing of human consciousness through music. Indeed, the very choice of the Romantic style as the basis for film music scoring has been attributed by some to this shared goal. Caryl Flinn, for example, suggests that the 'classical perception of film music … like that of [R]omanticism, insists that it bear the marks of a subjectivity, the stamp of a human presence'.[49] The use of the 'outdated' Romantic style of music therefore 'evokes the idea of a lost humanity' in a classical cinema that 'displays an almost obsessive concern with establishing the presence of some kind of human agency'.[50] Whereas the conventional source of human presence and interiority in concert music would presumably be the composer, however, film must surely transfer this affect onto the characters with whom the music becomes most strongly associated.

Both Hollywood and British cinema of the 1940s tend to gender narratives that foreground 'emotional' subject matter according to a conflation of the feminine and the female. The attendant gendering of music then becomes something of an accepted fact. As Claudia Gorbman, for example, examines music and audience identification in a crucial scene from *Now, Voyager*, she stops short of questioning the extent to which this identification is equally distributed between the male and female characters involved.[51] While in this particular case, of course, the generic specificity of the film may account for our primary interest being in the female protagonist's emotional trajectory, it must nevertheless be acknowledged that similar scenes in connection with male characters—in whatever genre—are comparatively rare. Indeed, a possible gender-musical distinction begins to arise in Gorbman's comparison of music and what she terms 'epic feeling' in *Mildred Pierce* (1945) and *The Young Mr Lincoln* (1939), as well as in Royal S. Brown's account of the meaning attached to the 'romantic' theme of *The Sea Hawk* (1940). These distinguish between an alignment of musically represented and universalized female social/personal/domestic and male social/political/historical emotion.[52] Brown's analysis also demonstrates the continuation of gendered musical semiotics, with the male hero represented by spirited and strong music such as fanfares and brass orchestration and the heroine's 'charming but frail, high-pitched' theme associated with 'a shimmering orchestral accompaniment that includes celesta, harp, and vibraphone'.[53]

Brown seems to accept this gendering of music without questioning its effect on the construction of the characters or their place within the narrative. Kathryn Kalinak's examination of musical representations of opposing constructions of femininity, however, does begin to suggest some of their possible ramifications for female characters. Although she does not refer to any such history of musical equivalents, the ancient figures of the Siren and the Muse manifest themselves in the codes of Kalinak's 'fallen woman' and 'virtuous wife'.[54] These more contemporary

49 Flinn, p. 31.

50 Ibid., p. 49.

51 Gorbman, pp. 65–6.

52 Ibid., pp. 81–2; Brown, pp. 102–9, 112–17.

53 Brown, p. 104.

54 Kathryn Kalinak (1982), 'The Fallen Woman and the Virtuous Wife: Musical Stereotypes in *The Informer*, *Gone With the Wind*, and *Laura*', *Film Reader*, **5**: 76–82.

characterizations demonstrate how the options for behaviour, action and reaction open to female characters can be delimited through an association with particular musical features. The musical styles that Kalinak finds aligned with specific types of female character in film reflect—according to the sexual and social implications of the siren/muse dichotomy—the codes from opera, dramatic music and earlier ideas of musical 'decency' already discussed in this chapter. She suggests that the 'classical [film] score frequently encoded otherness through the common denominator of jazz'.[55] The 'fallen woman'—rebellious, not respectable, sexually independent—could therefore be characterized through 'an association with the so-called decadent musical forms such as jazz, the blues, honky-tonk, and ragtime'. As a result, she was marked 'harmonically, by the inclusion of unusual harmonies, chromaticism, and dissonance; rhythmically, by the use of dotted rhythms and syncopation'.[56] The use of such styles clearly offered a popular equivalent to the meaning evoked through earlier uses of 'disruptive' and 'dissonant' codes in classical music and opera. The 'virtuous wife'—mother, sister, 'decent' woman—could then be represented in stark contrast by respectable, classical music 'with strong positive associations. Her instrumentation was orchestral, with the violins usually carrying the melody; the harmonies were lush, based on late nineteenth-century models; the rhythms were even and lyrical; and the melodies often had an upward movement, or included upward leaps in the melodic pattern'.[57]

Having established these polar opposites, Kalinak's model then moves beyond them to make clear that women can be characterized in more complex ways. In so doing, she suggests other interactions and implications that may be in operation between female characters and their styles of music. The distinctions that she draws, for example, between Katie and Mary (Margot Grahame and Heather Angel) in *The Informer* (1935), and Scarlett and Melanie (Vivien Leigh and Olivia de Havilland) in *Gone With the Wind* (1939) reveal their sexuality to be inextricably linked to their physical strength and fortitude. Virtuous Mary emerges as a far weaker character in all other respects than the fallen Katie, but Katie is still subject to a musical characterization determined purely by her sexuality. While Mary's theme is typical of Kalinak's virtuous wife convention, Katie's features dotted rhythms, syncopation, minor tonality and 'low strings, woodwinds, and brasses'.[58] In a similar way, Melanie is described by her own husband as '"frail and gentle"' in contrast to the '"fine and strong and beautiful"'—but also ruthlessly independent—Scarlett.[59] As Kalinak points out, both of these women are respectable in their actual sexual behaviour, and are therefore not as distinct in that respect as Mary and Katie. Although as a result they are both scored according to the codes of the virtuous woman, however, Scarlett's less acceptable attributes are still subtly registered in her music. Kalinak argues that the dotted rhythms and chromaticism of her theme suggest the fallen woman codes,

[55] Kalinak (1992), *Settling the Score: Music and the Classical Hollywood Film*, Madison: University of Wisconsin Press, p. 167.

[56] Kalinak (1982), pp. 76–7.

[57] Ibid., p. 77.

[58] Ibid.

[59] Ibid., p. 79.

even if not completely surrendering her to them, and that in this case, the music 'makes another distinction based on their sexuality: Scarlett is not a traditionally passive female; Melanie is'.[60] It seems possible, therefore, that acceptable sexuality may be considered indivisible in such cases from a more extensive and perhaps even partially negative sense of emotional passivity, dependence and consequent social submissiveness. A more uncontrolled and dominating sense of sexuality, on the other hand, may in turn suggest a stronger, more independent and perhaps even more productive and resourceful woman.

On examining the related musical and emotional representation of the female character in melodrama and the woman's film, the possible permutations of this formulation therefore need to be taken into account. What is at stake is a socially accepted codification that allocates particular narrative roles and possibilities to women, rather than any essential connection between music and female emotions, sexuality and subjectivity. This should not, however, imply formulaic simplicity, as Kalinak suggests a considerable degree of complexity in the interaction between different styles of music. Tying this together, furthermore, with points made earlier in this chapter, such potential for musical meaning must always be considered alongside the crucial relationship of the female character to her own voice and the ability or right to speak, her narrative agency, and her place and movement within patriarchal social and familial structures. In order to understand the full ramifications of the relationship of the female character to music, therefore, it is necessary to look even further than the style of music and the emotional construction of the woman. These concerns will only be fully meaningful if read within the context of the overall narrative and social dynamic in which she is placed.

Conclusion

What arises from this initial contextualization of music and female characterization in film is a clear picture of a history of both cultural ideas of women, and their dramatic representation, sharing a common preoccupation with 'over-investing' the female with qualities of the feminine. Women are defined according to their emotions and the effect of the expression of these emotions on themselves, as well as on men and patriarchal society in general. A respectable and socially desirable woman is capable of both emotional and sexual self-control, while a more dangerous model of femaleness threatens uncontrolled and destructive—but perhaps exciting—emotionality and sexuality. Particularly as music becomes conceptualized as representative of transcendent levels of 'feminine' emotion, however, its relationship to actual women is problematized by the perception of their physical weakness in the face of the sublime. The idea of female creativity at the same level as a male artist implies an undesirably 'masculine'/male level of strength and sexuality. Without this undesirable connotation of masculinity, however, the expression of 'excessive' and uncontrolled levels of feminine emotion signals potential insanity. As the perceived

60 Ibid., pp. 78–9.

excess of female emotionality becomes a point of curiosity, pathos or danger, women are therefore dissuaded, for their own safety, from its active musical expression.

When this is translated into melodramatic representation in film, the female character becomes subject to a particular dynamic of expression and repression/control in which non-diegetic music plays a defining role. Her musical–emotional representation, reduced to the perceived level of the sentimental and the romantic, demonstrates the dangerous and unrealistic levels of femininity that must be controlled in an ordered society. Perhaps because of this, and perhaps to avoid a confrontation of the question of whether women would in fact control themselves even if there were no such constraints placed upon them, she is habitually shown in social situations that demonstrate her enforced silence, control and containment. Her non-diegetic musical–emotional 'voice', countering this containment, then resonates with the sense of a universal emotional and moral 'truth' that transcends her social and historical context. While the music remains at the non-diegetic level, however, such resonances are potentially lost on other characters and known only to the film audience. In fact, an apparently inherent and inescapable circularity distinguishes women's relationship to music. The female character's representation through non-diegetic music in particular suggests that her words and actions are suffused with an emotional depth and veracity that male characters often seem to find difficult to match. This emotional profundity removes female characters in some sense from the social restrictions and codes that dictate their actions, so that they achieve a kind of transcendence that universalizes their experience. At the same time, however, the very fact that it is non-diegetic music that realizes their potential for such transcendent emotion highlights its very inexpressibility in the diegetic world. This seems to rue the impossibility accorded by the inadequacies of language or society to the female character's full expressive capacity. The eloquence of her silence is thus both enabled and regretted by the dynamic of her musical and diegetic representation. In short, the female musical–emotional voice is heard not only in order that the necessity of its control can be demonstrated, but also, importantly, in order that the cost of its containment to the woman does not go unrecognized. The dynamic of non-diegetic music and narrative and social context marks the melodramatic female as both the most powerful and the most powerless of cinematic characters.

Chapter 2

Music and the voice in the woman's film

'There's nothing I need to say to him.'
Henriette (Bette Davis) in *All This and Heaven Too*

'"I love you" is such an inadequate way of saying "I love you".'
Louise (Joan Crawford) in *Possessed*

Given its apparently sympathetic focus on female psychology and its aim to appeal specifically to female audiences, the woman's film offers the most obvious place to examine more deeply the dynamic of narrative and social agency, access to self-expression and musical emotionality that characterizes the melodramatic female. Its female-centred approach may suggest a positive development away from the less sympathetic operatic model or film melodrama's denigrating label of 'sentimentality' explored in Chapter 1, so that one might suppose that the woman's film would herald forward-looking changes in female musical–emotional characterization. What actually emerges may not be so categorical as this; it does, however, demonstrate ways in which the potential complexity of the woman's individual relationship to music may be maximized in order to achieve bolder representations of positive female subjectivity.

Women, Emotion and Subjectivity in the Woman's Film

Jeanine Basinger suggests that the success of the woman's film came from the fact that it 'worked out of a paradox. It both held women in social bondage and released them into a dream of potency and freedom'.[1] This balance of subversion and restriction offered the female audience a double identification—allowing them to indulge in exciting escapist fantasy on the one hand, while also, on the other hand, ultimately reminding them of the folly and even the mortal danger of seeking such freedom and independence. What Caryl Flinn terms the 'partial utopias' of the woman's film may therefore 'propose the beginnings of a difference from the status quo', but stop short of advocating true subversion.[2] The mediated access to subjectivity involved in this demonstration of the pitfalls of female agency is reflected in the kind of crisis that Mary Ann Doane locates in attempts to represent the visual point of view of the female protagonist. Pam Cook suggests that the emotion and desire central to

[1] Jeanine Basinger (1993), *A Woman's View: How Hollywood Spoke to Women, 1930–1960*, London: Chatto & Windus, p. 6.

[2] Caryl Flinn (1992), *Strains of Utopia, Gender, Nostalgia and Hollywood Film Music*, Oxford and Princeton: Princeton University Press, p. 150.

the construction of the female protagonist's point of view problematize the validity of femininity as a subject position.[3] Doane finds accordingly that the woman's film invests the female gaze with various symptoms of instability, weakness and danger. These undermine its authority and validity through narrative structures that continually evoke the '"feminine condition[s]" … [of] masochism, hysteria, neurosis, [and] paranoia'.[4] In some cases, as Janet Walker points out, the only point of view available to the female character may be a paradoxically passive 'look *back*' at the male gaze—be it individual or institutional—that actively strives to dissect and decipher her [emphasis in original].[5]

A further extension of this comes through frequent recourse to what Doane terms 'the medical discourse', based on Freudian models of psychoanalysis.[6] These narratives manifest women's difficulty in supporting a subjective position as an actual, identifiable illness. Such a condition can only be 'cured' by the woman's diagnosis at the hands of the male doctor to whom she confesses all, and her subsequent return to the 'normal' status of the object of a loving male gaze. The same threat of social disgrace, physical or psychological illness to which nineteenth-century women unable to control or subdue their 'excessive' femininity were subjected also, therefore, awaits the female protagonist of the 1940s woman's film—facilitating a narrative structure similar to Susan McClary's double framing operatic text (see Chapter 1 of this book). The emphasis on controlling the excesses of femininity—vital in any era to the maintenance of patriarchal control—now, however, takes on a historical specificity that at least partially mitigates the redefinition of its audience. Female emotionality, once again positioned as a perhaps ghoulishly stimulating spectacle to be enjoyed before being neutralized, is now principally addressed to a female audience who must learn to control *themselves* in the wartime absence of men as well as after their post-war return.

Women and the Voice in the Woman's Film

Particularly in the light of the continued relevance of McClary's operatic formulation, the question of self-control must also be considered in terms of the relationship that the woman's film grants its female protagonist to codes of speech, access to the voice, and vocal control. The generic emphasis on self-expression highlights the processes of communication, and just as Michel Chion argues that mutism may be considered 'a corollary

---

[3] Pam Cook (1983), 'Melodrama and the Women's Picture', in Sue Aspinall and Robert Murphy (eds), *BFI Dossier 18: Gainsborough Melodrama*, London: BFI Publishing, p. 16.

[4] Mary Ann Doane (1987), 'The "Woman's Film": Possession and Address', in Christine Gledhill (ed.), *Home is Where the Heart Is: Studies in Melodrama and the Woman's Film*, London: BFI, p. 285.

[5] Janet Walker (1987), 'Hollywood, Freud and the Representation of Women: Regulation and Contradiction, 1945–early 60s', in Gledhill (op. cit.), p. 209.

[6] Doane (1988), *The Desire to Desire: The Woman's Film of the 1940s*, Basingstoke and London: Macmillan Press, Chapter 2.

and condition of speech',[7] Peter Brooks suggests that muteness is the 'corresponding sensory deprivation' of melodrama.[8] Developing the melodramatic idea that the mute gesture represents some kind of 'original' and immediate language, mutism as a feature of characterization takes on a very particular weight of meaning. Chion suggests that although the mute character in melodrama is rarely a central figure, his or her presence can be key to the drama and inherently disturbing to the other, speaking, characters. Such a character not only indicates that the text incorporates a secret, but that it is this secret on which the story will turn. The position of 'knowing the truth' that this assumes for the mute character is in turn often extended to their assignment as the moral conscience of the narrative—the omniscient arbiter and source of truth 'next to [whom] everyone feels guilty'.[9] This role, as Chion suggests, positions the mute character as particularly powerful, paralleling 'the bodiless voice of the acousmêtre':

> In both cases … the character … is taken as more or less all-seeing, all-knowing, often even all-powerful. In both cases, the limits of his being and his body generally go undefined (even for the limits of the mute character's body, strange as this may seem), and thus also the limits of his role, his position, his power. And in both cases, unveiling either his voice, or his body and face, has the effect of breaking the spell, re-assigning the character to an ordinary fate, taking away his mythic aura and putative powers.[10]

When Doane suggests, however, that in the woman's film, 'the muteness which is constantly attributed to the woman is in some ways paradigmatic for the genre',[11] important questions arise as to the implied gender of Chion's characterization. It may be possible to bring to mind examples of male mute characters who exercise something like the kind of power Chion suggests, such as John (Art Smith) in *Letter from an Unknown Woman* and the nameless boy (Dickie Moore) in *Out of the Past* (1947). There is, however, no pressure for these characters to (learn to) speak. The curiosity value of how their voices would sound and the threat of such a revelation to their omniscience are therefore not really at issue. As I discuss in Chapter 5, even when a male character is compelled to 'tell' his story, his privacy within the narrative can still be protected by the confinement of his narration to his own imagination. In the case of the female mute, however, who, particularly in the medical discourse, naturally tends to occupy the central narrative position, the whole narrative turns on

---

[7] Michel Chion (1999), *The Voice in Cinema*, ed. and trans. C. Gorbman, New York: Columbia University Press, p. 98.

[8] Peter Brooks (1984), *The Melodramatic Imagination: Balzac, Henry James, Melodrama, and the Mode of Excess*, New York: Columbia University Press, p. 57. This sentence makes a slippage between the terms 'muteness' and 'mutism'. Whereas, as Chion points out in *The Voice in Cinema*, p. 96, the first condition is physical and the second psychological, I feel that in terms of film narrative, the effect in relation to self-expression is sufficiently similar to make the common use of the term 'mutism' acceptable.

[9] Chion (1999), pp. 96–7.

[10] Ibid., p. 100. 'Acousmêtre' is Chion's term for the unseen narrator of a voice-overled film. The relationship of the female character to this mode of narration is examined more closely in Chapter 3 of this book.

[11] Doane (1988), p. 66.

the inducement of the woman actually to *speak* within the diegetic space. This aim has the very purpose of returning her to a socially desirable construction of Chion's 'ordinary fate'.

The silence of the woman in the woman's film occurs primarily on one of three levels. 'Muteness' shows the woman as being physically unable to speak whatever happens, as is the case, for example, in *Johnny Belinda* (1948). 'Mutism' renders the woman silent for psychological reasons but allows her to be induced to speak—whether through persuasion, hypnosis, medicine, or the advent of absolute life-or-death necessity.[12] Examples of such cases occur in *The Seventh Veil* (1945), *Possessed* (1947) and *The Spiral Staircase* (1945). The third level of silence, which might be termed 'selective mutism', however, is perhaps the most interesting and complex. This shows a woman who is fully able to speak—and has something to say—but who consciously chooses to remain silent on a crucial issue. The second condition in particular suggests the silencing of the woman by various manifestations of social, domestic or emotional oppression. Instances of this, and the much less common physical muteness, inevitably lead to more specialized narrative patterns, usually placing the woman at the centre of Doane's medical discourse. In this case, the point of the story often becomes a gendered variation on Chion's 'Debureau effect'[13]—the curiosity to hear the woman's voice—in this case in order to understand her story and perhaps thereby to discover the reason for her mutism.

Freeing the woman's voice in this way is, however, a rather more contentious route to establishing her subjectivity than may be imagined. As Doane points out, the result of the nature of the psychoanalytical narrative process is that the woman's voice becomes the 'gift' of the male doctor.[14] Since she can only talk as freely and for as long as she is permitted, her discourse can be segmented, framed and controlled by its division into manageable chunks. In such films as *Lady in the Dark* (1944), *The Seventh Veil*, *Possessed* and *The Snake Pit* (1948), therefore, intermittent male analysis can help to guide the spectator towards a particular diagnostic interpretation of the woman's innocently straightforward storytelling. Once again as with the operatic 'double frame', the deviance of the female psyche can thus be 'viewed' from a safe distance, whether for the ends of jealous pleasure, sensuous enjoyment, disgusted horror or scornful disdain. Although this usually limits the female subject largely to flashback narration, films such as *Gaslight* (1940), *The Locket* (1946) and *Caught* (1948) demonstrate in different ways how the woman can be a completely non-complicit, or even deceptive and resistant, 'patient' in the present.

This renders the third condition of 'selective mutism' particularly significant for the woman's own choice in the matter. Even if she feels compelled to make her decision to remain silent as a result of undesirable social pressures or emotional

---

[12] I am borrowing Chion's distinction between the two terms here. He defines 'muteness' as 'a physical condition that prevents the subject from speaking (such as a lesion, or a destroyed nerve center or phonic organ)', and 'mutism' as 'the refusal to speak, for so-called psychological reasons, with no physical damage to nerves or organs', Chion (1999), p. 96.

[13] Ibid., pp. 102–3.

[14] Doane (1988), p. 56.

circumstances, this can evince a certain kind of power and control—perhaps of the only sort open to her. Since her silence often results in self-sacrifice of one sort or another, the element of conscious choice marks this as a state of simultaneous constraint and incredible strength and self-discipline, and this is perhaps the reason why this particular kind of silence structures some of the definitive moments of women's films. It signifies apparently glorious and transcendent moments of self-sacrifice, as well as marking the most extreme points of frustratingly inexplicable character motivation. Although tragic in affect, for example, the greater good of the innocent other can motivate painful selective mutism or the self-conscious use of 'wrong' words to conceal the truth. This occurs in maternal melodramas such as *Imitation of Life* (1934), *Madame X* (1937), *Stella Dallas* (1937) and *The Old Maid* (1939), as well as love stories such as *Dark Victory* (1939) and *All This and Heaven Too* (1940). Heroic selective mutism becomes more problematic, however, when those being protected are rather less innocent, such as undeserving daughter Veda (Ann Blyth) in *Mildred Pierce* or adulterous Walter (John Boles) in *Back Street* (1932). Finally, it becomes annoyingly inexplicable when it can lead to little but misunderstanding and pain, such as in Myra (Vivien Leigh)'s refusal to reveal the reported death of her fiancé and, later, her own descent into prostitution, in *Waterloo Bridge* (1940), and Lisa (Joan Fontaine)'s secrecy over her child and her own identity in *Letter From an Unknown Woman*.

Non-verbal melodramatic codes—notably music—may, however, sometimes be allowed to 'speak' the emotions, thoughts and memories of these diegetically silent characters. In Chapter 1, I suggested a basic paradox in the representation of the usually female 'victim' of the melodramatic narrative. In the woman's film, the essential oppositions of this 'circular' system of expressivity and non-expressivity are highlighted in order to make some of the most painful and frustrating points about society and femaleness, which arise from the genre's concentration on the female protagonist's social position in the context of her emotional or moral constitution. The parallel relationships of female vocality to silence, power to powerlessness, and propriety and social expectation to personal desire therefore become primary issues for consideration.

Non-diegetic Music and Emotion in the Woman's Film

The physical separation of non-diegetic music and diegetic speech or silence may ordinarily be accounted for as a matter of form. The particular context of the woman's film, however, highlights what is in fact an inherent, and somewhat paradoxical, shift between narration through silence and sound. The predominant association of music with the principal female character renders our experience of her story distinct from that of all other characters and marks her emotions as particularly important. The separation of music from the diegetic space, however, means that it becomes—as opposed to diegetic music—simultaneously *mute* and *audible*. This allows the film audience actually to 'hear', and therefore interpret, what the other characters can only guess at or, in truly melodramatic fashion, completely fail to understand about the mute woman. Thomas Elsaesser's idea of the 'silence made eloquent'[15] therefore proves a highly evocative description of female expressivity in the woman's film. Making the woman's silence so painfully and audibly eloquent ultimately serves more than anything else to highlight the reality, and fullest possible social and personal meaning, of her silence. At the same time, however, the essentially symbiotic nature of the relationship of music, silence and expression must be noted. While the lack of access to, or refusal of, verbal self-expression seems to necessitate music, it is nevertheless the presence of music as part of the film narration that *allows* and *facilitates* this particular kind of female silence. The woman does not need to be able to speak for us to understand something of what she might say if she could. If she consciously chooses to withhold her voice, the film may allow the non-diegetic music to speak for her while she remains enigmatic within the diegetic space. In her most heightened emotional state, as Martin Rubin suggests in relation to *Back Street*, the woman may even return the film to a wholly 'silent' state. She can remove speech altogether to represent 'pure' transcendent emotion through the combination of what Rubin sees as 'the two purest of the soundtrack's four voices—pure sound (music) and pure image (silence)'.[16]

This potential for the explicit representation of the woman's emotional state may also undermine any attempt the film makes to distance her from the power to narrate. Doane argues that the Hollywood sound film 'operates within an oscillation between two poles of realism: that of the psychological (or the interior) and that of the visible (or the exterior)'.[17] Within this schema, '"[k]nowledge" of the interior life of the individual can be grounded more readily on the fullness and spontaneity of his or her speech doubled by the rhetorical strategies of music and sound effects (as well as *mise-en-scène*)', as a result of which, '[t]he ideological truth of the sound track covers that excess which escapes the eye. For the ear is precisely that organ which opens onto the interior reality of the individual—not exactly unseeable, but unknowable within the guarantee of the purely visible.'[18] The woman's film capitalizes on the psychological 'realism' of female emotions and their validity as a source of motivation, so that whatever the film may do to try to frame the woman's speech can be circumvented by the freedom and veracity of her musical–emotional representation. The woman's film may therefore be attempting to represent a *specifically female* relationship to femininity. It seems to suggest a very particular idea of subjectivity that, rather than just showing how women feel, actively demonstrates a certain frustration with the inadequacy or impossibility of verbal self-expression. While this frustration can be painful, it can also register the intangible depths of female emotions in more pleasurable situations. As Louise says to David (Van Heflin) in

[15] Thomas Elsaesser (1987), 'Tales of Sound and Fury: Observations on the Family Melodrama', in Gledhill (op. cit.), p. 66.

[16] Martin Rubin (1985), 'The Voice of Silence: Sound Style in John Stahl's *Back Street*', in Elisabeth Weis and John Belton (eds), *Film Sound: Theory and Practice*, New York and Chichester, West Sussex: Columbia University Press, p. 284.

[17] Mary Ann Doane (1980), 'Ideology and the Practice of Sound Editing and Mixing', in Weis and Belton (op. cit.), p. 59.

[18] Ibid., p. 61.

Possessed, '"I love you" is such an inadequate way of saying "I love you"'. This sense of frustration in turn leads to a more specific understanding of how music can work in conjunction with the female character's emotions, at least when it is clearly attached to her individual trajectory.

In order to ascertain the role that music plays in the construction of female subjectivity, it is therefore necessary to move beyond the idea of the potential powerlessness of the non-diegetic space and the framing of musical–emotional representation within the 'rational' masculine discourses of medicine, psychiatry, respectable love and marriage. Female musical–emotional representation is much more intricate than this, with a very particular sense of female subjectivity being located in the close interaction of meanings conveyed by the woman's words, behaviour and non-diegetic music. A more specific idea of what this may mean for an individual female character becomes apparent through the following study of *Now, Voyager*, in which this approach begins to redefine the female protagonist's position in relation to narrative and narration. Since non-diegetic music allows her relationship to the strictures of language, propriety and medical analysis to be mediated, whatever she says—or is made to say or does not say—must be evaluated in terms of the accompanying music. Her point of view therefore emerges through the way in which she actively deals with, or behaves within, the context of emotions and desires that she knows to be 'unacceptable' or socially/respectably 'inexpressible'.

Now, Voyager and the Star Image of Bette Davis

Now, Voyager is a particularly rich text through which to examine the interaction of female emotions, the voice and music. It presents us with a woman who develops from a complete lack of emotional self-control to the conscious ability to either withhold or most eloquently express her own voice, thoughts and emotions. It also, however, incorporates the inherent potential for a powerfully subversive representation of womanhood promised by the star image of Bette Davis. Andrew Britton argues that Davis does not usually play feminist characters, since 'she *does* relate to men: she is located within the "private realm", the traditional sphere of female competence, but is for some reason incompatible with its norms'. He illustrates this by pointing out that she 'repeatedly plays … women who *wish* to be married, but whose marriage is prevented by some external impediment' [emphasis in original].[19] Alternatively, when she 'plays a woman who occupies a position of great social power (*The Private Lives of Elizabeth and Essex* (1939)), or who commits herself to professional self-definition outside of marriage (*Old Acquaintance* (1943), *All About Eve* (1950)), the film invariably stresses the ultimate barrenness of her achievement, its irrelevance to her "real" needs'.[20]

The question that arises from the specific casting of Davis in such roles, however, is the particular emotional effect of her ever-present capacity for playing '"wicked"

[19] Andrew Britton (1995), *Katharine Hepburn: Star as Feminist*, London: Studio Vista, pp. 162–3.

[20] Ibid., p. 164.

women and "bitches"',[21] which had been central to her persona since her earliest starring role in *The Cabin in the Cotton* (1932). This clearly remains a part of most, if not all, of her performances in some form. In a similar way to the operation of the star image of Margaret Lockwood in *Love Story* (see Chapter 4), this sense of a very different person within, with strength, dogged resolve, and sometimes selfish determination, informs even her most apparently 'girlish', delicate and/or defeated characters. It may therefore be supposed that audiences, familiar with Davis's previous roles, would read each new character in the light of this earlier experience. Some of the sense of unbelievably violent self-constraint in a film like *The Old Maid*, and at the beginning of *Now, Voyager*, for example, must come from knowledge of her 'true' sexuality, energy, strength or capacity for selfishness and/or wickedness displayed already in films such as *The Cabin in the Cotton*, *Jezebel* (1938), *The Letter* (1940) and *The Little Foxes* (1941), and which would be seen again in countless later films including *Mr Skeffington* (1944) and *Beyond the Forest* (1949). Knowing what lies within her, the power required to restrain herself becomes all the more astounding, and her agreement to be subjugated all the more suspect.

It is this monumental inner strength that comes to the fore in *Now, Voyager*, allowing her to come, in Britton's estimation, 'nearest to a feminist self-definition'.[22] Although crucial to many of her characterizations, it is here that her characteristic portrayal of an almost overwhelmingly powerful interiority becomes the issue of the whole story. Her desires are more fully expressed, and either accepted or condemned, in films such as *The Cabin in the Cotton*, *Jezebel*, *The Great Lie* (1941), *Mr Skeffington* and *Beyond the Forest*, and overtly repressed in others such as *The Old Maid*. *Now, Voyager*, however, challenges her to define herself against a series of equally viable social, sexual and emotional options. The necessity for her to understand and take control of her own desires results in an unusually intricate dynamic between strongly felt interior and exterior states. This is expressed to a significant degree in the interaction between the diegetic (sound and visual) elements and the non-diegetic music of the film.

Re-playing the Past: Emotion, Memory and Music in *Now, Voyager*

> 'As long as I can remember that fire has never been lit.'
> 'High time it was then Lloyd.'
> Lloyd (Ian Wolfe) and Charlotte (Bette Davis) in *Now, Voyager*

Now, Voyager—so commonly referenced in terms of both its narrative content and iconic images—is difficult to contest as a quintessential woman's film. Notoriously hard to pin down in terms of exactly what it is saying to its female, or indeed male, audience, it pits a complex of sub-generic patterns against Davis's powerful star image and famous ability to suggest profound depths of interiority through facial expression, tone of voice and physical gesture. Perhaps naturally, therefore, readings of the film are often contradictory, as theorists strive to make sense of exactly why

21 Ibid., p. 162.
22 Ibid., p. 164.

the heroine acts as she does and where this leaves the other characters and the film audience.

This is also a film veritably saturated in music, with rarely a scene that does not contain either diegetic music or non-diegetic scoring. What seems amazing about such an intensely scored narrative is the degree to which the non-diegetic music centres almost exclusively on Charlotte Vale, the main protagonist, and constitutes a comprehensive map of her developing relationship to her own emotions. Perhaps more than any other film, the score of *Now, Voyager* intricately charts the changing dynamic between a woman's emotional life, behaviour, speech and self-expression. It registers the place of memory and imagination in the construction of her psychology, and marks the crucial generic distinction between undesirable repression and conscious self-control. Davis's star persona, and its dynamic relationship with Charlotte's characterization, may account to some extent for this unusual approach to scoring. Despite the apparent association of themes with other characters, particularly Mrs Vale (Gladys Cooper), Dr Jaquith (Claude Rains), Jerry (Paul Henreid) and Tina (Janis Wilson), there actually seems to be a rather paradoxical lack of musical relevance to anyone other than Charlotte herself—although the closeness as characters of Charlotte and Tina may blur this distinction somewhat. Ultimately, it appears that the other characters exist largely in the capacity of catalysts for Charlotte's development, representing various issues in her earlier troubled life and the means of overcoming them. Although, therefore, her final situation locates her between the various people who have positively affected her, it is somehow more her relationship to the emotions and memories that constitute her own sense of selfhood that is most at stake.

Despite sharing the vital common element of the influence of others on the self, this singular self-focus marks *Now, Voyager* as distinct from other films in related sub-genres identified by Doane as the medical discourse, maternal melodrama and love story.[23] Charlotte's maternal relationship to Tina, for example, is balanced against her experience with her own mother. As well as taking on the aura of a more abstract commentary on the nature of motherhood through successive generations, therefore, it also pivots around Charlotte's transformation of the maternal role, rather than being just about either specific pairing of mother and daughter. Maria LaPlace also makes the extremely compelling suggestion that, as she is inflected by 'the connotations of the Davis image', Charlotte's desire for independence may supersede her desire for a husband or children of her own.[24] Remembering also her rejection of the well-meaning but overbearingly respectable Elliot (John Loder), it may therefore be that Jerry, as her lover, acts as barely more than a bridge for Charlotte. In order to win the right to dictate her own existence that she really craves, she must pass over him rather than become emotionally dependent on him. As LaPlace suggests, it does seem of paramount importance, after all, that '*he* loves *her*' [emphasis in original][25] rather than vice versa—although this is clearly also the case. Charlotte cannot really

---

[23] Doane includes a chapter on each of these in *The Desire to Desire*.

[24] Maria LaPlace (1987), 'Producing and Consuming the Woman's Film: Discursive Struggle in *Now, Voyager*', in Gledhill (op. cit.), pp. 164–5.

[25] Ibid., p. 145.

make an active choice over her potential romantic/sex life until it is absolutely clear that one is available to her. The real issue seems to be the achievement of the 'state' of desirability, beyond which an actual physical relationship seems almost unnecessary. The added bonus in this case is the promise of 'eternal desirability', thanks to Jerry's permanent commitment and re-naming of his daughter Tina as 'Our child'. This works even despite the denial of a physical relationship which, as a truly bizarre subtext to the film, seems to persuade characters, audiences and critics alike that there is no 'real' infidelity involved to his wife.[26]

The personal and social progress of Charlotte is reflected in her relationship to her mother, psychiatrist, lover and lover's daughter, as well as in her personal expression through her style of dress and appearance, and her apparent self-control and sense of her own sexuality. On the surface, this appears to present the straightforward metamorphosis of the woman—a transformation made successful through the combined efforts of Lisa (Ilka Chase) the benevolent sister-in-law, Dr Jaquith, Jerry and, unknowingly, Tina—which results in her achieving a kind of fantasy family life without being an actual wife or mother. By the end of her story she is desirable, rich and successful, and has reached a position where she can make sophisticated and assertive choices. Even at this level, however, readings of the film interpret the issues and questions raised in subtly different ways. This is exemplified by the fact that the real crux of the film's meaning, offered in its closing scene, becomes the site of disagreement, not so much as to what happens but why it happens.

Stanley Cavell poses what is perhaps the basic question of *Now, Voyager* and indeed all similar narratives that seek to 'cure' the woman of whatever ails her, when he questions what it means for a woman in such a compromised situation to be redeemed by a man:

> This demand for education has to do with the woman's sense that she stands in need of creation, or re-creation. Now comes the moral cloud. Does creation from, even by, the man somehow entail creation *for* the man, say for his use and pleasure and pride? If not, how does the woman attain independence; how does she complete, as it were, her creation? [emphasis in original][27]

As Charlotte is taken up and re-created by the narrative, therefore, a process that she herself desires as she begs Dr Jaquith to help her, a crucial problematic arises. This concerns the question of whether she can become a person in her own right, or whether she is merely transformed into a form of womanhood more acceptable to men in which she herself can also find some degree of pleasure, if not complete happiness. Cavell considers that Charlotte does achieve her own re-creation, and that this is indicated in her transformed responses to Jerry's inability to free himself from

---

[26] This is not to say that Jerry has not been guilty of actual physical infidelity prior to this point. Such infidelity is strongly implied both during the night that he and Charlotte spend together on the mountain after their car accident and by their conversation and embrace on the hotel balcony.

[27] Stanley Cavell (1996), *Contesting Tears: The Hollywood Melodrama of the Unknown Woman*, Chicago: University of Chicago Press, p. 116.

his wife to marry her.[28] Whereas during their holiday together she expresses tearful gratitude that he would even consider the idea, by the end of the narrative she flies into a fury as he seems unable to comprehend that she could possibly want anything other than a husband. Jerry seals his own redundancy in Charlotte's trajectory, Cavell suggests, when he talks of her self-sacrifice in caring for Tina on her own rather than finding 'some man who could make [her] happy'. Through her angry and amazed rebuttal of his 'conventional, pretentious, pious' attitude, Charlotte renders Jerry 'simply superficial'.[29] This denies the possibility that she is 'sacrificing herself to or for Jerry's world' by her very revelation that this is only true in so far as 'this is essentially the way Jerry wishes to comprehend her'.[30]

In vindication of the new strength being exhibited by Charlotte over Jerry at this stage, Cavell also points to the disappearance of Charlotte's nickname 'Camille' from Jerry's speech.[31] *Now, Voyager* is a text that espouses the power of names to delineate and determine identification—the family name; the names and titles that signify the famous psychiatrist and the spinster; the specificity of nicknames used by spouses, friends and illicit lovers. This disappearance therefore suggests Jerry's realization of his loss of power over his ex-lover—the woman whom he once instructed to call him by the shortened name (from Jeremiah) used specifically by his friends. Lea Jacobs, however, picks up on this very point as an expression of the failings of Charlotte's final narrative moments. Seeing Charlotte as 'alone in her mother's house' and having to 'repress her desire and live without a man',[32] Jacobs considers that 'Jerry's position within the couple is filled by a girl who is the double of Charlotte herself',[33] his daughter, Tina. The confirmation of this transfer comes from the slippage in naming that results in both Charlotte and Tina adopting Jerry's nicknames for each other (Tina shortened from Christina, and Camille). They therefore, Jacobs suggests, come to 'speak to each other through his language',[34] so that Tina, and the 'stars' of Charlotte's final line of dialogue, become merely 'replacements for the man'.[35] There is indeed little doubt that Charlotte's comparison of the stars to the moon does imply a compromise, and something less than absolute happiness or fulfilment. This is also a compromise, however, that she decides they must both make: 'Don't let's ask for the moon, we have the stars.' Charlotte and Jerry remain locked in a trajectory even if it is neither ideal nor a conventional sexual relationship. What is most important, however, is that it is *Charlotte* who has made the undoubtedly reluctant decision over its terms. A broad definition of Charlotte's desire is therefore necessary to a recognition of the sophisticated and subversive degree of active choice that she is clearly exercising. Whether she likes it or not, she recognizes that she cannot have everything if she wants to remain faithful to her own

[28] Ibid., pp. 129–30.

[29] Ibid., p. 129.

[30] Ibid.

[31] Ibid., p. 131.

[32] Lea Jacobs (1981), '*Now, Voyager*: Some Problems of Enunciation and Sexual Difference', *Camera Obscura*, **7**: 102.

[33] Ibid.

[34] Ibid.

[35] Ibid., p. 103.

emotions. She therefore chooses what she sees as the most satisfactory way forward and resigns herself and Jerry to it. Her strength in resisting her own still evident desire for Jerry therefore becomes the most crucial point of the final scene.

Both Cavell and LaPlace actually seem to see the relationship between Charlotte and Tina as more telling of the film's message than her relationship with Jerry. Charlotte may have claimed some kind of independence, even if, as LaPlace points out, she 'must exercise it from within her home'.[36] Her positive mothering skills, however, nevertheless involve recreating for Tina the very approach to self-image that Charlotte herself apparently seeks to challenge. Cavell once again poses the vital question about this relationship when he suggests that it 'may be regarded either as the most disturbed or as the most therapeutic of all we are shown; as the one in which the conditions of unhappiness in this world are perfectly synthesized and reproduced for another generation, or in which they are specifically relieved, or modified'.[37] A difficult question to answer; the apparent advantages of the situation for both females are extremely complex. As LaPlace states, the discovery of Tina constitutes the beginning of 'the final movement of [Charlotte's] journey … By becoming the good mother to Tina—thus by identification, to herself—Charlotte achieves mastery both of herself and in the world'[38]—including, of course, mastery of Jerry. The repetition of her own physical transformation in Tina, however, happens despite Charlotte's new modern-minded independence. She herself has become much less concerned with the excesses of glamour that preoccupied her earlier transition from being her mother's 'ugly duckling' to the ideal of 'everyday' womanhood that she represents at the end of the film's 'how-to-be-beautiful' consumerist project.[39]

This difficulty is perhaps reflected in the actual appearance of Charlotte's transformed Tina, which does seem to suggest the potential ugliness of glamour. Although it is unclear whether this is the film's intended effect, the idea sits surprisingly comfortably within the text as a whole. Despite being an attractive girl, actress Janis Wilson is made to look somewhat uncomfortable and over-fussy in her long frilly party frock—a style of dress that also puts her out of kilter with the more casual mode of dress of the surrounding party guests in her final scene in the film. Although undoubtedly a highly fashionable dress for a girl of her age at this time, it nevertheless seems to emphasize her lack of adult shape, complete with a rather too 'grown-up' hairstyle that lends to the strangely awkward appearance of her usually bespectacled eyes. Likewise, the height of Charlotte's foray into 'borrowed' glamour during her holiday cruise seems designed more to express the bad fit between her unconfident state of mind and her sophisticated outward appearance. Her clumsily heavy evening gown and cape lend her an unflatteringly swamped and round-shouldered shapelessness. This stands in sharp contrast to her later stylishly simple and understated outfits, which draw attention to her new 'ideal' figure and self-confident poise. Cavell suggests that the glamour of many films lies in their evocation of 'real' beauty as arising from the possibility of attaining 'the

[36] LaPlace, p. 164.

[37] Cavell, pp. 142–3.

[38] LaPlace, p. 163.

[39] Ibid., p. 141.

courage to become the one you are'.[40] Perhaps, therefore, in passing through to the other side of 'standard' glamour, a woman can achieve what Charlotte herself would call 'a kind of beauty'. It would then be possible to argue that Tina is merely in transition, with a view to ending up as sophisticated and 'deeply' beautiful as her surrogate mother. The fact remains, however, that in terms of the film's structure, her uncomfortably superficial glamour and her new-found 'lovable' selfhood appear, rather worryingly, to coincide as a triumphant conclusion to her own lonely story. Most pertinently, the truth of her final state may be read between the lines of her reunion with Jerry. In seeking his verbal assurance of his feelings for her in response to her new incarnation, she reveals her sense that her appearance alone is the key to being liked, even, unbelievably, where her own father is concerned.

Finding a way through this veritable minefield of seemingly contradictory values and ideas leads to perhaps more basic questions concerning the nature not only of personal transformation, but also of happiness. Barbara Creed suggests that a key element of melodrama is that '[t]he ending of the heroine's story is never an unconditionally happy one', in evidence of which she cites Charlotte as a prime example as a woman who 'relinquishes her dreams of a marriage and family'.[41] Although I cannot wholly agree with Creed's interpretation of Charlotte's final choices, this does throw open the question of whether there is any real meaning behind such a phrase as 'unconditionally happy', particularly in the context of narratives that seek to negotiate the impossibility of women's social positioning. Rather than bemoaning the necessity for compromise, therefore, a more productive route may be to examine the exact nature of Charlotte's negotiation of her own narrative and social possibilities. This also opens up the question of what transformation really means in the context of her story. As a result, *Now, Voyager* becomes more of an honest confrontation of what it actually means to live with painful memories and fantasy on a daily basis, and a measurement of ongoing behaviour against this background. The story therefore goes beyond the potential points of romantic narrative closure with either Jerry or Elliot and contests Doane's contention—perhaps too simplistic in this case—that the regaining of the woman's health coincides with her 'transformation ... into a specular object'.[42] Instead, it swiftly bypasses the usual intricacies of the psychoanalytic process to focus on what happens in the long months afterwards, demonstrating how Charlotte's cure continues throughout the film. The search at the heart of the narrative is not for the original source of her problems, with the rather fantastic but surprisingly common idea that this discovery will deliver instant mental health. Instead, it seeks a way in which she can bring herself forward from what is only the starting point offered by Dr Jaquith.

Outwardly, Charlotte's transformation is little short of radical. Various constructions in the film, however, including the relationship of her behaviour and her voice to the musical score, suggest that she is still negotiating ghosts from different stages of her past right up until—and undoubtedly beyond—the final

---

[40] Cavell, p. 122.

[41] Barbara Creed (1978), 'The Position of Women in Hollywood Melodramas', *Australian Journal of Screen Theory*, **4**: 28.

[42] Doane (1988), p. 41.

scene. Her later sophisticated clothes, for example, as Richard Dyer points out, recall the pattern of her original frumpy dress combined with the style of her interim journey into glamour.[43] Such circularity also informs the development of her verbal communication with Dr Jaquith. In the beginning, she cannot look at him while she speaks, and delivers her opening words—'Introverted, Doctor'—in a sarcastically clipped tone. After a transitional phase, however, during which she references him more indirectly as a respected source of wisdom, through flashback, verbal references and a letter, she is rendered able to communicate with him in the most relaxed and familiar way. In the final party scene, most notably, she looks him directly in the eye and asks in an affectionately mocking tone: 'What are you looking at, Dr Owl?' She thus turns the very process of his examination back on him and gently undermines the authority previously signified by his title and name. At the same time, in recalling their original clinical relationship, she confidently lays bare the real question behind her initial barbed parody of self-analysis. Charlotte's transformation is therefore emphasized as a re-negotiation with her physical and emotional surroundings and her memories, rather than a miraculous shift between polar opposites. Therapy has not wiped her memory clean, but has given her the tools to re-fashion herself. Even though she still contains her old self, she is therefore different. Accordingly, her developing interaction with her emotions must be reflected through a new verbal and behavioural relationship to her own non-diegetic musical representation.

The importance of music to such an emotion- and memory-centred narrative is clear. It is through the score that elements of the past, and the various influences that affect Charlotte, can be kept alive and present. At the same time, musical variation can transform the past, and the particular dynamic of music to action and voice can recontextualize memories and influences and chart her current position in relation to the past. It is therefore impossible to understand the crucial role of interiority in this narrative, and the relationship of interiority to outward behaviour and appearances, without examining the score.[44] Such an emphasis on the past and emotional development is indicated in its densely thematic structure. Kate Daubney in fact suggests: 'Steiner's methodical interpretation of action through placement of musical themes can … be read as hyper-explicit, leading us on a journey through the story as explained by the different themes.'[45] It also seems, however, that the very musical construction of each theme indicates elements of its narrative bearing, including its significance in relation to the connotations of other themes. The musical themes themselves, through the particularity of their similarities and differences, therefore contain a kind of narrative of their own, establishing and working through interrelated emotional concerns in a purely musical way. Since the first appearances of most themes precede a full development of the narrative elements with which they are associated, music therefore becomes a vehicle of the characteristic omniscience of the melodramatic spectatorial position.

---

[43] Richard Dyer (1998), *Stars*, second revised edition, London: BFI, pp. 110–12.

[44] An excellent musicological analysis of the score of *Now, Voyager* is offered by Kate Daubney in *Max Steiner's* Now, Voyager*: A Film Score Guide*, Westport, Connecticut and London: Greenwood Press, 2000.

[45] Ibid., p. 46.

In order to examine the musical–emotional development of the film, I have divided it into four sections. Each of these marks a new stage in Charlotte's progress in terms of the two most important elements of her life: the maternal—whether as daughter or mother—and the potential marital relationship. Within each section I focus on key episodes that crystallize Charlotte's state of mind by presenting and re-presenting her interaction with various narrative themes and characters. This involves firstly considering the particular musical themes used in each scene in terms of their past and present significance, and secondly examining Charlotte's speech and behaviour in conjunction with these themes and their accumulated meanings. It is through this twofold approach—as I suggested in Chapter 1 and earlier in this chapter—that the specificity of Charlotte's version of female subjectivity ultimately emerges. Various repeated narrative motifs punctuate these episodes. Charlotte's four-part (re-)positioning in relation to the act of descending stairs, for example, marks her physical transformation, her mother's physical and metaphorical fall, and her final reincarnation through her 'daughter'. References to her mother, likewise, and most particularly her use of the term 'mother' itself, offer a periodic measure of her ongoing relationship to the original source of her repression and thus her quest for independence. Alongside such recurrent motifs, the interaction of musical themes and their relationship to other textual elements develop between the sections in ways that may initially seem incongruous. Often together with notable changes in the themes themselves, however, this actually allows a more sophisticated understanding of the subtle differences in the types of emotion, need and influence that inflect Charlotte's various relationships at different times.

While this segmented approach means that many music cues are not included in the analysis, this should not imply their irrelevance to the emotional meaning of the text, but merely that every minute nuance of Charlotte's development cannot be recorded here. There are also reasonably long sections of the film where composer Max Steiner uses non-thematic music both diegetically and non-diegetically. This fulfils more general place- and mood-setting functions, most significantly during Charlotte's two holidays. It is my contention that relevant themes are purposefully eschewed on such occasions in order to allow for a sense of time passing and experience being gained through which Charlotte can develop towards her next significant moment. As well as protecting the audience from complete emotional overload, this lends a greater emotional import to those occasions that are thematically scored. The main exception to this is examined in my analysis of the third section of the film, concerning Charlotte's engagement to Elliot Livingston.

The Main Musical Themes

The main musical themes are introduced in connection with Charlotte in her own view (henceforth the *Charlotte* theme), in her mother's view (the *Mother* theme), in connection with Jerry's initial kindness (the *Gift* theme), their subsequent relationship (the *Jerry* theme), and finally with Tina (the *Tina* theme).[46] The particular way in which each of these themes is constructed strongly suggests both their individual and related narrative connotations. At a very basic level, all the themes incorporate a similar pattern of repeated descending movement between pairs of notes. The *Mother* and *Tina* themes move primarily in close stepwise intervals, repeating pairs of notes sequentially with only a limited amount of deviation from this pattern. The *Charlotte*, *Gift* and *Jerry* themes, however, elaborate the movement between the notes, regardless of the width of the interval between them, retaining the emphasis on the framing pair of notes through accenting and longer note duration (Examples 2.1a–e show the melody lines of the main themes with the note pairs bracketed). While this may appear to suggest a relatively restricted emotional palette, it also evokes the idea of the presence of the same personality at the centre of each emotional response. This not only indicates how much density of emotion can be contained within one individual character, but also, and perhaps most importantly, the way in which those emotions can be closely related and even interdependent. Each emotional state experienced by the central character is not separate from all her other feelings, but is informed and constructed according to them. It is therefore possible that the subtleties of the musical–emotional relationships of the story, and the development of the main character, will be suggested in the dynamic of similarity and difference between all the themes. Before embarking on a more detailed examination of the musical and narrative development of each theme, therefore, it is instructive to note how the relationship between the themes may work in broader overall terms.

Example 2.1a Max Steiner, *Now, Voyager*, p. 1. The *Charlotte* theme

[46] If listed in strict chronological order, the first appearance of the *Tina* theme actually precedes that of the *Jerry* theme. It is such an isolated initial statement, however, that I have listed it in this context as appearing later. I have also named these themes based on my interpretation of their narrative significance; they are not so named in Max Steiner's score, nor on his cue sheet. I am indebted to Kate Daubney for access to her copy of this cue sheet. I am also indebted to her for access to her copy of Steiner's manuscript short score for *Now, Voyager*, which I have used as a source for both the musical extracts quoted and all references to Steiner's organization of and precise markings in the score made throughout this chapter.

Example 2.1b Max Steiner, *Now, Voyager*, p. 13. The *Mother* theme

Example 2.1c Max Steiner, *Now, Voyager*, p. 76. The *Gift* theme

Example 2.1d Max Steiner, *Now, Voyager*, p. 85. The *Jerry* theme

Example 2.1e Max Steiner, *Now, Voyager*, p. 73. The *Tina* theme

In terms of the basic similarity of movement between pairs of notes, the *Charlotte*, *Gift* and *Jerry* themes represent more elaborate and extended versions of the *Mother* and *Tina* themes. This elaboration raises the question of movement and the journey between two points as much as the beginning and end points/notes in themselves. If such a musical distinction can be read in narrative terms, it may be possible to say that the basic pair of notes represents the problematic maternal issue at the heart of Charlotte's story. The more melodically extended themes then indicate her experience of her own passage through life, and specifically the developments that facilitate her movement between daughterhood, adulthood and motherhood. This may explain why, although the *Mother* and *Tina* themes operate to resolve the original source of all Charlotte's narrative dilemmas, the story is actually framed by the *Charlotte* and *Jerry* themes.

Elements of similarity between the *Mother* and *Tina* themes (Examples 2.2 and 2.3) suggest the close proximity of Charlotte's relationships to her mother and Tina, a closeness that is also echoed in other textual elements. At the same time, however, pertinent differences between the themes lend them very distinct narrative properties and roles in relation to one another. The pairs of notes in each theme feature the repeated use of narrow descending intervals—major seconds in the *Mother* theme and alternating major and minor seconds in the *Tina* theme. The harmonic and rhythmic context of this unit, however, differs in such a way that the *Tina* theme offers a kind of 'answer' to the *Mother* theme. In its initial form, the *Mother* theme suggests a peculiar feeling of both stasis and instability. The sense of stasis comes from the almost monotonous repetition of the melody line and supporting chords. The slight deviation of the melody line into an ascent by the still narrow interval of a minor third seems only to emphasize this by its immediate return to the original note pairing. The melodic notes are tied, however, over the strong beats of the 6/8 metre in anticipation of the (further accented) supporting chords, which fall on the strong first and fourth beats of each bar. The overall rhythm therefore suggests a slightly unstable, 'rocking' or undulating effect. This is further emphasized by the countering of the melodic notes in the inner voices of the chords, so that as the melody moves from D# to C#, these voices move from C# to D#. Daubney points out that 'the effect of the music is only generated by the interaction between melody and accompaniment, and the theme would be ineffective without the combination of both elements'.[47] This construction of mutual dependence is central to the theme's narrative signification and thus my decision on how to name it. It suggests the restriction and confinement to which Charlotte is subject, as well as the precarious balance of her emotional state. It also contains within its own structure, however, the repressive mirror that Mrs Vale holds up to her daughter, convincing her of her own worthlessness. There are thus two people held within this theme, pushing against each other, so that each time the theme is heard, we are returned to the memory of Mrs Vale's opinion or depiction of Charlotte and its effect, rather than just Charlotte herself.

As Charlotte's relationship to her mother is replaced by her relationship to Tina, this instability is countered by the more stable rhythm, pointed harmonic direction and more urgent sense of movement and progression of the *Tina* theme. The undulation of the *Mother* theme's 6/8 rhythm and rhythmically weak, tied melodic notes is 'steadied' into a 3/4 metre with rhythmically strong appoggiatura notes. The particular effect of 'leaning' into the harmony that these notes offer suggests a yearning for resolution. The poignancy of this effect is emphasized by the notes that deviate from the paired pattern (i.e., the C in bar 2 and the F in bar 3 in Example 2.3). These leave the subsequent appoggiatura notes unprepared, which heightens the effect of their dissonance. These notes are resolved, but this resolution is nevertheless undermined by the constant upward chromatic movement of the bassline—which also delays the full resolution of bars 1 and 3 until the D of the third beat—as well as a frequent resolution onto seventh chords. The 'leaning' notes of the *Tina* theme foreground the resolution of dissonance through a figure that poignantly imitates the very sound of the young girl's name. The frequent resolution onto seventh chords, however, retains a sense of yearning and a lack of completeness within the repeated promise of a more satisfactory solution. In narrative terms, this seems to encapsulate both the possibilities and the difficulties of seeking to resolve the dissonance of the initial maternal relationship, Charlotte and her mother, through its replacement, Charlotte and Tina. What the *Tina* theme indicates most strongly in relation to the *Mother* theme, therefore, is the positive *potential* for change and the correction of past mistakes offered by the representation of Charlotte's first few steps into motherhood.

---

[47] Daubney, p. 59

Example 2.2 Max Steiner, *Now, Voyager*, pp. 7–8. The *Mother* theme

Example 2.3 Max Steiner, *Now, Voyager*, pp. 73–4. The *Tina* theme

In a similar way, the *Jerry* theme may ultimately offer a positive 'antidote' to the *Charlotte* theme, and in this context the *Gift* theme acts as a kind of transitory representation of the necessary interim inflation of Charlotte's spirits and self-confidence. All three themes, in elaborating the movement between notes, seem more concerned with the *way* in which Charlotte travels, as it were, rather than what her voyage is ultimately about. They seem less focused on the maternal issue itself, referring instead to the broader personal development that must happen in order to enable her to transform from daughter/child into mother/adult. If it is possible to say, therefore, that the *Mother* and *Tina* themes represent Charlotte as a daughter/mother, the *Charlotte*, *Gift* and *Jerry* themes refer to her as a person/woman. The salient differences between these latter three themes in this context may therefore be located in the style of movement between the framing notes.

This suggestion of a musical–narrative journey via thematic construction recalls Daubney's conception of the score as determined by an overarching movement from chromatic to diatonic harmony. She states:

> [The *Charlotte*, *Mother*, *Therapeutic*, *Vale* and *Jerry*] themes are key stages in a score-wide strategy of harmonic suggestion, created by the relative presence of chromatic and diatonic language. The progression from the chromatic to diatonic across the five themes noted above, mirrors the emotional and psychological experiences of the film's main character, Charlotte, in a way which is more far-reaching than could have been achieved by the development of a single theme.[48]

In light of this, it is tempting to suggest that the statement of the *Charlotte* theme that accompanies the main titles incorporates something of the emotional trajectory of the whole film in its own extremely compact development. It opens in a style imbued with turbulence, but after a relatively subdued middle section returns to a more harmonically stable version of its own opening material and ends in a major key before segueing into the story itself. It is the first four bars of the theme that may therefore suggest Charlotte's position at the outset of the narrative (Example 2.4). The framing pairs of notes in each of the phrases of the theme fall on the—further accented—strong first beats of the bar, giving the theme a definite sense of shape and movement. A further sense of urgency is added by the tying of the melodic notes at the beginning of bars 1 and 3, so that the underlying chords seem to be forcefully striving to push the melody onwards. A sense of dramatic tension is created by the musical tension between major and minor tonality—an effect that is exacerbated by the laborious semitonal movement of notes between the chords as well as their harmonic complexity. The intervals of the melody are relatively narrow, giving a sense of drama to the suddenly expanded descending interval between the final two notes.

The pessimistic turbulence implied in these forcible shifts and complex harmonies is underlined by aspects of orchestration and performance. The full symphonic rendition is heralded by a brass fanfare and a rapidly ascending string glissando. The melody is played in a strong, marked style in the strings and echoed by a similarly accented countermelody in the brass and cellos. The first, third and last note of each repeated phrase is marked by the timpani, and the use of rubato emphasizes the weightiness of the movement towards the final descending interval. The second statement of the theme begins at a higher pitch and is once again emphasized by glissando notes, this time ending on a cymbal crash on the first melodic note. The strident style and emphatic use of glissandi and percussion thus evoke the sense of a powerful emotional struggle between potential defeat and the continual striving for something seemingly beyond the limits of the music. Such an emotionally charged and truly melodramatic musical opening seems to match the accompanying image of a massive liner in transit.

---

[48] Daubney, p. 71. Daubney's interpretation of how the themes relate to characterization is different in several places to my own. For the purposes of clarity, therefore, I have changed the names of the musical themes to my own. In this particular quotation, the themes as she lists them are: 'Voyager, Charlotte, Dr. Jaquith, Mrs. Vale and the love themes'.

Example 2.4 Max Steiner, *Now, Voyager*, p. 1. The *Charlotte* theme. Opening title sequence

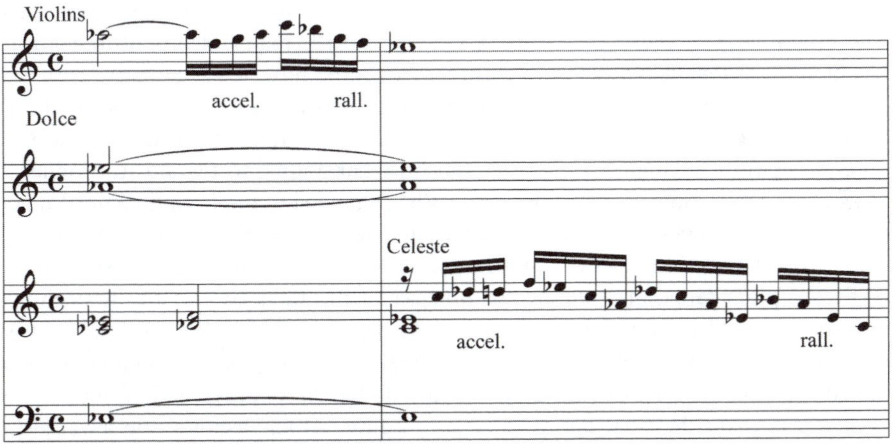

Example 2.5 Max Steiner, *Now, Voyager*, p. 76. The *Gift* theme

Example 2.6 Max Steiner, *Now, Voyager*, pp. 85–6. The *Jerry* theme

The *Gift* theme follows a very similar overall pattern, but eschews the turbulence and drama of the *Charlotte* theme's first appearance in favour of smoother melodic movement and less complex harmony (Example 2.5). The contour of the melody follows a more consistently smooth rise and fall of predominantly stepwise intervals, with a narrower interval between the framing pair of notes. The major tonality, lighter texture and more fluid movement—including the celesta that replaces the brass and cello countermelody of the *Charlotte* theme—supersede the previous sense of pessimism with a feeling of excitement.[49] This is compounded by the second statement of the theme beginning at the same pitch as the first, but with the passage of notes reaching a minor third higher, and the framing interval being narrowed. The modulation of the theme from A flat major to E major also contributes to a brightening of tone and a sense of the music 'opening out'.

The *Jerry* theme pares down the detail of the previous themes while retaining their basic overall shape (Example 2.6). It maintains the positive tone of the *Gift* theme, but further simplifies the melodic line, harmony and texture to produce a more serene and controlled final version. While the idea of the framing pair of notes remains, this is smoothed into a descending line of even narrower intervals than in the *Gift* theme. The melodic movement between the framing notes uses a more restricted pitch range and number of notes, and the final note of the first phrase is also sustained to become the first note of the second phrase. Each of the first two phrases ends by emphasizing upward rather than downward movement, with an added touch of lightness being given by the dotted rhythm. Ascending movement is accentuated in the final optimistic rising figure, which seems to be a variation on the initial ascent of the countermelodies of both the *Charlotte* and *Gift* themes. The lack of such a countermelody gives the *Jerry* theme a less complex and more homogenous texture. The seventh chord at the highest point of the ascent, however, yearns for the resolution that only follows from the transition into a new key for the theme's repetition.

The movement from the *Charlotte* to the *Jerry* theme therefore suggests that Charlotte's discovery of desirability and romance gives her the capacity to chart a less troubled and turbulent course. The *Jerry* theme moves with a kind of grace that, in the terms described in Chapter 1, might be more associated with acceptable,

[49] Steiner uses the spelling 'celeste' rather than 'celesta' in the short score. I have used his spelling in the extracts quoted.

rather than dangerously excessive, femininity. It retains a similar overall shape to the *Charlotte* and *Gift* themes, but eschews their sense of either turbulent drama or fluttering excitement. The chromaticism and major/minor tension of the *Charlotte* theme, although eventually 'tamed' within the title sequence, is more permanently resolved in the more straightforward harmonies and progression of the *Gift* and *Jerry* themes. Where the *Charlotte* theme is also characterized by struggle, with any attempt at upward movement always eventually defeated by further descent, the *Jerry* theme places greater emphasis on ascending movement, which in turn suggests both lightness and a transcendent sense of yearning. As Charlotte realizes her own desirability, therefore, she achieves a maturity and sense of inner calm that eradicates anything that might be considered extraneous or unnecessarily elaborate in her musical–emotional representation.

The two remaining themes, designated according to their respective narrative associations as *Therapeutic* and *Vale*, appear less centred on Charlotte's interiorized response to influences than on the influences themselves. The most important of these is the *Therapeutic* theme. Although this is originally associated with Dr Jaquith and the Cascade institution, it often appears independently of the mention of either. In so doing, it becomes more indicative of the therapeutic influence in a general sense. In the same way that the story's maternal issue becomes universalized, therefore, the power of recuperation becomes an effect that shifts between characters, which seems to comment as much on the nature of relationships as on Charlotte's personal cure. Both of these themes, perhaps because of their initial representation of attempts to contradict the flow of Charlotte's life, accentuate ascending movement. It is the strength offered by the ascent of the *Therapeutic* theme (Example 2.7) that prepares Charlotte for resisting the power of the *Vale* theme (Example 2.8).

Example 2.7 Max Steiner, *Now, Voyager*, pp. 17–18. The *Therapeutic* theme

Example 2.8 Max Steiner, *Now, Voyager*, p. 142. The *Vale* theme

'My mother! My mother! My mother!': The Introduction of Charlotte

The basis of Charlotte's problems, and the relationship to music, sound and vocality that initially defines her position in relation to her mother, marriage and her potential cure are established through the interaction of the three major elements of the first section of the film—the opening title music, which I describe above, Charlotte's current situation in her Boston home, and her own view of herself in the past.

The Vale household, in direct opposition to the musical turbulence of the main titles, is a monument to the repressive control of sound—the ultimate mark of the omnipotence exercised by Mrs Vale. With 'ears like a cat'[50] she can monitor other characters without need of sight—Charlotte through a squeaking stair-tread, the noise made by party guests and the doorbell, for example, and Dr Jaquith through the tapping of tobacco from his pipe. The equation of such control with the repression of self-expression is symbolized by the formally measured and functional chiming of the grandfather clock—the first sound heard after the opening title music—which also allows Mrs Vale to know the time without looking. The grand piano in the drawing room is reduced to nothing more than a piece of furniture and, very unusually, is never played. Most important to this sonic landscape, however, is Charlotte—the personification of her mother's regime. Her initial complete inability to speak evokes the idea that she has been historically 'silenced', actually and metaphorically, by her mother's view of her. Indeed, as she first appears before her sister-in-law, niece and Dr Jaquith, her mother compounds her vocal inability by drawing attention to her silence. It is symbolic, given the description of her own particular brand of hearing quoted above, and her depiction in the same scene of Charlotte as a 'moulting canary', that she asks her: 'The cat got your tongue?' Charlotte's lack of vocality is thus presented as the result of a violent appropriation, with Mrs Vale and her daughter playing out the roles of predator and prey. So powerful is her control over her daughter's self-expression that she is able to speak about her in her presence, without Charlotte even having the ability to respond. When Charlotte flees from the room, however, it is to the accompaniment of sequentially rising music that suggests her growing distress despite her continued lack of speech. Accordingly, when Dr Jaquith says that he likes (noisy) pipes because they are 'messy things', he becomes representative of Basinger's opposite lifestyle choice for Charlotte.[51] As he breaks Mrs Vale's regime, so he will free Charlotte's voice. His influence will present her with the possibility of a life that eschews the symbolic silence of socially sanctioned repression, for a more philosophical embracing of unconventional, disordered and complicated individuality.

Although Charlotte's condition is introduced through dialogue, the truly horrific extent of her mother's emotional power only becomes clear through the particular combination of image, sound and music that marks her first actual appearance. As she is called from her bedroom to join her mother in the drawing room, the ivory carving on which she is working is spoiled by a slip of the hand. Immediately, the reappearance of the theme from the opening titles constitutes Charlotte as the 'voyager' of the film's title, while simultaneously registering the emotional impact of her current situation. The previously strident style is reduced in scale and tempo to a plaintive solo cello line, supported by sparse strings rather than the solid sound of the brass. The use of rubato now gives a feeling of hesitancy and the end of each

---

50 This description of Mrs Vale comes much later in the film and is the assessment of her nurse, Dora Pickford (Mary Wickes).

51 Basinger, pp. 19–21.

phrase is no longer marked by strongly accented chords. Instead, the final note of the melodic phrase leads straight into a slow, chromatic rising and falling variation on the original countermelody. Despite the higher pitch on which the second phrase begins, the sense of striving of the earlier version is undermined by the feeling of tentative, indecisive, defeated movement.

In order to explain the weakness suggested by this transformed *Charlotte* theme, the *Mother* theme follows immediately to accompany Charlotte's first descent of the staircase. This suggests her mother's definition of her as the root of her problems, linking her visual unattractiveness—suggested initially by our view of only her feet and legs clad in ugly heavy shoes and stockings—with her current lack of voice.[52] The nature of this relationship is achieved not only through the *Mother* theme's musical structure, however, but also by a pointed manipulation of the whole soundtrack. The only diegetic sound accompanying her descent is her mother's voice, amplified into a consistently audible voice-over. This psychologically motivated volume ignores the changing spatial relation of Charlotte, or indeed the film audience, to the actual sound source, in order to privilege the centrality of her mother's opinion to her identity. The attachment of the non-diegetic music's chords to each of her footfalls—together with the cage-like mise-en-scène of the heavy wooden spindles of the staircase behind which she is seen—suggests an emotional proscription that pens every aspect of her plodding, aimless existence within her mother's words and opinions. As she nears the bottom of the stairs, she hesitates and makes to retreat as her mother describes her as her 'ugly duckling'. The significance of the music is then ultimately linked to Dr Jaquith's implication that Charlotte was an unwanted child.

The construction of this theme as a constricted version of the *Charlotte* theme, however, already begins to suggest what is later confirmed in her self-defining flashback. Charlotte has always contained and still does contain within her the self-confident, sexually attractive and active woman that she will become once again in the future. This therefore proves that her current appearance is neither her true self-image nor indeed her true self. As she is trapped and constrained by her mother, so is the expansiveness of her theme and, accordingly, during her flashback, the use of the *Charlotte* theme reiterates both the contrast and its process of development and fragmentation. Charlotte's vision of herself as a young woman on a holiday cruise, in love with the ship's Wireless Officer Leslie Trotter (Charles Drake), begins with a light celesta glissando leading up to a string and vibraphone statement of the theme. The orchestral texture is lighter, with strings and woodwind replacing the previous brass in the supporting chords and countermelody. The performance style is more lyrical and smooth, and is marked in the score as 'appassionato' and 'expressivo' (*sic*) as opposed to the opening statement's 'broad'. Together with a lack of the previous heavy accenting, this counters the dramatic tension with which the opening statement imbued the shifts in tonality and final falling intervals. As the young and carefree Charlotte approaches her mother for the first time, however, the negative maternal influence becomes apparent. The *Charlotte* theme fragments as she is forced to make herself conventionally unattractive by wearing her spectacles and is denied permission to socialize with the other passengers (Example 2.9). Despite the

---

52 LaPlace, p. 142.

theme's triumphant return as she and Leslie defy her mother within the flashback, therefore, the retention of its more negative form as she returns to the present is firmly associated with her imminent nervous breakdown.

Example 2.9 Max Steiner, *Now, Voyager*, p. 25. The *Charlotte* theme, Charlotte's flashback

Charlotte's flashback establishes what is perhaps the primary contention of the narrative—the potential disjuncture of outward appearance and interior emotion. Her silencing and de-specularization are indivisible. Indeed, even in her finest moment, when Leslie publicly declares his love for her, she defies her mother's resistance to their relationship more by proxy than directly. Despite Charlotte's declaration that she doesn't care that they have been discovered, it is Leslie who really confounds Mrs Vale with his speech, and her command that Charlotte return to her room is met with pride, but nevertheless silent compliance. Her mother's appropriation of Charlotte's voice—nascent here, but about to grow and strengthen—parallels her control of her emotions and sexuality. As a result, in contrast to her mother's absolute control of sound in the present, the depth of Charlotte's repressed emotions means that any attempt at their verbal expression overwhelms her and induces a breakdown into angry shouting, tears or further strained silence. The non-diegetic music, evidencing the magnitude of the repression that her mother has effected, emphasizes her inability to break productively its associated silence. Her narration of her own flashback, therefore, describing and representing her rebellious feelings alongside surging music, demonstrates her true emotional as much as physical potential. This promise of an eventual return to the more familiar Bette Davis face and persona allows greater concentration on the longer and more complex process of Charlotte's inner development, which is represented through the gradual realignment of her speech and behaviour with her musical–emotional representation and most notably in her progression from 'being silenced' to 'remaining silent'. The temporal disjuncture between her physical and emotional correction is expressed visually in the repeated difficulty of characters in recognizing her in her transformed state. This perhaps accounts for why she herself does not seem to convincingly settle into her new life until the last scene.

At the same time as the film establishes Charlotte's repression by her mother, and contrasts past and present to reassure the film audience of her natural but stymied feelings towards men, it also presents her escape route. Dr Jaquith follows Charlotte upstairs in her flight from her mother's barbed comments and the invasive discussion about her mental health in the drawing room. Although the *Mother* theme reappears at this point, his refusal to allow her emotional retreat effects the detachment of the theme from Charlotte's steps. This freeing of her movement in turn seems to enable her self-expression so that she can break her silence, albeit in a rather clipped manner, for the first time. A sudden shift in shot construction, however, signals a continuing difficulty. As she proffers her sarcastic self-diagnosis—'Introverted, Doctor'—she is abruptly placed in profile at the right hand foreground of the frame, looking off-screen while Dr Jaquith regards her in astonishment. Since the focus has previously been on Charlotte's gaze as she tentatively watched Dr Jaquith, this change of shot suggests that her gaze, voice and music are still very much out of kilter and cannot yet co-exist. The potential that Dr Jaquith's freeing of her movement offers, however, is nevertheless confirmed by the *Therapeutic* theme, which appears as his fascination with Charlotte's ivory craftwork prompts her profession that he is 'the least clumsy person [she has] ever met'. At this point, thanks to his benevolent persistence, she is able to exercise her first extended gaze in the present—something that her flashback reveals was not a problem in the past.

It is only after the flashback that Charlotte can begin to speak with any eloquence, but even then this is only in a very particular musical context. Prior to her flashback, her emotional outbursts in front of the doctor were accompanied firstly by a repeat of the music that suggested her distress during her flight from the drawing room, and then by the *Charlotte* theme, returned to its original stormy state, as she opened her photograph album to begin telling her story. After the end of her flashback, however, her current feelings towards her mother are finally expressed, over a long crescendo chord. She becomes increasingly agitated and finally reveals the root of her repression as she cries: 'My mother! My mother! My mother!' Having given expression to these feelings, she can at last speak clearly as she asks Dr Jaquith for his help. Rather than this taking place against the background of the *Charlotte* or *Mother* themes, however, it is accompanied by the *Therapeutic* theme. Under Dr Jaquith's influence, we now understand that she will be able to speak and express herself. Dr Jaquith's approach to psychoanalysis is therefore represented as a branch of humanity rather than medicine. He does not have to force, persuade or drug Charlotte into speaking, but enables her voice and begins to change her relationship to her own emotions—and therefore to her non-diegetic music—by his genuine benevolent interest. Charlotte's cure can therefore remain in her own control by arising from her own desire for help, allowing her inner 'Bette Davis' to confront the doctor with Charlotte's problems.

'I was thinking of my mother': Charlotte, the Cruise and Jerry

Charlotte's second staircase descent begins the next stage of her emotional development—the holiday cruise on which Dr Jaquith advises her to be 'interested in everything, and everybody'. Recalling the scene of her original oppression, she is awaited and watched with equal interest by the other passengers, including the next man in her life. Now, however, her previous unattractiveness has been magically eradicated, with the camera revealing stylishly clad feet and legs before moving up the body of an *apparently* very different Charlotte. The music, following the ascending camera movement, surrounds her in admiration rather than restriction. The *Mother* theme accompanying her descent is played at a higher pitch and the timbre is lightened by the addition of harp, celesta and vibraphone to the strings.

Even though it follows the same rhythm as before, it clearly does not coincide with her footfalls. The patterns of the past therefore continue in the present, inviting reflection on Charlotte's transformation so far. The nature of her first descent has been stylistically modified by the effect of her staircase ascent with Dr Jaquith, which began to loosen the musical–emotional maternal grip. This time we watch Charlotte, rather than just her feet, and the transformation of the music seems to reflect her physical and emotional progress. At the same time, however, there is a suggestion that this 'normal' appearance is still largely a façade. She has clearly moved beyond her previous state, but her introduction through a false name suggests a continued difficulty with identity, particularly since we learn that she has clearly made no effort to correct the mistake and has barely been out of her cabin so far. As if in explanation of this as she first appears, her hesitation, the doubtful expression on her partially obscured face, her very brief speech, and the fact that the *Mother* theme remains with her despite its own transformation, attest to the memories that still battle to inform her concealed self-image.

During the holiday and Charlotte's discovery of romantic love, the *Charlotte* theme is gradually superseded by the *Jerry* theme via the *Gift* theme. The score then focuses on the 'traffic' between the *Mother*, *Jerry* and *Therapeutic* themes, and the implications of this for the passage of Charlotte's emotions and self-definition. Despite therapy, she begins her journey without having moved beyond her mother as a touchstone influence. Her initial moments of independence or defiance therefore take place against this memory. Even when redefined by Jerry's presence as a desirable 'wife', she still remains otherwise defined as a daughter—the imposed eternal child/virgin role and most obvious sidestepping of motherhood that underpins her outwardly adult status as spinster 'Aunt Charlotte'. Towards the end of her journey, however, the direct link between the *Jerry* and *Therapeutic* themes renders Jerry her new recuperative influence. This shift gives her the strength to face the past in a different way when she returns to Boston.

During Charlotte and Jerry's first conversation, Charlotte recalls the influences of both Dr Jaquith and her mother. The reminiscence of Dr Jaquith's advice is accompanied by an ethereal version of the *Therapeutic* theme, played by high-pitched strings supported by harp, celesta, piano and vibraphone. The delicate timbre of this orchestration, as well as the smooth melodic line and chordal texture, suggests his continued positive influence. By stark contrast, her recollection of her mother returns us to her earlier flashback and is accompanied by the same fragmentation, a semitone higher, of the *Charlotte* theme (see Example 2.9). The comparatively shrill sound of the flute and clarinet triplets and the chaotic nature of their hasty descent place her once again in the context of her youthful distortion. Her two basic emotional—and musical—influences are now placed in direct conflict for dominance over her behaviour. The transfer of her contemptuous tone of voice from her original encounter with Dr Jaquith to her verbal reference to her mother, however, as she tells Jerry, 'I was thinking of my mother', offers another glimpse of Bette Davis—this time with a surprisingly strong recollection of her capacity for bitchiness. This not only demonstrates Charlotte's desire to reject the past, but allows her to express contempt for her mother and her opinions—at least those on travelling—against the musical background that signified the original effect that these had on her. This is a more than marked improvement on the guilty and evasive tone with which she asked after her mother at Cascade when Lisa came to collect her and dispatch her on the cruise, and having achieved this, she immediately agrees to see as many tourist sights as Jerry wishes—a direct contravention of her mother's earlier instructions. While this shows strong signs of progress, however, Charlotte is still not able, in their following conversation, to utter her own name without becoming clearly upset—this taking place even without any non-diegetic themes to face her overtly with her memories or insecurities.

As Jerry shows Charlotte his family photograph after she has helped him buy presents for his daughters, the close juxtaposition of the *Tina* and *Mother* themes suggests both Tina's future role as resolution to the maternal dilemma and Charlotte's current unreadiness for the salvation of 'motherhood'. Mrs Vale's future absence from the text is necessitated by Charlotte's still unrelinquished musical–emotional 'daughter' self-image, represented by the *Mother* theme's appearance as she recognizes Tina as an unwanted child through the similarity of their experiences and attitudes. At the same time, before the question arises of a relationship between Charlotte and Jerry, his emotional influence is represented as more paternal, equating her to Tina with a benevolent, seemingly platonic concern. This allows his later romantic interest to replace Dr Jaquith in the narrative's 'recuperation cycle'. Despite the difficulties represented by the appearance of the *Mother* theme, however, Charlotte's verbalization of Tina's plight in fact represents a progression in terms of her self-expression. She appears to surprise herself with her ability to voice her own dilemma, and this is indeed an unusually strong moment since it takes place against the music that signifies that dilemma. However, this is mitigated by the expression being once again by proxy. Although we know that Charlotte is talking at least partly about herself, she is of course actually referring to Tina. At this point, therefore, she can express her own dilemma against the music that signifies it only in terms of its applying to someone else. This stage of her vocal development is also reflected in her tendency to allow Jerry to speak for her or tell her what to say. Apart from the fact that he renames her, of course, she also defers to his choice when asked what she would like to drink, he speaks almost entirely on her behalf when they meet Deb (Lee Patrick) and Mack (James Rennie), and when he tells her not to give him an answer to his initial romantic overtures, but to say 'I'll see', she dutifully replies, 'I'll see'.

When Charlotte later shows Jerry her own family photograph it reveals—as her earlier holiday photograph and account of herself did to Dr Jaquith—what really lies behind her current disguise. Just as her memory of her own youthful emotional strength precipitated her breakdown in front of the doctor, so the memories associated with the *Mother* theme, and the necessity of verbalizing references to both her mother and herself, now cause her loss of control and confessional self-revelation to Jerry. Her continued daughter/spinster/aunt self-image becomes evident, laying bare her limbo state of being neither 'the fat lady with the heavy brows and all the hair' nor that mythical ideal of sophistication whose identity she has partially borrowed through her name, her place on the cruise and her clothes: 'Renée Beauchamp.'[53] This incongruity of musical theme and exterior appearance makes sense of the intervening non-thematic holiday music, which serves to withhold the reality of her confusion over her own identity and makes a rather ironic coincidence of Mack's initial excitement that she might be 'the famous Beauchamp … the one who does all the imitations'.

Jerry responds sympathetically to her revelation, however, prompting Charlotte to offer a full list of all the kind things he has done and to credit him profusely for making her feel 'much better'. The *Gift* theme has already suggested Jerry's dramatically positive effect on her self-image when he gave her a gift of perfume. Now, the delicate string orchestration and lilting rhythm of the *Jerry* theme consolidate this as Charlotte speaks her words of gratitude. The music at this crucial turning point, however, introduces Jerry's benevolent paternal rather than romantic role. The turbulent version of the *Jerry* theme in the subsequent montage suggests Charlotte's restless night of confused identity and desire, which ends with a segue into a 'calmed' version of the *Mother* theme as Jerry writes to Tina (Example 2.10). While Charlotte's personal identity remains in crisis, Jerry is unwittingly forging her destiny. The poignancy of his letter—with music played according to Steiner's customized 'schmaltzo' marking—lies partly in its shared assessment of both Charlotte and Tina. Jerry comes to understand his own daughter more fully as a result of his sympathetic concern for Charlotte. At the same time, a steadier rhythm is effected by more sustained supporting chords, and the theme reaches a harmonic resolution as his letter ends and the screen fades momentarily to black. This suggests a positive future in the mutually beneficial grouping of all three characters.

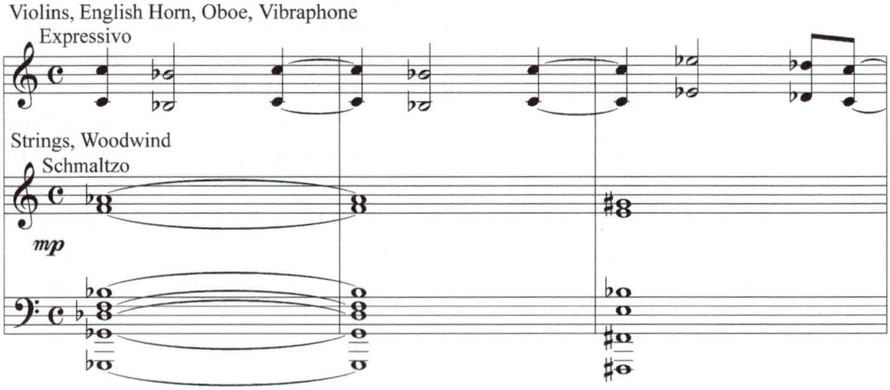

Example 2.10 Max Steiner, *Now, Voyager*, p. 89. The *Mother* theme, 'calmed' version

[53] The first description is Jerry's unwitting comment on her old incarnation in her family photograph. Renée Beauchamp, as the friend whose place Charlotte takes on the cruise, offers a spectre of glamour and sophistication through the clothes and accessories that she lends Charlotte for the trip and the instructions on how to dress and co-ordinate outfits that she has pinned to various garments. Since she is never actually seen, however, she seems at first to represent an ideal to which Charlotte simply cannot aspire.

Jerry's appropriation of the caring role, which shifts the power of recuperation from therapy to love, is finalized in the development of Charlotte's responses to his romantic overtures across two scenes, the first on their hotel balcony and the second at the airport. As Jerry approaches her on the hotel balcony Charlotte appears to regress to her former terse and evasive self, unable to converse in a properly relaxed way and avoiding his gaze. When Jerry begins his declaration of love, the *Jerry* theme represents the effect of his love on Charlotte. She is silenced once again, but this time by the tears that signify the former impossibility of such a moment. As we see that she has started to cry, the *Therapeutic* theme appears, before being replaced once again by the *Jerry* theme. The delicacy of the theme's first appearance is developed into fuller 'appassionato' chords and a more insistent tempo as Jerry notices what she calls her 'tears of gratitude ... for the crumbs offered' and they kiss. In the following scene, however, we see the real effect of Jerry's love on Charlotte. On the balcony Jerry still took vocal control, telling her in response to her self-deprecation: 'Don't talk like that.' She, on the other hand, was finally able to say exactly what she felt about herself, under the influence of being loved, and her attempt at vocal empowerment when she asked that he 'let [her] go' was clearly not heartfelt. At the airport, however, she is at last returned to the passionate woman of her first flashback. She gazes directly and intensely at Jerry and speaks openly. She takes control of their conversation and reminds him of their agreement that they are 'both to go home'—even though her voice falters at the very mention of her destination—and they kiss as romantic equals. Charlotte can now speak and express herself confidently against the backdrop of the *Jerry* theme. Knowledge of being loved has moved her to the next stage of her development.

Removal from home has allowed Charlotte a rapid 're-visiting' of the conventional adolescent progression from one kind of love to another, which was stymied during her own physical transition into womanhood. The development of Jerry's feelings from friendly through benevolent paternal to adult romantic love therefore moves her further from the past in a way unavailable to Dr Jaquith. Since Jerry's marital unavailability means that Charlotte is still unable to escape her mother's domestic setting, however, she must instead use her new desirability as a source of personal strength with which to confront her past. Returned to the same attractive, marriageable state that she occupied in her own first flashback, the only remaining obstacle to her full psychological entrance into adulthood is her mother.

'I'm not afraid, mother': Charlotte's Return to Boston

Charlotte's return from her holiday to Boston marks the third stage of her emotional development. This is characterized by a precarious oscillation between almost compromising her desires in order to conform—to the expectations of her mother, society or both—and her growing sense of self-sufficiency and independence. The latter is propelled chiefly by Jerry, despite him being more or less absent throughout, and is signified through her eventual decision not to marry and have her own family—a vital preparation for her ultimate self-styled appropriation of the maternal role. The musical–emotional influences that have altered her relationship to her self and the maternal/parental role while she was away empower her in direct combat with her mother's attempts to reinstate her oppression. As Mrs Vale weakens, Charlotte becomes more self-confident.

Initially, however, her self-assurance with the memory of Dr Jaquith's advice, and the *Therapeutic* theme, does not quite seem to prepare her for withstanding the tirade of abuse with which her mother greets her return. As she enters her mother's room, Charlotte occupies a dominant place in the frame, stands over her mother as she greets her, and speaks in a confident and forthright manner. Mrs Vale, of course, can doubtless sense the performance of such a demeanour and wastes no time in breaking it down. She immediately repositions Charlotte as the object of her critical gaze, instructing her in exactly where and how to pose and move as she examines her. As she pronounces that Charlotte's state is 'worse than Lisa led [her] to suppose, much worse', the lowering of Charlotte's eyes indicates that her mother's instinct was correct and there is every chance that Charlotte can be once again brought under complete maternal control. Her mother now dominates the frame as she is seen looking at Charlotte, with the reverse shots showing Charlotte caught in the full glare of her mother's gaze—reduced to a small, vulnerable figure in the middle of the floor, framed between the sturdy wooden posts of the bed in which she was born, her head bowed and her hands fiddling awkwardly with her glamorous hat.

Similarly, just as the house remains a sonic testament to Mrs Vale's control—true to form, she heard the doorbell and knew that Charlotte had arrived before she could be told—so she now also re-appropriates her daughter's voice. Charlotte's initially confident speech is silenced firstly by the humiliating catwalk display to which her mother subjects her and then under the power of her final verbal tirade and the inevitable reappearance of the *Mother* theme. Beginning with an exact repetition of its original statement, this time marked 'triste' in the score, this registers the sad possibility that things may merely return to their previous state, or at the very least that her mother may wish them to. Daubney points out that Steiner actually employs three consecutive statements of the theme here, 'falling a major third each time … giving the sense of descent into gloom'.[54] Both the narrative associations of the theme and its particular musical treatment therefore contribute to the precarious feel of Charlotte's state of mind at this crucial moment. Indeed, she seems to be leaning towards capitulation over wearing her old, unflattering dress for the evening's dinner party, as her mother has planned, when she indicates to the maid that the seamstress may come to her room later to make any necessary alterations. Victory is snatched from the jaws of defeat, however, by the timely arrival of the camellias that signify the desirable 'Camille' alter ego given to Charlotte by Jerry during their affair. As she sees the flowers, the *Jerry* theme reappears for the first time since her holiday ended. Also returned to its original key, orchestration and style, this recalls for both Charlotte and the film audience the first time that the full therapeutic effect of Jerry's loving support became clear. The pain of their physical separation is therefore superseded. While he is no longer with her in person, the flowers offer evidence of his continued love, and so promise the survival of Charlotte's positive self-image.

In order for Charlotte finally to speak up against her mother's financial and emotional influence, however, she must initially absent herself in some way from

[54] Daubney, p. 78.

the latter's direct gaze or presence. When her mother visits her room to challenge her for a second time, Charlotte speaks confidently and assertively to her, but turns her back and looks at her primarily through reflection in the mirror or hides out of shot to change her clothes as she speaks. Her underlying emotional development from one speech to the next is then registered in their thematic accompaniments. The first speech comes in response to Mrs Vale's attack, following the delivery of the flowers, on Charlotte's status as a guest in her mother's house. This attack introduces, in the face of obviously waning personal influence, the austere *Vale* theme's representation of the social and financial power of the family name. Charlotte is able to resist her despite the continuation of this theme, and following this, as her mother asks about the flowers, the *Gift* theme implies her return to the excitement of her interim development through Jerry's kindness and attention and suggests his influence as the strength behind her resistance. As Charlotte attempts to lay down new rules for their mother–daughter relationship, this theme signifies that she stands halfway between her old and new positions with regard to her mother. Her mother then rebukes her once again, expressing her grave disappointment in Charlotte as a daughter. This time, Charlotte's resistance constitutes an even more significant development for her, as she maintains her stance even against the backdrop of an ominous, heavily accented version of the *Mother* theme. Marked 'slow and heavy' in the score, this registers the personal power of her mother's opinion. It continues as Mrs Vale responds to her daughter's new resilience with her symbolic, self-induced fall down the very staircase that originally signified her oppressive power. At this point, the tempo of the *Mother* theme is held back further to prepare for its dramatic culmination in a sustained, dissonant, fortissimo chord as Mrs Vale 'stumbles'. The progress of this same theme faltered during Charlotte's initial descent of this staircase in response to her mother's hurtful words. Now, its interruption marks the narrative conclusion of her power, thus enabling a further stage of Charlotte's transformation of the maternal influence. As she subsequently walks from the stairway into the gaze of the family and friends assembled by her mother to greet her return, including, of course, the next significant man in her life, she therefore does so with her appearance and personality one step closer together.

The ultimate success of this first social test on 'home territory' allows the next key stage of her vocal and musical–emotional relationship to her use of the word 'mother', with her evangelical realization, to the accompaniment of the *Mother* theme: 'I'm not afraid, mother.' The relatively high pitch, light orchestration (strings and celesta) and faster tempo of this version seem to suggest the literal lightening of the burden of maternal tyranny. This leads in turn to Mrs Vale's first demonstrable loss of control over the sonic environment of the house. Thanks to the alcohol in her hot toddy and nurse Dora's head massage, Mrs Vale begins to doze, but still attempts to add to Charlotte's sense of guilt by heaping praise on her nurse for her superior care and good sense. Dora is able to fool her patient, however, by telling her that Charlotte has already left the room and so cannot hear her mother's words. Following Dora's direction, Charlotte slips unheard from the room as her mother becomes increasingly groggy. Her movements within the house are, therefore, finally out of her mother's aural control, if only temporarily and if only thanks to the help of another proponent of benevolence as therapy.

Charlotte's subsequent relationship with Elliot Livingston, despite appearances to the contrary, actually seems to represent her second and most important moment of oscillation towards potential defeat. This in no way equals the fate of repressed servitude that her mother originally had in mind for her, but does nevertheless represent a serious compromise through which she can be reconciled not only with her mother but also with 'normal' women and society in general. As Daubney points out, however, the music that characterizes this relationship is not only, as it were, 'borrowed', but also exists solely in the diegetic realm.[55] This therefore presents a musical–emotional echo of the borrowed and inappropriate identity that both signalled and concealed her difficulties during her holiday cruise. Since Charlotte now understands all too well that 'borrowed wings' do not suit her, it seems clear that although all may appear to be well in a superficial sense, her story cannot possibly end here. Like the heavy evening gown of Renée Beauchamp, this emotional bad fit must also be discarded in order for Charlotte to return to the veracity of her non-diegetic musical–emotional representation and, accordingly, find her own individual conclusion to her story.

The use of the *Therapeutic* theme as Dr Jaquith reads Charlotte's letter telling of her imminent engagement to Elliot might suggest that marriage and children will supersede Jerry as the final stage of the therapeutic cycle. There is certainly social desirability in marrying Charlotte off to a Livingston; as her mother says, 'I'm only so astonished that you of all the family should bring such a feather to the family cap'. Both this and Charlotte's rather abstract desire for the domestic set-up that she believes 'almost every woman wants' are, however, ultimately confounded by the pestering memory of the selfhood and love that she discovered on her holiday cruise. The hopelessness of her relationship with Elliot is actually made clear from the outset by its very representation. In a similar way to the opening section of the film, this makes a stark and dynamic contrast of past potential and present repression through a pointed mobilization of memory, music and sound. Charlotte's only chance of surviving marriage to Elliot would have rested on her tolerance of leading a double life, contenting herself in her bored repression with the memory of her secret love. Her evident technical ability to conduct such a charade lies in the new relationship to her voice and to music that follows her partial appropriation of her mother's power. It is this same vocal, emotional and narrative power, however, that ultimately allows her to face up to and reject her attempt to play at conventionality. In this instance, therefore, sound and music are used to demonstrate emotional distance rather than proximity.

Charlotte purposefully manipulates the use of voice and language in order to delineate and control Elliot. Her letter to Dr Jaquith has a decidedly uncommitted tone that his bemused expression suggests he has also detected, and her later descriptions to Jerry of both her relationship and her fiancé are framed in a negative light by being compared to their own affair. When he asks if she loves Elliot, she replies: 'Not like we do. Not like us. I thought it might grow to be, or something like it.' Similarly, when asked what kind of man Elliot is, she reveals yet more compromise: '[He is] like you [Jerry] in many ways. Oh, not your sense of humour nor your sense of

---

55 Ibid., p. 87.

beauty nor your sense of play, but a fine man, and the kind of refuge I thought I could never have.' It is her control with Elliot himself, however, which is most telling of her conscious compromise and secrecy. She is cleverly evasive when questioned about Jerry's camellias so as to retain her private 'Camille' identity, and during their car journey to a pre-concert party, she even manages to accept his marriage proposal while simultaneously relegating him to the position of the necessary father of her future child, rather than her husband. The fact that Elliot happily accepts this registers her vocal and behavioural skill—thanks to her ability to conceal her real feelings and simulate enough contentment to convince him, Elliot remains blissfully unaware that there is anything amiss.

Charlotte's commensurate ability to control her speech and language in order to conceal her real emotions may in fact have continued to hide the reality of her proposed marital compromise. However, an encounter that seems to mimic the function of her earlier crucial flashbacks disturbs this potential course of action. Since her holiday romance with Jerry is ostensibly over and she now lives openly—in any case as far as the film audience is concerned—with his memory, it seems that something more than a flashback is required in order to confront her continuing emotions and make her see the error of her current course. Jerry's melodramatically coincidental appearance at the pre-concert party, immediately following Charlotte's acceptance of Elliot's proposal, therefore represents a kind of heightened flashback, re-animating the past in the most literal way possible. Now, diegetic music and voice both speak her feelings and enable her deception. A presumably diegetic performance or recording of Cole Porter's *Night and Day* plays at the party—with the lyrics conveniently missing to avoid conflict with the spoken words of the illicit couple—before everyone leaves to attend a concert performance of the deeply passionate Tchaikovsky Symphony No. 6. Both pieces allow the double-registered conversation of the ex-lovers, concealing their private passion beneath a social façade. This contrasts with their relationship to diegetic music during their holiday, when their emotional and physical proximity was permitted through the acceptable conventions of dance. Now, the couple's discussion of their feelings against the backdrop of what Daubney terms 'culturally constructed passion'[56] emphasizes the anomaly of publicly sanctioned representations of essentially private emotions. Elliot may take his fiancée's hand as he listens with polite attention to the orchestral performance, but it is Charlotte and Jerry's exchange of looks and whispered words over her corsage of camellias that holds the key to the real passion of both the film and the music. Both also allow Charlotte to betray Elliot, but to hide this through her vocal dexterity. It seems particularly poignant that he does not notice her actions in the concert hall, given his close proximity and the otherwise silent audience. At least in this case, however, Charlotte is cognisant of the possibility, and glances briefly at him to check that she has not lost her touch. Preparing for the return, after the concert, of the *Jerry* theme for Charlotte and Jerry's torrid exchange at the railway station, the public concert, like the later radio broadcast of the Tchaikovsky Symphony, confirms what the score has suggested from Elliot's very first appearance. In this film, a lack

[56] Ibid., p. 87.

of non-diegetic music, and even a seemingly uninvolved relationship to diegetic music, signifies an unacceptable, if harmless, absence of real emotion.

The strength that Charlotte has gained by the end of this episode, evidenced by the new stance on marriage that sees her reject both Elliot's actual and Jerry's hypothetical proposal, also precipitates her final transformation of the maternal relationship. In response to her mother's renewed contempt at her plans to remain '*Miss* Charlotte Vale', she resolves the circumstances of their very first confrontation, now finding herself able to lay bare the hard facts of their relationship against the same sequential musical pattern that accompanied her initial hysterical silence in the face of her mother's scornful gaze and vicious comments. In direct contrast to that initial confrontation, it is now Charlotte's speech that silences her mother. Mrs Vale therefore appears to die from the shock of Charlotte's very vocality, a complete reversal of the original expression of her mother's power that leaves Charlotte in a position to assume the maternal role.

'Our child': Charlotte, Jerry and Tina

When Charlotte coincidentally encounters Tina at Cascade, she is once again saved from despair—this time resulting from her mother's death and posthumous influence—and so begins the final stage of her emotional development. The sadness of Tina's broken childhood spirit is emphasized as Charlotte first sees her by the slow rendition of the *Tina* theme, with the celesta marked by Steiner to be played like 'a sad music box – sort of thing'. The fluid interaction of the *Tina* and *Mother* themes during their first conversation confirms the emotional veracity of Charlotte's identification with Tina, as well as finalizing the symbiotic collapsing of their lives into the same maternal issue. Charlotte can now relive her childhood, using her doctor/parent role to reverse her own mother's misdemeanours. Accordingly, the traffic between themes that previously indicated the therapeutic influences of Dr Jaquith and Jerry finally marks her as both agent and beneficiary of the recuperative process. In a quietly understated iconoclastic stance against Miss Trask (Katharine Alexander)'s enactment of maternal oppression, Charlotte takes control in the face of music that recalls her own flights from her mother's tyranny, but which now represents Tina's growing distress in a similar situation. She therefore re-enacts Dr Jaquith's original role in her own life and, accordingly, is 'given' the *Therapeutic* theme by Miss Trask as she is advised on how to treat Tina. Charlotte then usurps the authority of both Dr Jaquith and Miss Trask to recreate Jerry's role in transferring the emphasis of therapy from medicine to love.

The dominant use of the *Tina* theme establishes the forward-looking nature of this new maternal relationship. The *Mother* and *Jerry* themes remain, however, seemingly to register Charlotte's consciousness of the need to change her relationship to Jerry if she is to help Tina, long before Dr Jaquith could have drawn any parameters for their future behaviour.[57] This is most clearly seen in the two instances when Tina

[57] Both Charlotte's refusal of Jerry's hypothetical proposal of marriage at the station and her refusal of the first opportunity to speak with him on the telephone when she calls him for Tina precede her conversation with Dr Jaquith about their relationship.

telephones her father. The *Tina* theme suggests Charlotte's maternal solicitude as she helps Tina to make her first call. The held chord as she hears Jerry's voice and silently hands the receiver to Tina gives way to the theme as Tina begins to talk. Its continuation, however—over the perhaps more obvious choice of the *Jerry* theme—as she listens to their subsequent conversation, reveals the meaning behind her visually evident suffering. Making the ultimate choice between her own love story and maternal melodrama, Charlotte denies herself the desired musical–emotional connection to Jerry with a painful strength of resolve. This is underlined when, even in the face of the *Jerry* theme's actual appearance during the next telephone call, she actively resists the opportunity to speak to Jerry that Tina so pressingly offers her.

Only following this ultimate display of strength and her time spent as 'mother' to Tina can the conclusion of Charlotte's story revisit the pattern of the film's opening sequence through the filter of her fullest re-negotiation of space, sound, music, emotion, and the behaviour of herself and others. This reverses the original problematic presentation of the Vale household and its oppressed daughter. As Dr Jaquith arrives at the Boston house with Jerry, he prepares him for its gloom—an image emphasized by the reappearance of the weighty *Vale* theme. Charlotte, however, has made her home into a light, bright place. It is full of young people centred around a hearty fire—a pertinent reminder of her earlier confrontation with her brother, when he warned her: 'As long as I can remember that fire has never been lit.' Perhaps most significantly, however, there is also cheerful dance music spilling out of the drawing room into the hall. Charlotte has taken control of space in the way most contrary to the dictates of her mother. She has given it, and herself, life and 'fire', most notably through the negation of the symbolically oppressive silence of the house. Now she can choose her own sound environment, a point most strongly underlined as she later closes the door in order to speak with Jerry in the library. This blocks out the diegetic music, not only to allow silence for their conversation to be heard, but also to emphasize the later return of non-diegetic scoring.

As Charlotte, Jerry and Tina meet together for the first time, the traffic of themes underlines the shift in power relations. This focuses particularly on the emotional conflict with which Jerry unwittingly confronts Charlotte, but which she is now able to resist and control. The transformed Tina appears at the top of the stairs and is instructed on how to descend without tripping on her dress by Charlotte—a genuinely caring mother. Tina first walks then runs down the same staircase that saw Charlotte's initial forced, defeated descent, her mother's fall, and Charlotte's adult social 'rebirth'. We are therefore returned to the beginning of Charlotte's story through her own re-creation of daughterhood. At the same time, Tina's excited and proud descent from privacy into the public gaze replays the spectacle of Charlotte's first appearance on the cruise ship in junior form, restoring the spirit that it sorely lacked. Resolving the issues of Charlotte's dystopian youth, Tina now has a loving mother and (sometimes present) father, freedom of movement, and the right to enjoy her own appearance and emotions. The *Tina* theme therefore becomes subject to the same kind of heralding that Charlotte's own theme enjoyed at the beginning of the film and in her first flashback. She falls into her father's embrace as a rapidly ascending string glissando leads to a sforzando chord. This is then sustained by tremolando playing until breaking into a fast, light, string and celesta version of her theme as she talks excitedly to Jerry.

The attempt of the *Tina* theme to consolidate this idyllic 'family reunion' is undermined, however, by both Jerry and Tina's revelation of its inherent incongruity, which Charlotte must face as the final hurdle to her independence. Its bright sound and fast tempo are interrupted when Jerry directs his crucial expression of love for Tina over her shoulder towards Charlotte. This suggests his (generically naïve) belief that the different kinds of feeling that define the love story and maternal melodrama can successfully co-exist. The *Jerry* theme evidences Charlotte's continuing feelings when this declaration halts her staircase descent as effectively as did her mother's original expression of contempt. Charlotte is able, however, to rally herself and resist the possibility of their love, even with Tina unwittingly hammering the point home by asking if Jerry may call her Camille, the nickname she too has chosen for Charlotte. With the independence that her unconventional maternal status offers, however, Charlotte can consent to be renamed without the commitment that Jerry might presume. Accordingly, in her subsequent private meeting with Jerry in the library, Charlotte's self-styled re-negotiation of the apparently incompatible maternal love, romantic love and independence allows her to confront and control the uncomprehending Jerry against a musical background of memories and emotions in painful conflict with her decisive actions and words. Despite the misery of denying herself romance, however, her choice between the conflicting desires that offer several potentially 'correct' decisions marks the triumphant culmination of her self-development. Beyond all doubt, she is now in command of her own voice whatever the influences, opinions, needs and desires of others.

Jerry's frustration at Charlotte's failure to realize that he is not 'in tune' with her new outlook on life—as she innocently asks if his antagonism towards her relationship with Tina is something to do with their own relationship—introduces an agitated version of the *Jerry* theme. As a direct repeat of the music that accompanied Charlotte's earlier pursuit of Jerry to the railway station to explain her engagement to Elliot, this once again signifies a moment of crisis in mutual understanding inevitable in such a clandestine and difficult relationship. Now, as then, Charlotte is violently confronted with the disjuncture between her actual interiority and the effect on Jerry of her apparent detachment from past and present emotions. The smooth flow of the theme is therefore interrupted and repeated in ascending sequence almost as obsessively as the music that earlier represented both Charlotte and Tina's rising distress in the face of their respective maternal figures. Unfortunately for Jerry, the *Mother* theme's appearance in conjunction with his conclusion that Charlotte should be seeking a husband recalls not only his earlier benevolent, and now somewhat patronising, parental role, but also Mrs Vale's belief in her daughter's shameful worthlessness as a spinster. At last winning her struggle to be defined as something other than a potential wife, and particularly defying her previous submission to Jerry on this issue, Charlotte rallies in the most forcefully vocal way. Confounding his limited view of her, she repeats back to him his own notion of 'some man who will make [her] happy', thereby turning his opinion of her around on him in utter contempt, just as she did previously with both Dr Jaquith and her mother. She thus firmly places his power over her as a thing of the past.

The poignancy of this crucial power shift is marked, however, by its accompaniment by the *Jerry* theme, so that she expresses her profound disappointment in Jerry against music that nevertheless recalls her feelings for him. In a reversal of the earlier scene on the hotel balcony where they first kissed, their mutual emotions are now under Charlotte's, rather than Jerry's, control. He tries to kiss her in presuming the continuation of their affair. Her repetition of her earlier half-hearted insistence, 'please let me go', however, now heralds a successful ability to resist his advances that she was previously unable to sustain. Despite a continuing mutual attraction, therefore, their behaviour in the face of their own emotions is reversed. Jerry previously kissed the tearfully grateful Charlotte after tempering his declaration of love with the proviso that he could not possibly leave his wife. Now he clamours rather desperately while she exercises complete control over both their fates. She still has tears in her eyes as he tries to kiss her, but they now attest to what she knows she could have—and indeed wants—but must resist, rather than her inability to believe what she is hearing. This monumental display of vocal and behavioural control then allows her to determine not only her own future, but also Jerry's and Tina's. As even Jerry appears to realize, Charlotte's superior strength has allowed them a much greater degree of emotional intimacy than he could have expected. Rather than merely sharing a bed, they now share a child. Jerry's redefinition of Tina as 'our child', although gratefully received by Charlotte, is, therefore, really only a verbalization of a decision that she has already made.

As she tells Jerry of Dr Jaquith's expectations of their relationship, her accompaniment by the *Therapeutic* theme finally closes the therapeutic circle of the narrative. Charlotte has at last become the agent of her own recovery. In speaking on behalf of Dr Jaquith, she enables the safe continuation of her independent maternal role, thereby ensuring her control over future events as far as possible. As Jerry exercises little more than Hobson's choice in agreeing to her redefinition of their relationship, the *Jerry* theme returns to triumphantly herald Charlotte's fully assertive and desirable selfhood. She stands confidently alone in the face of love, men and domesticity, and enigmatically withholds her emotions in answer to Jerry's final question: 'And will you be happy Charlotte?'

Conclusion

Now, Voyager raises two important issues for the consideration of the woman's relationship to emotion and music. The first centres on the exact and subtle meaning that can accrue to a particular musical theme, either in itself or in relation to other themes. Musical patterns and techniques may be used to reflect on the specifically personal significance to an individual character of broader narrative concerns. Themes interact with other elements of storytelling to predict and recall important connections between events and characters. They may therefore inflect the text with an emotional resonance that lies beyond the full understanding of the characters. A theme's meaning may also involve traffic or interaction between characters rather than merely signalling the distinct characteristics or outlook of a given individual. A theme can, for instance, 'hold' one character in another's gaze, so that it reflects less on the represented character themselves than on the perhaps influential opinion of someone else—a possibility that is most evident, of course, in *Now, Voyager*'s use of the *Mother* theme. Even at the most apparently simple level of 'character + theme', therefore, the creation of meaning can be extremely complex. Secondly, by extension, it is clear that there is limited scope in considering music's role in characterization in isolation from myriad other representational elements. It is in the dynamic between diegetic behaviour and diegetic or non-diegetic music, rather than solely in the music itself, that the character's relationship to their own emotions can be traced. It is also the divide between audible vocal expression and 'mute'—that is to say non-diegetic musical—expression that registers the crucial (im)possibilities and (in)adequacies of verbal self-expression and communication. The way in which words, silence, actions, behaviour or aspects of mise-en-scène interact with the implied meaning of non-diegetic music must therefore be considered.

The woman's emotional construction is therefore at least partly determined by the relationship between the emotions suggested by her 'own' non-diegetic music and her effective vocality. At the beginning of Charlotte's trajectory, the music has two important connotative functions. It both represents Charlotte's current emotional state and emphasizes the powerful emotions and sexuality that she is forced to repress. She is, however, unable to communicate her emotions verbally without pushing herself to breaking point. Charlotte's extreme state therefore suggests the danger of a woman who cannot express herself in a reasonable way in the face of her own emotions, but instead, being overwhelmed by the power of her own emotions, is prone to psychological illness. Her degree of effective and 'proper' self-control, no matter how strong her underlying feelings, may therefore be gauged by her level of verbal eloquence and behavioural self-restraint in the face of her 'personal' musical accompaniment. This balance of individual emotionality and control, in the terms of Chapter 1's historical survey, ultimately becomes the yardstick by which her social and personal 'acceptability' as a woman is measured. The film thus presents the victorious nature of Charlotte's achievements in terms of self-expression and the control of her feminine interiority as effectively overriding the sadness of the necessity for romantic compromise. For, despite the fact that this victory is one determined by the gender codes of patriarchal society, it nevertheless allows her to defy that society, at least to some extent, by carving out a highly unconventional trajectory of her own choice.

Charlotte's achievement of this state is also significant in terms of her relationship to narration and the representation of her subjectivity. Since she is so emotionally distressed at the beginning of the film, she can only 'speak' successfully by recreating her younger self in flashback. While memory is a crucial part of her self-reformation, however, it is mostly accrued throughout her progress in the present, and our witnessing of events alongside her proves to us that her narration of her memories is entirely credible. That is to say, we believe that she sees things clearly and correctly and that she does not 'romanticize' events. The granting of such veracity to female subjectivity may be unusual, since, as was discussed in both Chapter 1 and this chapter, the reliability of female narration and female subjectivity is often represented as fraught with difficulty due to the woman's apparent emotional over-determination. The nature of the balance of musical–emotional representation and diegetic self-expression that informs the de- and re-construction of Charlotte's character therefore requires closer scrutiny. The most obvious way to tease out this relationship is to examine it in a more exposed state, and such a state is clearly achieved in those narratives that consciously foreground the relationship of women to—necessarily diegetic—music and the emotions that this music inspires. If a female character's emotions are linked directly to a diegetic musical stimulus, her representation must confront the problematic limitations of self-expression brought about by the Romantic inheritance. Examining how films deal with this very particular situation therefore brings us closer to the crux of the 1940s melodramatic view of music and femininity in relation to female characters.

Chapter 3

The female listener

> 'A French philosopher once listed three hundred ways of committing suicide, only he left one out—falling in love with an artist.'
>
> Monte Loeffler (Craig Stevens) in *Humoresque*

> 'The way she listened was more eloquent than speech.'
>
> Waldo Lydecker (Clifton Webb) in *Laura*

There are several levels of conscious involvement that a character may have with diegetic music in a film. The character who actually creates or performs music is perhaps the most active, followed by the character who makes a choice about what diegetic music will be heard, either by someone else performing or the use of recorded music. A further level is offered, however, by the character who listens to the diegetic music that someone else performs or controls, without any authority over its choice, meaning or significance. This creates a unique and yet problematic relationship between the character and their musical–emotional representation. The actions and reactions—and therefore the emotions—of the listener are contextualized by music that remains under the complete control of another character. The listener is therefore constructed, at least in the moment of listening, in response to the musician and the precise piece of music that they choose to perform, thus rendering them passive in terms of both narrative and emotional agency. Naturally, this disturbs the close relationship between character, emotion and music discussed in Chapter 2, and raises the question of how that relationship survives or develops when the music is removed from the implied interiority and privacy of the non-diegetic track and is instead made public within the diegesis as an acknowledged means of emotional expression or communication. What must then also be taken into account is the frequency with which such diegetic music is subsequently transferred to the non-diegetic level. This further complicates the position of the listener if that music becomes intimately associated with their emotions, as is often the case. The character positioned as the listener therefore requires closer examination on their own terms in order that the relationship found in previous chapters between characters and their non-diegetic musical–emotional representation may be appropriately refined and developed.

Female Emotions and Male Music

Given the musical–emotional proximity of these paired characters, it is hardly surprising that the key to understanding the listener should begin with an account of the musician. There are many possible explanations for the proliferation of musician characters in Hollywood and British film in the 1940s. As well as fulfilling a useful role in terms of contemporaneous attitudes towards classical music in film,[1] they seem to have offered an especially attractive model of artistic creativity. What is most interesting about this characterization, however, is the way in which it relates to gender, with a clear distinction transpiring between men and women in relation to musical creativity and performance. While the majority of musician characters at this time are male, they are often not the main emotional concern of the narrative. Instead, leaving the musician himself relatively unexplored, the primary concern in most cases is with the representation of the effect of his musicianship on surrounding characters, particularly women. The predicament of the woman positioned as a listener to the male musician then often results from his inspirational association of the music with her. This might in fact suggest that his emotions actually are central to the narrative, but while, in one sense, this is true, it is only in so far as these emotions are received by and reflected in the woman. This is because, rather than focusing directly on the emotions that the woman inspires in the man, the narrative of the male musician–female listener is primarily concerned with the emotional effect on the woman of being positioned as a passive and relatively powerless muse.[2] This relationship therefore suggests a Romantic construction of gender in terms of both musicality and emotionality. A range of film narratives conceptualize this in different ways and to varying degrees. The most extreme examples, however, represent the perceived female tendency to 'romanticize' through music and the musician as tantamount to a psychological disorder. This suggests both the Romantic idea of the woman's inability to contain or control her own emotions, as well as the resultant denigrated concept of 'romanticization' when applied to female ideas of love and men that I discussed in Chapter 1. This excess of irrational 'femininity' may even demonstrably throw the very reliability and stability of the woman's overall

---

[1] The use of classical music in British film is considered by many composers and critics at this time to offer a valuable opportunity for developing the musical taste and knowledge of the cinema audience. Both exposure to the work of 'serious' contemporary composers writing specifically for film and the use of existing concert repertoire are seen as important in this respect. Muir Mathieson, Music Director of the Rank Film Organization, commends the brave forays into 'the realm of serious music by some of the bolder film producers'. Reflecting on the influence of such music in film on 'renewed interest in concert works', he suggests that film 'mirror[s] popular taste … yet at the same time add[s] a stimulus of its own'. Mathieson believes that experience of serious music through cinema-going results in a gradual increase in the music's own independent popularity. Cinema at this time, he suggests, is 'doing more for serious music, and so for the cultivated taste of more people, than it has ever done or been able to do before', Mathieson (1948), 'The Film and Musical Taste', *Look and Listen*, **2**(5): 93. John Huntley, however, also highlights a potential problem with the use of existing classical music. He states: 'The work of popularising serious music through the medium of the cinema … is an excellent scheme and provided that the music can *occur naturally* in the picture, it should be developed as a contribution from the art of cinema to the art of good music' [my emphasis], Huntley (1947), *British Film Music*, London: Skelton Robinson, p. 18.

[2] This chapter uses the term 'female listener' to denote the diegetic female character who watches and listens to the male performing musician. This should not be confused with the female cinematic audience.

subjectivity into question. It must therefore, as ever, be contained and neutralized by the framing devices of the text.

Perhaps most importantly in terms of the musical–emotional relationship of character and narrative, is the tendency for pieces in this context to 'serve double duty'[3] at both the diegetic level and as part of the narrative, non-diegetic score. Irene Kahn Atkins suggests that the diegetic placement of music, particularly, of course, when either drawn from the Romantic repertoire or imitative of that style, 'assumes an importance as a statement about the *personality of the … composer*. The style of the work is a reflection of his (or her) own emotional life-style, or ideals and aspirations' [my emphasis].[4] Further to this, Claudia Gorbman points out how the transference of such a personal musical statement to the non-diegetic track 'insistently links the character's subjectivity with the spectator's'.[5] Whether the story is based on a real or purely fictitious musician, their music may therefore be used as a means of moving beyond the isolated occasion of composition or performance, in order to imbue the whole story with a very particular subjectivity. The idea that a character can be allowed, albeit unwittingly, to exert such an influence over the way in which the spectator perceives the narrative suggests that this particular musical transfer may at some level be imitating the function of a first-person voice-over narration. Not only, it seems, can the emotional point of view of the musician inform our view of events as the narrative progresses but, as Gorbman points out, the music-related memories of any character can also adopt this 'meta-diegetic' function, initiating flashbacks or recalling previous episodes to the present.[6]

The significant power of the emotional 'voice' that is constituted by the diegetic musical performance may therefore recall the configuration of the performer–audience relationship forwarded by Richard Poirier and Edward Said. Following Poirier's ideas on 'performance' in literary creativity, Said conceptualizes the act of live musical performance as an exercise of power and control over the audience. Poirier suggests that performance constitutes a process 'at first so furiously *self-consultative*, so even narcissistic, and later so eager for publicity, love, and historical dimension. Out of an accumulation of secretive acts emerges at last a form *that presumes to compete with reality itself for control of the minds exposed to it*' [my emphasis].[7] Said balances this by pointing to 'the listener's poignant speechlessness

---

3 Claudia Gorbman (1987), *Unheard Melodies: Narrative Film Music*, Bloomington: Indiana University Press; London: BFI, p. 151.

4 Irene Kahn Atkins (1983), *Source Music in Motion Pictures*, Rutherford, Madison and Teaneck: Fairleigh Dickinson University Press; London and Toronto: Associated University Press, pp. 89–90.

5 Gorbman's observation is specifically in relation to *Hangover Square* (1945), the representation of fictitious composer George (Laird Cregar)'s psychological disorder and his more twentieth-century style of composition. See Gorbman, p.152. Despite the differences in the specifics of the film, however, this practice can easily be seen as common across many more typical male musician–female listener films.

6 Ibid., pp. 22–3. I use Gorbman's definition of meta-diegetic music throughout this book.

7 Richard Poirier (1992), *The Performing Self: Compositions and Decompositions in the Language of Everyday Life*, New Brunswick, NJ: Rutgers University Press, p. 87.

as he/she faces an onslaught of such refinement, articulation, and technique as almost to constitute a sadomasochistic experience'.[8] Although Gorbman, Atkins and Poirier focus explicitly on the act of composition as the expression of the artist's personality, Said's comments suggest the potential for similarly powerful self-projection in the performance of existing repertoire. The mark of personality, in this context, can lie as much in the realization and interpretation of a piece of music as in its original creation. As a result, the experience of musical performance relies on the balance of 'the performer's interpretive and histrionic personality fenced in by his or her obligatory muteness' and 'the audience's receptivity, subordination, and paying patience'.[9]

Placing such a powerful performance within a specifically diegetic context also alters the music's function and capacity for meaning in relation to the conventions of non-diegetic music. Diegetic music can be designed to accommodate the mood of a scene in much the same way as non-diegetic scoring so that, as Gorbman points out, music in a nightclub scene may be expected to reflect the emotions of a film's dancing/courting protagonists.[10] There is no way, however, that this nightclub music could 'know' what was happening between the main couple. The music in this case must be seen either as purely an aspect of mise-en-scène or a factor that actively, but unknowingly, influences the actions or mood of the characters. The position of omniscience that non-diegetic music can necessarily imply over character interiority is not realistic as a diegetic device. Unlike non-diegetic music, however, which is 'bound', to whatever effect, to the emotional resonances of narrative events, diegetic music has the potential for a very particular kind of emotional independence. This allows the music unparalleled freedom to 'comment' on the situations of characters in a relatively distanced and objectifying way, while nevertheless avoiding the alienating effect of non-diegetic music that is used to this end. This technique is often used to what Michel Chion describes as 'anempathetic' effect.[11] In this instance, rather than expressing sympathy with the emotions of a character or situation, the music emphasizes its—and therefore the world's—'indifference'.[12] Taking such a technique to its emotional extreme, there is, as Max Steiner suggests, 'no greater counterpoint … than gay music underlying a tragic scene, or vice versa'.[13] The power accorded to the affect of the diegetic musical performance may therefore be invested in a potentially dubious event. Although, as with Gorbman's nightclub example, it *may* concur exactly with the emotions of the characters it involves or affects, this cannot be relied upon to the same degree as non-diegetic music. The position of the performer in this particular context is possibly even more powerful,

---

8 Edward W. Said (1991), *Musical Elaborations*, New York: Columbia University Press, p. 3.

9 Ibid., p. 11.

10 Gorbman, p. 23.

11 Michel Chion (1990), *Audio-Vision: Sound on Screen*, trans. C. Gorbman, Paris: Editions Nathan; New York and Chichester, West Sussex: Columbia University Press, p. 8. Gorbman examines Chion's idea in *Unheard Melodies*, pp. 24 and 159–61.

12 Chion (1990), pp. 8–9.

13 Max Steiner (1938), 'Scoring the Film', in Nancy Naumburg (ed.), *We Make the Movies*, New York: W. W. Norton and Co., p. 225.

and the position of the transfixed listener even more precarious, than Poirier and Said suggest.

Both Poirier and Said leave the question of gender largely open, although most of their examples of musical performers are in fact male. The cinema, however, rehearses and examines this power relationship most frequently in terms of a female listener to a male musician. The male musician, whether in the biopic or fictional narrative, is often positioned as the object of a kind of female adoration marked by such devotion that, in certain contexts, it can easily transform into love or even obsession. The source of this slippage often lies in the fluidity of meaning allowed within the diegetic musical performance. Following a particularly Romantic ethos of the emotional constitution of the musician, the man's musical 'voice' in performance signifies much more to the woman than merely a talent or profession, and the perception of an unusual depth of feeling and sensitivity combined with the potent masculine strength of artistic expression proves, perhaps unsurprisingly, his most powerful and fascinating attraction. Such emotional overdetermination of the musical performance can be signalled by the specific way in which the woman listens. The collective 'mesmerized' gaze of Paganini's female listeners, identified by K.J. Donnelly in *The Magic Bow* (1946),[14] is typical of the fixated, almost hypnotized listening mode of female listeners in numerous diegetic performance scenes, such as can be found in, for

---

[14] K.J. Donnelly (1997), 'Wicked Sounds and Magic Melodies: Music in 1940s Gainsborough Melodrama', in Pam Cook (ed.), *Gainsborough Pictures*, London and Washington: Cassell, p. 165. This clearly touches on the realm of the biopic, which brings into play actual accounts of the effect of musicians such as Paganini on his female audiences (see also my comments on Liszt and Paganini in Chapter 1). The 1940s are of course populated by a mixture of 'real' and fictitious characterizations of classical composers and musicians. Despite the pretensions of the composer/musician biopic to represent actual figures, however, it often has much in common with its fictitious counterpart. George F. Custen suggests that the primary concern of the biopic may be an exploration of the general nature of 'fame and its relation to the ordinary individual', Custen (1992), *Bio/Pics: How Hollywood Constructed Public History*, New Brunswick, NJ: Rutgers University Press, p. 18. Film producers—Custen refers specifically to the policies of Darryl F. Zanuck in this context—seem often to have felt that only '[p]ersonal narratives of the famous rendered them understandable to the average viewer, though the construct "understandable" most often meant the producer's notion of what a viewer would understand', Custen, p. 19. This concentration on the private lives and experiences of real musicians/composers facilitates the elaboration and/or exaggeration of areas such as their charisma. Such an approach undoubtedly makes for compelling melodrama. For some, however, it impinges to too great an extent upon the 'true' representation of the musician's creativity and relationship to their own music. Critics who habitually champion the diegetic foregrounding of classical music often find the liberties taken with actual historical figures so ridiculous that the entirely fictitious counterpart becomes preferable. Hubert Clifford, for example, following the model of the Chopin biopic *A Song to Remember* (1944), wryly suggests the potential for a biopic of Mendelssohn starring Frank Sinatra, Bing Crosby and Dorothy Lamour entitled *A Song Without Words to Forget*, Clifford (1945), 'Music From the Films', *Tempo*, **10** (March): 11. Likewise Ernest Irving, in response to *The Magic Bow*, offers the opinion that '[t]here is nothing in the slightest degree diabolical about [Stewart] Granger and if he should now take up music seriously I should recommend some lessons on the bass-tuba', Irving (1946), 'Film Music', *Tempo*, **2** (December): 27.

example, *Intermezzo* (1939), *Dangerous Moonlight*, *Humoresque* (1946), *Deception* (1947) and *Interlude* (1957). The simultaneous sense of aloof distance and power of attraction of the man that this suggests can also be represented more literally, and therefore in fact emphasized, through the particular representation of the woman's physical stasis and/or movement during his performance. While the hypnotic power of the performance may freeze the woman in fascinated stasis, it may also induce her to move towards the performer. Musical and emotional attraction therefore translates into a literally 'magnetic' physical attraction. The representation of the first diegetic performance, in particular, frequently incorporates the idea of music motivating the woman's crossing of a physical and/or emotional distance between the characters. In films such as *Dangerous Moonlight* (within the flashback sequence), *Night Song* (1947), *Humoresque* and, in effect at least, *Deception*,[15] the woman is physically—and emotionally—drawn across space by hearing the musician play.

While the man may not *fully* realize the power of his music over the woman, he may also not be completely innocent in the creation of its effect. The particularly dedicated nature of the woman's attraction to the musician is sometimes at least partly a product of the musical thoughts or creativity that he claims she inspires in him. Regardless of whether or not he is the original composer of the piece, he may therefore adopt a crucial ownership over its emotional meaning within the context of the film—a process that can mislead or confuse the woman as to his real feelings. In *Possessed*, for example, Louise's psychological problems derive from the irreconcilability of her apparent capacity to inspire David to play romantic music by Schumann, with his subsequent refusal of emotional commitment. In *Dangerous Moonlight*, Carol (Sally Gray) is veritably hypnotized by the intensity of Stefan (Anton Walbrook)'s gaze as he composes the melody of his *Warsaw Concerto* in response to her. She later makes the rather crucial discovery, however, that she is not the sole source of his inspiration or emotional dedication. In *Intermezzo*, Holger (Leslie Howard) describes Anita (Ingrid Bergman) in terms of a Viennese waltz, and in *Interlude*, Tonio (Rossano Brazzi) uses an anecdote about Mozart writing music for a woman he loved as a means of implying the depth of his attachment to Helen (June Allyson). Both Holger and Tonio, however, are already married to other women, and their existing emotional responsibilities must ultimately be honoured—even though it is the beloved illicit woman who makes the noble decision on the man's behalf in each of these cases.[16]

---

15 In this case, strictly speaking, Christine (Bette Davis) is heading towards the concert because she has seen it publicized. Although, therefore, she is not actually drawn by the sound of the music, the scene constructs her movement towards Karel (Paul Henreid) in this way, and we do not learn of how she actually came to be there until later. The same kind of construction occurs twice more in the film, as Christine returns home to find Karel practising, and later when she visits Alex (Claude Rains) at his request. In each case, she is obliged after her apparent drawing in by the music to wait, watch and listen at a respectful distance, until the man has finished playing.

16 An alternative to this kind of power is offered when the man's strength is compromised in such a way that he clearly *needs* the woman to lend him her own strength or support if he is to continue as a musician at all. In this case, the woman may be almost as much a part of the creation or performance as the man himself, but once again, of course, only in so far as she

Thus when such diegetic pieces as are involved in these situations are transferred to the non-diegetic level, it results in an apparently incongruous musical–emotional configuration. The male musician remains the actual diegetic source of the music, while his female listener is positioned by—among other things—her representation by this music at the non-diegetic level, as the emotional centre of the narrative. Just as the music inspired by the fictitious 'Mary' in *Night Song* remains diegetically with Dan to remind him of what she means to him,[17] therefore, the music that transfers across narrative levels to represent the interiority of the 'muse' woman in the non-diegetic score must always still *belong* in some sense to the male musician. The woman may have inspired its composition or performance, but as an expression of emotion it can only ever exist for her as something 'given'. Mary Ann Doane suggests that a formal diegetic involvement with music counters, to some extent, the potential feminization of the man involved in this genre. She states: 'In the love story, the male undergoes a kind of feminization by contamination—in other words, he is to a certain degree emasculated by his very presence in a feminized genre.'[18] Making him an actual musician therefore 'recoups some of the male's inevitable losses' by rationalizing his involvement with music in any form or at any narrative level.[19] It seems, however, that the sense of masculinity that Doane suggests is returned to the male character by his diegetic musicianship does not fully account for the extent of its effect. Rather than just being re-masculinized in himself, the effect and deployment of his music within the narrative actually extends to giving him a broader controlling 'voice' in the woman's emotional trajectory. While his 'gift' of emotional representation may appear similar to the doctor or psychiatrist giving the woman access to speech in the medical discourse, however, the very point of the musical exchange is often to be found in the couple's mutual misunderstanding of its actual emotional significance. The most common misunderstanding centres on the nature of the emotions that are either apparently or actually contained in the performance. The woman either misinterprets the emotional depth that the music implies in the man, as in *Possessed* and *Letter from an Unknown Woman*, or overestimates her sole claim on those emotions, as in *Intermezzo*, *Dangerous Moonlight* and *Humoresque*. The man, on the other hand, fails to recognize the potential problems caused by the depth and sincerity that his music is bound to convey. Such is the case, for example,

---

enables his 'genius'. Accordingly, in both *Deception* and *Night Song*, the genuine dedication of the woman is demonstrated by her active self-construction as the man's life-changing source of support and inspiration. Christine and Cathy (Merle Oberon) respectively put aside or use their own musical ability and knowledge in order to prioritize the nurturing of Karel and Dan (Dana Andrews)'s apparently greater or more important talents.

[17] Cathy, the rich self-appointed saviour of blind composer Dan, poses as the blind 'Mary' in order to gain his trust. After successfully returning him to his composition and, following an operation, also to his sight, she engineers a relationship with him as her real self, leaving poor 'Mary' behind. The memory of his blind muse, however, is too strong for Dan, and he resolves to return to her. Everyone seems happy as he discovers that Cathy and 'Mary' are in fact one and the same.

[18] Mary Ann Doane (1988), *The Desire to Desire: The Woman's Film of the 1940s*, Basingstoke and London: Macmillan Press, p. 97.

[19] Ibid.

in *Intermezzo*, *Dangerous Moonlight*, *Possessed* and *Letter from an Unknown Woman*.

The disjuncture between the woman's romantic fantasy of what the performance implies, and the diegetic reality of its status as a 'performance', therefore marks the musician–listener relationship as one of potential misrecognition. As a result, at the non-diegetic level, this music can be invested with a particularly complex conflation of emotional subjectivities—namely, and respectively to each particular narrative situation, the man's real feelings for the woman, the feelings that he claims the performance is intended to convey, the emotions that the woman believes are conveyed by the performance, and whatever she believes can consequently be understood of the man and his feelings towards her. Complicating this is the question of whether the performance actually reflects the man's real emotions or whether it is merely a performance of emotion, and to what extent this is acknowledged in the woman's reaction. Most importantly, however, is the idea that the woman's emotions, as they are represented by the non-diegetic music, become as a result less a reflection of her own independent personality than of her emotional configuration by the man and her consequent dependence on his continued admiration. It is hardly surprising, therefore, that this music can represent what happens to the female protagonist in peculiarly ambiguous ways. In *Possessed*, for example, the representation of Louise's emotions by various non-diegetic manifestations of the piece played for her by David—*Chopin*, the twelfth piece from Schumann's *Carnaval*, Op. 9—not only expresses her self-torture as she descends into serious illness, but also appears to take an active part in this psychological downfall. As his music follows her gradual breakdown, particularly her aural and visual hallucinations, it therefore marks her as an emotional 'product' of the man. The danger of female 'romanticization' suggested by the film is therefore most violently expressed not through Louise's eventual murder of David, but through the temporary ability of her hallucinations to take over the seemingly objective representation of the film. When both the film audience and Louise believe for a few moments that she has killed Carol (Geraldine Brooks)—only to discover this as being purely the product of her crazed imagination—the precariousness, emotional overdetermination and consequently unreliable nature of female subjectivity is made abundantly clear.

The extent to which a female fascination with the man through his music can grow into a complete distortion of perception is ultimately encapsulated in the confusion of the man with his iconic musical instrument. In *Letter from an Unknown Woman*, Lisa appears to relate to Stefan (Louis Jourdan)'s piano as if it were the man himself, with this physical manifestation going one step further than his representation through the sound of his music alone. In *Intermezzo*, Margit (Edna Best) walks in on Anita gazing at and caressing Holger's violin, and looks as shocked as if she had discovered them locked in a passionate embrace. Where such extreme distortions of perception are concerned, there often seems to be no possible conclusion but the destruction or self-annihilation of the woman. In both *Possessed* and *Deception*, although it is actually a male musician who is murdered (in *Deception* to protect the sanctity of the woman's listener relationship to another male musician), the real importance of the murders appears to lie with the denial of a future that they bequeath to Louise and Christine respectively. Anita in *Intermezzo* and Helen in *Interlude* sacrifice themselves emotionally by insisting that Holger and Tonio return to the greater need of their wives and families. Helen commits suicide in *Humoresque* and Lisa in *Letter from an Unknown Woman* conveniently dies of typhus at the point where Stefan's ignorance of her is finally clear. Even *Night Song*, in which the couple are eventually united, achieves this only as a result of the film's doubling of Cathy/'Mary', which allows each woman to be partially killed off in their combined creation of Dan's ideal woman.

Female Narration and Male Music

Films such as *Possessed* and *Letter from an Unknown Woman*—and even to some extent *Brief Encounter* (1945), although the stimulus to narrate here is a gramophone record—place the issue of the relationship of the woman's subjectivity to her non-diegetic musical–emotional representation under the closest possible scrutiny by actually allowing the woman to narrate her own view of events. The question of female subjectivity can therefore be highlighted not only by examining her representation by the man's music, but also through questioning the particular type of voice to which she is given access. Sarah Kozloff points out that women's narration in the fiction film is largely restricted to the first-person mode.[20] One reason for this, which she suggests along with Kaja Silverman, lies in an apparent problem with granting the female the kind of authority that the more traditionally male third-person narrator (Chion's 'acousmêtre' in Chapter 2 of this book) enjoys. By only allowing women to tell stories in which they also appear as characters, the narrative film restricts them to relating only 'their own life stories or their own memories … their area of knowledge is generally constricted to what they have personally experienced'.[21] Since this mode of narration is embedded, furthermore, within the overall framework of the film as a subjective flashback, it 'embodies' the woman's voice, containing it within what Silverman terms a 'hyperbolically diegetic context'.[22] The woman is thus returned to the kind of double operatic frame discussed in Chapter 1.

Both George Custen and Maureen Turim suggest that the individual subjectivity stressed by the flashback format can never operate independently of its 'present-day' contextualization.[23] Indeed, as Custen observes, 'One of the functions of the flashback … [as has already been seen in the case of Charlotte's flashbacks in Chapter 2's examination of *Now, Voyager*] is to retell history from the vantage point of a particular narrator. This privilege allows the narrator to frame the life not just in terms of the order and content of events, but to frame its significance.'[24] The persistence of the 'double frame', however, leads to certain complications with this

[20] Sarah Kozloff (1988), *Invisible Storytellers: Voice-Over in American Fiction Film*, Berkeley, Los Angeles and London: University of California Press, p. 99.

[21] Ibid., p. 100.

[22] Kaja Silverman (1988), *The Acoustic Mirror: The Female Voice in Psychoanalysis and Cinema*, Bloomington and Indianapolis: Indiana University Press, p. 45.

[23] Custen, p. 183; Maureen Turim (1989), *Flashbacks in Film: Memory and History*, New York and London: Routledge, Chapter 4.

[24] Custen, p. 183.

narrational vantage point where female narrators are concerned. Firstly, the targeted use of other elements of narrative representation within the woman's flashback, such as mise-en-scène and music, allows the film the possibility of commenting on her point of view and undermining the reliability of her subjectivity. Further to this, the containment of her flashback within a present-day context that emphasizes the error of her romantic ways—she has, after all, been brought to some kind of unfortunate end as a result of her past actions—also potentially points the film audience towards its own negative assessment as the narrative progresses. It then only remains for the optional diegetic male voices, usually of doctors or psychiatrists, to be given the 'clarifying' and authoritative right of retrospective interpretation, as is the case, for example, in *The Seventh Veil*, *Possessed*, *Caught* and *The Snake Pit*.

This particular kind of present-day contextualization thus allows the flashback to undermine the woman's vision of her own past through her evident inability to perceive 'reality'—so that she has ended up, for example, as an errant wife/mother, a psychiatric patient or a rejected lover. Interventions of 'objectivity' and 'reality', in whatever form, reveal the woman's view as *excessively*, and so dangerously, subjective—a point highlighted by her own frequent confusion over the events she recalls and the images she sees. She therefore, for example, suffers the extensive hallucinatory episodes of Louise in *Possessed* or makes the false connections of Virginia (Olivia de Havilland) in *The Snake Pit*. She may even, like Nancy (Laraine Day) in *The Locket*, wilfully resist the accurate narration of her own story, until the greater power of the film bombards her with unwelcome and overwhelming memories, eventually proving her psychological illness against the initially questionable sanity of the film's multiple male narrators.[25] The woman's autobiographical retelling of events may therefore lead her unwittingly to enable a reading of her life to targeted ideological ends. On the one hand, the presentation and content of the flashbacks may reveal the kind of alternative narrative that Turim sees concealed in *Possessed*. 'In this "other" film,' she states, 'one hears more of Louise's subjective experience, more of the functioning of the unconscious, more of the social circumstances that limit a woman's options to deviant behaviors. Implicitly, *Possessed* exposes some of what might possess a female psyche to strike out with violence'.[26] The structural status of the flashback, however, demonstrates the containment and regulation of such impulses. As a result, the woman's past can be safely presented in a cautionary light, while the female audience can nevertheless enjoy the vicarious experience of temporarily living a socially forbidden, but perhaps desirable, alternative life.[27]

Considering my earlier discussion of the relationship of female emotions to male music, it is possible to see how the male musician–female listener narrative adds its own peculiar twist to the various issues already associated with female narration.

---

[25] See Doane (1988), pp. 58–9 for a full description of the narrative structure of this film. Doane points out, in fact, that 'it is the hallucinatory voices heard by a madwoman which act as a verification of the narratives told by the men. The film is structured so that her madness confirms their sanity'.

[26] Turim, p. 160.

[27] See Jeanine Basinger (1993), *A Woman's View: How Hollywood Spoke to Women, 1930–1960*, London: Chatto & Windus.

As long as the female narrator's memories are accompanied by non-diegetic music sourced from the man's diegetic performance, not only must her emotions be informed as much by his attitude as by her own, if not more so, but so must our reading of both her narration and her narrative. Whether or not the woman is fully aware of the man's feelings, these therefore remain a necessary part of the narration. She narrates her story verbally, but the man 'narrates' musically through either the woman's, or the film's, constant recollection of his attitude to both the music and her. While this may serve to undermine further the reliability of her subjectivity, both in the present and the past, an interesting paradox arises from our ultimate identification with her point of view, encouraged, perhaps particularly, by her representation through non-diegetic music. This is because, according to the tenets of the melodramatic mode, the emotional veracity of non-diegetic music, whatever its source, makes it difficult to condemn her for any possible misunderstanding or resultant misdeed. While the man's 'rational' diegetic music proves a minefield of potential misunderstanding or overdetermination for her romantic sensibilities, her 'irrational' emotions are at the very least guaranteed to be pure, genuine and unadulterated. Any thoughts or actions based on such genuine emotions are thus lent an interesting and persuasive credence.

'Are you crazy?': *Letter from an Unknown Woman*

> 'Tell me, when you climb up a mountain, what then?'
> 'Then you come down again.'
> Lisa and Stefan in *Letter from an Unknown Woman*

Letter from an Unknown Woman offers a complex take on the male musician–female listener narrative. Its use of the conventions of voice-over narration to comment on the subjectivity of its female protagonist are conspicuous, but at the same time surprisingly subtle in effect. It eschews a position of absolute judgement in favour of a more gently objective and even sympathetic contextualization of the woman's emotions, thoughts and actions. The film's most striking quality, however, comes from its presentation of the origins of the woman's musical–emotional predicament. Rather than allow the male musician to assign an association with music to her, *Letter from an Unknown Woman* observes the woman as she does this for herself. Unbeknown to the musician, therefore, she becomes a unique combination of his dedicated listener and self-styled muse, creating an attachment to an imaginary ideal that can only be properly reciprocated after her death.

The film centres on Lisa Berndl's life of dedication to concert pianist Stefan Brand, of whom she constructs a romantic vision during adolescence by listening to him practise and gazing at his possessions. The piece that she associates with him, Liszt's Concert Study in D Flat (*Un Sospiro*), becomes the main source material of the non-diegetic score. The very presence of music in this narrative, and particularly the exact way in which it initially bonds Lisa to Stefan, is integral not only to the creation of its essential dynamic between objective reality and romantic fantasy, but also the continually ambiguous attitude to both of its main characters. Most importantly, however, it predicts the impossibility of romance in anything other than the realms of, in the end, either Lisa or Stefan's imagination. Music therefore plays a significant role in setting the terms of the narrative and the parameters within which the characters can operate, as well as offering a certain logic for the film's enigmatic closing moments. The ability of the score to encompass such conflicting meanings lies in its presentation of three points of view on the narrative, simultaneously representing events through the opposing filters of blind emotional fantasy and objective reality, as well as the eventually more persuasive power of subjective emotional truth.

Much of the existing writing on *Letter from an Unknown Woman* centres on the articulation of the difference between the narrating position of Lisa and the broader narrational 'voice' of the film. In a similar way to Laura (Celia Johnson) in *Brief Encounter*, Lisa is never subject to the obvious prying eyes of diegetic medical analysis, leaving her free to tell her story more or less interrupted. The questioning disruption of her romantic vision is, however, concealed within the images that purport to represent her own narration. No matter how much inducement there is to believe that Lisa's letter/voice-over is the source of the images, we are constantly recalled to the more knowledgeable or objective view of the film itself.[28] In this way, as Robin Wood points out, '[Lisa's] narration is allowed its own integrity, which he [Ophuls] respects, even venerates: it is, as far as it goes, "the truth." But it is *her* truth, not his [Ophuls's/the film's]' [emphasis in original].[29] This dynamic, and the film's subtly sophisticated commentary on Lisa's subjectivity, suffuses the film even at the broad structural level, where the narrative incorporates an objective view of events of which Lisa could not be aware and therefore could not describe in her letter.[30]

Above all, the film is imbued with rhythms that offer a fatalistic commentary on the inescapable passing of time in the lives of all the characters. Lisa's sense of time is dictated by the emotional significance of events, a framework also reflected in the structure of the musical score. For her, the past exists in the present as much as it will in the future. Stefan, on the other hand, is represented as more spontaneous and above all free, with his less active attention to past events and the accumulation of memories being particularly notable in his inability to recognize or remember his former lover. This crucial temporal distinction is expressed at the broadest level through the simultaneous expansion and compression of time offered by the eponymous letter itself. The flashback structure

> … allows Ophuls to counterpoint the passing of the years in Lisa's narrative with the passing of the hours as Stefan reads her letter—the two time-schemes at last converging

[28] Sarah Kozloff discusses this process in general in *Invisible Storytellers*, p. 48. Robin Wood discusses it in specific relation to *Letter from an Unknown Woman* in (1976), *Personal Views: Explorations in Film*, London: Gordon Fraser, pp. 127–9, and (1993) '*Letter from an Unknown Woman*–The Double Narrative', *cineACTION*, **31**: 6–7.

[29] Wood (1993), p. 6.

[30] Many writers have focused on this point, including V.F. Perkins, Robin Wood, Andrew Sarris, Tania Modleski and Virginia Wright Wexman.

> and uniting in the closing minutes, as Stefan finishes the letter and the carriages arrive to bear him to the duel with Lisa's husband.[31]

As Lisa focuses Stefan on the idea of her life—and also *his* life—as being 'measured' by certain events that signify their relationship, in her eyes at least,[32] she therefore confronts him with the necessity of acknowledging a relationship to time that is alien to his own. Bringing him into line with her vision of life in this way then both precipitates and necessitates his death.

The difference at the heart of the film's mode of presentation, however, also marks the distinction between Lisa's personal experience of repetition and destiny and the film's more objective view of history repeating itself. The whole narrative resounds with a higher level of echoes, rhymes and ironies of which Lisa and the other characters remain completely unaware. Many critics note, for example, the twinning of shots that frames Lisa's return home with Stefan for their one night of passion within the context of her earlier adolescent observation of his return with another (unknown) woman.[33] Similarly, V.F. Perkins points out the specific placement of two phrases used as a framing device for her recounting of her life in Linz. He observes: 'The correspondence of "You who have always lived so freely" and "I told him I wasn't free" is constructed by the film and not observed by Lisa. What the film sees, and she doesn't, is the conflict between a man's freedom and a woman's lack of it.'[34] Lisa's imperviousness to such resonances seems literalized in aspects of both the presentation and content of story elements that are clearly intended for the sole view of the film audience. This is most strikingly manifested in those scenarios that Lisa literally could not have seen, and therefore could not have recounted. These represent the working-class support mechanisms of upper-class entertainment, and hence the very unromantic conditions that qualify the possible scenarios of romance—an element of reality that uniformly eludes Lisa.[35] It is the music that is so constantly foregrounded, however, which offers the film's most poignant commentary on its hapless female protagonist. Diegetic music fulfils a particularly ironic function, in terms not only of its direct correspondence with simultaneous visual events, but also, and undoubtedly most poignantly, in terms of its reflection on Lisa's excessively romantic interpretation of Stefan's musical performance. While the implications of Lisa's (mis)understanding of music are amplified in the following case study of the film's score, this requires some preparatory contextualization within the overall codes of musical signification constructed by the film.

---

31 Wood (1976), p. 131.

32 See V.F. Perkins (1982), 'Letter From an Unknown Woman', *Movie*, **29/30**: 62.

33 See, for example, Wood (1976), pp. 128–30, and George M. Wilson (1986), *Narration in Light: Studies in Cinematic Point of View*, Baltimore: Johns Hopkins University Press, pp. 103–4.

34 Perkins (1982), p. 71.

35 See, for example, ibid., pp. 65–6, and Virginia Wright Wexman (1986), 'The Transfiguration of History: Ophuls, Vienna, and *Letter from an Unknown Woman*', in (ed. with Karen Hollinger), *Letter from an Unknown Woman*, New Brunswick, NJ: Rutgers University Press, pp. 13–14.

At the broadest level, the romantic significance of Vienna, in terms of what it represents for Lisa, is marked by its musical contrast with Linz. As both Perkins and Virginia Wright Wexman point out, the music of Linz exists entirely in the public and diegetic space and is therefore diametrically opposed to the private and 'intimate' realm of non-diegetic music within which Lisa envisions her relationship with Stefan.[36] It seems to act, rather, in the manner of a powerful sanction of social regulation and strictly controlled emotion, with Leopold (John Good)'s unwelcome and extremely unromantic proposal appearing virtually choreographed to its overbearing physical and aural presence. This obviously recalls the similar section of *Now, Voyager* examined in Chapter 2, in which Elliot's association with diegetic music signified his lack of significance in terms of 'real' emotion. Thus, just as Elliot was clearly not the man to usurp Jerry, Leopold is no replacement for Stefan. The predominance of diegetic music signals the same absence of genuine passion, however well intentioned the young suitor may be. Lisa's stubborn fidelity to her romantic ideal therefore dictates that she must reject such socially conditioned and conditioning music, forcing her, as Perkins points out, to break through the boundary of the military musical parade to escape back to her idealized Vienna.[37] There is also a warning for Lisa in the music of Linz, however, if she did but know it. If she overestimates the 'feminine' qualities of Stefan's musicality, then the military musicians of Linz certainly overstate the very unromantic, commonplace aspects of a working relationship to music. The 'unsmiling grunts' and laborious approach of the pompous bandmaster[38] counter any possible emotion in the Wagnerian love song that the band performs.[39] Lisa's tendency to ignore anything in music but the romantic, however, prevents her from realizing the implications of this alternative 'underside' of music.

Most pertinently, as with all those other manifestations of work that she fails to see, the idea of Stefan's playing constituting only the routine practising of a professional musician completely eludes her. As he abandons this task in petulant frustration, in an early scene that we can see but she can only hear, it therefore seems one of the film's supreme ironies that it is the male musician's lack of serious musical commitment which, at least according to Lisa's physical response, is misread as an expression of the deepest emotional turmoil. Since Lisa is convinced that her emotional responses emanate not from within herself, but from Stefan's music and therefore from Stefan himself, she is compelled to see herself as emotionally dependent upon him. This over-identification with his musicianship then develops into a desire for his equal artistic/emotional dependence. Her greatest point of romantic hope is offered when Stefan considers that she appears to understand him better than he does himself and that, consequently, '[she] may be able to help [him]'. What Wood terms 'her

36 Perkins (1982), pp. 63–4; Wright Wexman, p. 5.

37 Perkins (1982), p. 66.

38 Ibid., p. 65.

39 V.F. Perkins discusses the full political resonances of the use of Wagner in this context and Ophuls's critical stance on both the composer and Linz; unpublished typescript, 'Ophuls Contra Wagner and Others'.

fantasy of vicarious empowerment'[40] therefore seems to position her, in the terms discussed in Chapter 1, as his self-constructed muse. In contrast to this, Stefan's lack of emotional commitment seems most clearly manifested through the diegetic use of Papageno's aria *Ein Mädchen oder Weibchen* from Mozart's *The Magic Flute* during Stefan and Lisa's reunion outside the Vienna Opera House. The preparation for this reunion with the call to the diegetic audience to return for the second act of the opera evokes the sense of an equally well-rehearsed performance in Stefan's second attempt to seduce Lisa—a performance that is, perhaps, matched in its contrivance only by Lisa's melodramatic flight from the auditorium as a means of 'innocently' attracting his attention. It certainly suggests that having apparently reached some sort of settled state in her marriage, no matter how much compromise this may have demanded, the whole sad ritual is in fact about to start up all over again. Stefan's words thus seem to sing along with the lovelorn bird-catcher's contemplation of companionship with 'a [any?] girl or woman'. While the nature of Papageno's desires offer a biting commentary on Lisa and Stefan's relationship, the optimism, energetic cheerfulness and humour of the aria chime ironically with Stefan's now sadly desperate, overbearing and somewhat tired seduction routine.

The relationship of a romantic sensibility to the more mundane aspects of harsh reality is yet further exposed in the film's dynamic of music, dialogue and sound effects. Lisa's romanticizing over Stefan, his music or his possessions is frequently interrupted by discordant and disruptive noise and, during her adolescent adoration, by the distinctly unromantic voice of her mother. She must, we assume, be as aware of the actuality of these disruptions as she is of the physical obstacles that often obscure her ability to see Stefan, but she seems to be similarly immune to their commentary either during their initial appearances or as they become relevant again at later points in the story. She evidently sees no irony, for example, in the particular nature of the interruptions to her inquisitive reveries over Stefan's possessions caused by his own harp. Firstly, its discordant noise while being unloaded from the removal van belies its conventional musical delicacy, and secondly, its ungainly physicality takes precedence over its exquisite beauty as it obstructs her illicit movement through his apartment.

Eventually, however, it may be that the film's ultimate irony is at the expense of the viewer, rather than Lisa. As Stefan reaches the end of Lisa's letter and finally—although only with the help of his servant John—realizes her identity, he rather dramatically chooses to accept the reframing of his own life that she has offered. Perhaps suggesting that at least some amount of truth lies behind his earlier protestation to Lisa that his life has been spent in search of his elusive 'goddess', her letter seems to give his life, especially in its current depleted state, a significance that it has previously lacked. Ultimately, he displays as much romantic idealism as Lisa. Indeed, as George Wilson points out,

> Through the vehicle of the letter, Brand assimilates Lisa's memory of the past—her memories fill that void in him—and comes to see her as the 'ideal woman' whom he had not recognized and now has lost irretrievably. This closure is satisfying in that it reverses

---

[40] Wood (1993), p. 10.

> the situation in which his music creates her vision of an 'ideal love' in the future, an ideal that, for other reasons, she was bound to lose.[41]

In the end, therefore, it is not just Lisa who is able to 'help' Stefan, but also he who 'helps' her. He finally fulfils her romantic fantasy by becoming the very personification of emotional depth and tragic passion that she always imagined him to be. At the same time, however, she is rescued from the risk of denigration to which her apparent excessive romanticism exposes her by his grateful participation in the scenario that she has created. The veracity accorded to her vision of past events is evident in Stefan's—and for that matter even John's—reverent reactions. As Wood points out, 'Lisa retains a yearning for a perfection unrealizable in life, yet the yearning confers upon life (even if posthumously) its highest dignity and value'.[42] Ultimately, Lisa's romanticism is redeemed by Stefan and the film to the heights of a Romantic—male—transcendent vision.[43]

The Creation of the Non-diegetic Musical–Emotional Fantasy

In order to chart both the nature and development of the relationship between Lisa's status as listener to Stefan, and her self-construction as his muse, my analysis of the score of *Letter from an Unknown Woman* takes an approach similar to that of the previous chapter in its focus on selected musical elements of four sections of the film. The first section takes Lisa from the beginning of the film up to her departure for Linz, and begins by detailing the way in which her image of Stefan is initially formed. It then shows the process by which her romantic fixation causes the appropriation of the diegetic music onto the non-diegetic track, and her attendant self-construction as Stefan's (unrecognized) muse. As she craves any kind of contact with Stefan, the non-diegetic score locks particular patterns in the music to her desire and begins to suggest the more objective musical codes by which it will comment on, or even condemn, her emotions.

The film is divided into a series of flashbacks, motivated by Stefan reading the eponymous letter that creates for him his history with Lisa. In the first of these flashbacks, Lisa tells of the basis of her attachment to Stefan after he moves into a neighbouring apartment. The only knowledge she has of him initially comes from gazing at his possessions and, most notably, from the sound of his piano-playing. The key to her very subjective reading of this is made clear through her own account of her thoughts and words at the time. As we first see her in the act of listening, it is apparent that Lisa is already in a fascinated state. Within her narrated account, our first view of Stefan is also determined primarily by his music, with the first shot showing his hands as he practises the Liszt Concert Study in D Flat. Seeing his hands before his face suggests that we are being offered a re-presentation of Stefan according to Lisa's belief that he can be determined and identified through his music. It is nevertheless true that we have already seen Stefan in the present-day opening of the film, and

41 Wilson, p. 123.

42 Wood (1976), p. 132.

43 Ibid.

therefore possess knowledge of his flippant and dishonourable demeanour that Lisa does not have at this stage. The direct juxtaposition of these scenes therefore presents the two conflicting views of Stefan central to the project of the film.

Lisa's romantic idyll is also contextualized, however, by the representation of her obscured vision. Her point-of-view shots of the outside wall of Stefan's apartment and the uselessly high and partially obscured window make it clear that she cannot share our more mundane view of what is happening within. While we witness that Stefan seems to see practice as rather strenuous and even irritating labour, Lisa hears an emotional depth to his personality that will later lead her to tell him: 'Sometimes, I felt when you were playing that, that you haven't quite found, I don't know what it is, what you're looking for.' Her remoteness from the actuality of the work of music allows her to deify the process. For her, music contains the key to an intimate understanding of Stefan that she undoubtedly believes—probably rightly—passes other women by. She is not in love with Stefan as he actually is, or at least as he appears to be from the evidence we are given up until the very final moments of the film, but rather with the man whose secret inner voice she thinks she hears within her own response to his musical performance.

As she listens, her movement already being dictated by the rhythm of the music to which she glides back and forth on a swing in the yard, she is also joined by her friend, who clearly does not share Lisa's developing fantasy. Like a last voice of reality before Lisa is lost forever to her romantic reverie, this girl places herself physically in the way of Lisa's gaze and serves to remind her of the cruder aspects of life and love. After denigrating his playing as mere 'noise', she interrupts Lisa's listening with the sound of her eating and a very down-to-earth account of her relationship with a local boy. As she reaches the point of implying that this relationship is becoming more physical than might be proper, however, Stefan's playing breaks down, and an opposition is set up between Lisa and Stefan's narrative and the girl's story through an association of the two males' hands. The girl talks of the boy being unable to keep his hands to himself and possibly having to 'do something about it', which is followed firstly by a musical disruption and then a shot of Stefan's hands stumbling on the keyboard. Since Lisa relates to Stefan as an ideal rather than an actual man, it seems appropriate that when confronted with the everyday reality of sexual relations, the imaginary auditory bond on which her fantasy is based breaks down. At the same time, however, this exchange between the two girls also acts as a precursor to what will turn out to be Stefan's behaviour with women, based on his own inability to 'keep his hands to himself', and Lisa's apparent power to 'do something about it' by bringing about his eventual death. Already, the film has presented the parameters of Lisa and Stefan's trajectory in the most concise and tragic way possible. It has also indicated the hopelessness of the situation both by the interplay of music and 'noise' and by the otherwise inexplicably knowing smile with which her friend responds to Lisa's shock when Stefan's playing suddenly stops. Lisa can neither 'see' nor 'hear' reality, and Stefan is completely unaware of her presence, let alone her feelings. His performance is not intended to be public, and so Lisa eavesdrops on a private musical moment rather than a personal communication to an ardent admirer.

The future of this mutual misrecognition, furthermore, is predicted in the repetitive pattern of the short section of music used, the incessant, imitative motion of Lisa's swing and the way in which the music ends. The diegetic performances of the Liszt Concert Study never progress beyond the first 38 bars, and it is material from this section of the piece on which the non-diegetic score is primarily based. Just as the diegetic performance of the piece never reaches its own end, the point at which Lisa's fantasy is initially disrupted is the point at which her story will effectively end. Her fantasy and her emotional state of mind are frozen in one adolescent moment in time, with each repetition of the music pulling the story back to this initial episode. Using the music that inspires the fantasy to chart its progression, without any significant musical development, serves to condemn it as redundant. Both the musical phrases and the swing therefore suggest a futility of movement and an impression of progress that actually constitutes stasis.[44] In a film replete with repeated visual motifs and narrative patterns, the relentless repetition of this musical segment continually restates that no musical progression signifies an equal lack of real emotional or narrative progression. By the same token, the violent disruption of the music—firstly by the abrupt halt of its rapid flow and then by the frustrated crash of Stefan's hands on the keyboard—mirrors the usual interruptions of Lisa's fantasizing by the sound or 'noise' of reality.

The silence of the non-diegetic track when Lisa subsequently sees Stefan for the first time—within the flashback at least—evidences both his emotional indifference to her and her own current lack of musical–emotional representation. The film's revelation of this lack, however, seems entirely purposeful, crucial as it is to contextualizing and marking the significance of the following transferral of music that takes place between the two characters. This transfer involves three interrelated aspects. Firstly, it allows Lisa to gradually reposition herself as the emotional instigator of Stefan's performances; secondly, it removes the music from Stefan's own diegetic level and relocates it to the non-diegetic realm, which seems, initially at least, to belong to Lisa alone; and thirdly, it encourages us towards a more sympathetic complicity with her fantasy. This third point is most obvious in the first stage of the transfer, when Lisa gets out of bed and creeps through her apartment in order to be able to hear Stefan's playing more clearly. This is the first opportunity for her uninterrupted fantasy, as she tells him that she imagined he was playing 'just for [her]' and that he was giving her 'some of the happiest hours of [her] life'. As she gets as close as she can to the source of the music, standing on the stairway next to Stefan's front door, and opens the small window into his apartment to hear as clearly as possible, the music reaches the exact point—the cadenza pattern of bar 37—where the disruption caused by her friend's story had previously led to Stefan abandoning the piece in frustration (Example 3.1a). The important difference at this moment, however, is that we are denied our previously privileged view of the music in practice and share instead Lisa's purely aural experience. Now, Lisa is uninterrupted by any suggestion of real human relations, and the film audience is undisturbed by the sight of Stefan's efforts to play the piece correctly. Her night-time privacy therefore allows the metaphorical parallel between his successful musical

---

44 Robin Wood identifies a similar instance of what he terms the film's 'movement/stasis opposition … in the "fake" railway train in the Prater, where the moving scenery gives the illusion of the movement of the train' (1993), p. 5.

Example 3.1a Franz Liszt, Concert Study in D Flat (*Un Sospiro*). Extract from bar 37

Example 3.1b Daniele Amfitheatrof, *Letter from an Unknown Woman*. The descending patterns of the Liszt cadenza and the *resolution* motif combined with the 'comment' of woodwind orchestration

performance and the imaginary fulfilment of her fantasy—and the film audience shares this moment with her.

Although Lisa clearly reacts emotionally to Stefan's music, however, its continuing status as diegetic denies it the role of representing her individual interiority. As the next stage of the transfer begins to associate Lisa with the music in a more personal way, it therefore appears at the non-diegetic level for the first time within the narrative.[45] At the same time, the nature of her fantasy and her projected future fate are expressed in an unusually exact way through the actual construction of the theme drawn out of the piece. Although as a professional pianist it must be assumed that she would have heard him practising a much wider repertoire—and she does follow his concerts through reading other people's programmes and newspaper reviews—Lisa only ever actually recounts Stefan as practising this one Liszt piece. From this the film score extracts the melody of bars 3 to 5 (Example 3.2a), and in terms of following Lisa's emotional trajectory, the narrative mobilizes the musical capacity of this theme to express anticipation and resolution by dividing it into two 4-note motifs. As Example 3.2a illustrates, the first half (henceforth the *anticipation* motif) ends suspended at a highpoint of non-resolution, with the second half (the *resolution* motif) providing the balancing resolution. This patterning becomes relevant in reflecting the idea of emotional anticipation and resolution as the story develops between Lisa and Stefan.

[45] It has of course already been heard at this level under the opening title sequence of the film, but disappears as the narrative begins.

The new flexibility of the music to Lisa's feelings, and the first suggestion of its connection to her desire for Stefan, begins with her illicit foray into his apartment. As she first enters the apartment, we hear her friend's offscreen voice asking: 'Are you crazy?' This is the final question she asks before disappearing completely from the film and, it could be argued, taking with her Lisa's last reasonable chance of facing reality. As she ignores her friend and progresses further through Stefan's rooms, three versions of his piece play successively on the non-diegetic track. Firstly, the whole theme is played in the original key over a pedal note accompaniment, keeping it relatively close to the memory of Stefan's performance despite its variation and string orchestration. The second statement of the theme continues the pedal note pattern and begins to fragment the melody line. This fragmentation suggests a new flexibility more conventionally associated with non-diegetic scoring and begins to reflect the gradual removal of the music from the world of Stefan's rehearsed and controlled performance to that of Lisa's private feelings, as well as from self-referential interpretation to an emotional focus on the 'other'. The omission of the expansive arpeggios surrounding the melody notes in the original piece also negates the idea of public display and (masculine) technical prowess. This leaves Lisa with a kind of simple musical 'essence' that reflects her concentration on a personal construction of Stefan from within the notes.

The final statement of the theme is delayed until Lisa is actually in the room with the piano—the most important iconic representation of Stefan. At this point, the grounding of the music through the use of the pedal note develops into the use of more sustained chords, enabling the freeing of the melody line for the improvisatory style of the solo violin as Lisa looks around the space of the piano (Example 3.2b). The elaboration of the melody and the extraction of an individual musical voice suggest the development of Lisa's fantasy as she sees more of the content of Stefan's world, and in keeping with this, the visual sources that she has to feed her fantasy are public representations of Stefan and his lifestyle rather than anything personal. The piano, standing as the main symbol, is surrounded by concert posters, instruments, piles of sheet music and portraits of famous classical composers. The theme is varied, however, in an extremely precise way. While the *anticipation* motif is virtually unchanged from the original, the *resolution* motif is extended and elaborated beyond the point where it might be expected to end. It is then left sharply incomplete as Lisa's reverie is brought to an abrupt and unresolved halt by the fall of a pile of sheet music onto the floor. This begins to suggest that the resolution of Lisa's fantasy anticipation of a relationship with Stefan will be problematic. The music is removed from the self-contained structure of Stefan's performance and is reflecting Lisa's flight from reality. Her fantasizing, improvisatory line is disrupted, however, by a final reminder of Stefan's actual relationship to his music. The printed music falling to the floor with an unmusical crash presents music as a concrete physical entity. This paper is only a representation of what music really entails, paralleling Stefan's diegetic and real working relationship to it, as opposed to Lisa's more romantic (over-) involvement. It is possible, from what we see of Stefan, that he and his music have little more than a relatively superficial emotional connection, which nevertheless translates in performance—particularly without sight of that performance—into a kind of passion and emotional depth that in reality he appears not to have. While Stefan is likely to be quite aware of his place in the equation, however, Lisa chooses to believe what she thinks she hears.

The theme next returns as Lisa runs in desperation from the railway station before she must leave with her family for Linz, her voice-over confirming her intention to both confess and offer herself to Stefan. As she reaches the apartment building and runs up the stairs to his front door, the *anticipation* motif returns. After its first two repetitions, its intervals are constricted from two sets of whole tones to two sets of semitones, emphasizing her frantically heightening expectation. Each of these short phrases is 'answered', however, by a similar rising figure in the brass, and it is alongside the last of these that Lisa realizes Stefan is not at home (Example 3.2c). The string and brass phrases are kept separate, and while the brass instrumentation appears to have supported Lisa's increasing excitement, it also underscores her first experience of the difficulty of a workable resolution to her desire. As she then makes her way to the back door of the apartment, two solo woodwind passages introduce a slightly dotted rhythm, which temporarily lightens the mood despite her sad defeat. Both of these instances, however, actually serve to introduce the 'realistic' function of non-string orchestration that will be foregrounded in the following Linz sequence, with its combination of weighty brass band music and the socially desirable but personally abhorrent prospect of conforming to her family's matrimonial expectations.

In order to assure her inescapable bond to Stefan and the past, and therefore to prepare for her abrupt refusal of Leopold's proposal in Linz, the film now has Lisa return to her old, now empty and desolate apartment. Here, she is accompanied by non-diegetic music that encapsulates her emotional trajectory so far. In a musical fusion of both the earliest and latest stages of the score, it confirms the continuing development as well as the inherent circularity, and ultimate hopelessness, of her romantic fantasy. The sound of the piano returns, playing bars 3 to 8 of the original piece, comprising two statements of the main theme (see Example 3.2a). Since Stefan is not at home, and the music is treated with the slight echo effect that conventionally signifies it as existing in a character's imagination, we may assume that we hear the piece because, as her voice-over makes clear, Lisa is remembering it. The sound of the piano, even though it is now outside the confines of diegetic performance, distinguishes this restatement of the theme as the fullest possible return to the original moment of Lisa's fantasy—a musical device that will be used only once more at the very end of the film as she pledges her unchanging love despite all that has happened. A soft, non-diegetic string accompaniment to the piano, however, re-establishes the element of fantasy in the face of the reality suggested both by the recent uses of brass and woodwind and by the possible recollection of the diegetic status of Stefan's original performance evoked by the return of the piano. It also marks the first time that elements of both Stefan's and Lisa's versions of the piece have been heard together. Although, in appearance, this mirrors the earlier scene when she left her bed to listen to him playing, Lisa now controls the appearance of the music and appropriates it in her own space. She has therefore appointed herself the instigator, albeit imaginary, of Stefan's music—reframing her, in her own mind, as the muse who inspires his playing. As Stefan subsequently returns to his apartment with yet another woman, however, a series of sustained string notes once again stymie the musical fulfilment of the fantasy, just as the advent of reality prevents Lisa from confronting the object of her affection.

The transfer that has occurred between the two characters now, ironically, leaves them equally bereft of direct access to musical–emotional representation. Stefan remains the technical source of the music, but has been distanced from his ownership of it by the transfer of the piece out of the (masculine and rational) diegetic space into the (feminine and irrational) level of emotional excess. This transfer has also removed the masculine control and power signified by solo self-containment and the virtuoso display of total mastery over the execution and interpretation of written music. In those moments when he is accompanied by its non-diegetic version, its strong re-association with Lisa means that it can only serve the purpose of gradually encompassing him in her emotional vision as he reads her letter. It is significant, therefore, that he will never be seen to play this piece again. Lisa, on the other hand, is represented by music that has been appropriated from Stefan. Since she has effectively constructed herself as the inspiration for his playing, she not only believes that Stefan is a man of great emotional depth, but that his music expresses an emotional response to her which only she can fully understand. The fact that this refers all her emotions back to him therefore reflects her conviction in their destiny as lovers. Although she fails to realize it, however, the music also contains evidence of the narrative's more objective contextualization of her fantasy. Firstly, its second-hand status means that it must always carry the marks of what we might call the 'real' Stefan, the professional musician and habitual womanizer who is initially completely unaware of Lisa and later evidences no real feelings for her—thus the basis in fantasy of her emotions. Secondly, the specific location of Lisa's misrecognition as a feature of her youth condemns her to an eternally adolescent psychology.

The Intrusion of Diegetic Music

The nature of Lisa's quest is slightly altered by the time of her return to Vienna and her engineering of the only whole evening that she and Stefan ever spend together. Now, she has actual adult contact with him, so that under normal circumstances a relationship might be considered feasible. Her vision of their mutually dependent destiny is so idealized, however, that Lisa needs Stefan to move beyond simple attraction. In order to fulfil her all-or-nothing view of their love, he must truly recognize her unique sympathy with his (presumed) interiority, and thereby realize and acknowledge her crucial role in his musical and emotional life.

Example 3.2a **Franz Liszt, Concert Study in D Flat (*Un Sospiro*). Bars 3–5, melody only. Anticipation–resolution pattern**

Example 3.2b **Daniele Amfitheatrof, *Letter from an Unknown Woman*. Extension and interruption of the *resolution* motif**

Example 3.2c **Daniele Amfitheatrof, *Letter from an Unknown Woman*. Repeated *anticipation* motif and introduction of brass instrumentation**

Example 3.2d **Franz Liszt, Concert Study in D Flat (*Un Sospiro*). Bars 9–12, melody only. Extended resolution pattern**

Example 3.2e **Daniele Amfitheatrof, *Letter from an Unknown Woman*. Extended resolution pattern**

Example 3.2f **Daniele Amfitheatrof, *Letter from an Unknown Woman*. Interruption of *resolution* motif for repetition of whole theme an octave higher**

Example 3.2g **Daniele Amfitheatrof, *Letter from an Unknown Woman*. Whole theme with extended resolution**

Example 3.2h **Daniele Amfitheatrof, *Letter from an Unknown Woman*. Compressed repetition of *anticipation* motif without final resolution**

Lisa has just returned from the world of Linz's diegetic music, which reflected her inability to separate herself—even had she wished to do so—from Stefan and her private fantasy world, and emphasized the lack of real passion in her potential relationship with Leopold. When she returns to Vienna and finally achieves her practical goal of eliciting Stefan's romantic attention, it therefore seems cruelly ironic that the feasibility of her fantasy is undermined by a continued predominance of diegetic music. As their relationship seems to come closest to constituting a matter of fact, therefore, the musical–emotional void of their very first encounter is recalled and they are denied an escape from the reality signified by diegetic performance. Only at one point does Lisa's fantasy manage to break through, but this poignant moment serves to demonstrate the even greater unlikelihood of their successful union by emphasizing the continuing adolescent nature of her idyll. As she and Stefan ride together in a horse and trap, her music makes a sudden reappearance on the non-diegetic soundtrack. A light variation of the main theme (see Example 3.2a) plays in the harp with orchestral accompaniment as they ride together and begin to talk. The theme then continues, however, through the rest of the melody of the original Liszt piece (Example 3.2d), although with a slightly altered rhythm, creating an extended resolution to the theme (Example 3.2e).[46] As this new non-diegetic thematic material appears, the orchestra swells and Lisa reaches out to Stefan. But this is not a reach towards an embrace; rather, she seeks only to tuck his scarf into his coat. This extended musical figure therefore becomes suggestive of the ultimately childlike nature of Lisa's actual fantasy. Her caring gesture paradoxically reveals her desire for an idealized, perhaps even non-sexual union—one based on an innocent, adolescent vision of emotional intimacy—rather than what Stefan has in mind. His pensive comment, 'It's a long while since anyone did that for me', reveals his recognition of the unusual nature of her action, and he responds by buying her a single white rose rather than the usual red roses that the flower-seller is obviously used to providing for him. The return of the solo violin line that has previously suggested Lisa's flights of romantic fantasy in turn suggests that she interprets this as an equally genuine—and perhaps even equally innocent—gesture of affection.

After this sadly isolated moment, however, the film returns to its succession of relatively frivolous diegetic pieces in public and commercial contexts, which suggests the continued construction of Stefan through an association of music, work, the social and the superficial. This is emphasized with particular irony as their evening draws to a close, thereby preparing for the subsequent ruin of Lisa's ultimate emotional moment. As the couple end the evening dancing in a small café, the bombastic bandmaster of Linz and his stiff military musicians are parodied in the humourless and tightly uniformed all-female musical ensemble. The only female musicians in the film—which makes its main protagonist such a slave to the Romantic ideology of music—are unromantic in the worst possible sense. They gulp pints of beer, chomp on huge mouthfuls of food, complain bitterly about their economic conditions, and express sour disdain for the loving but, they rightly assume, unmarried couple. As soon as they leave, Stefan goes to the out-of-tune piano at Lisa's request, and perfectly reproduces the waltz the band has just played, complete with the extra style, rubato, dynamic contrast and elaboration which marks him for Lisa as the only 'real' source of music. Her transition from listener to muse is, thanks to her own machinations, finally complete. Stefan now really is playing 'just for [her]' as she always imagined. She is therefore returned to the height of a little girl, sitting on the

---

[46] The melody shown in Example 3.2a is stated twice in the original piece before the appearance of the extended resolution pattern, as occurs in Example 3.2g.

floor at one end of the keyboard and watching his hands more than his face—as if she still believes that this is where his true emotions lie.[47]

The non-diegetic continuation of this music in the piano and orchestra as the couple return to his apartment recalls the similar orchestration of the music that accompanied Lisa's lonely night of reminiscence and waiting for Stefan before her reluctant departure for Linz. This suggests that this episode may offer a resolution to the ultimate lack of success of that night, so that Lisa will finally have achieved the object of her fantasy. Stefan, however, has turned the musical tables on her in his swift appropriation of the waltz from the female musicians. Although it becomes non-diegetic as they arrive at his apartment, it is, nevertheless, the *wrong* music. It therefore confirms Stefan's (perhaps unwittingly) false adoption of the romantic associations of music as part of a relatively standard and extremely real seduction routine. As they embrace, the last minute reappearance of Lisa's non-diegetic music—specifically the extended resolution pattern with its suggestion of her desire for a caring relationship—is suddenly suspended at a point of jarring incompleteness, making its affect abrupt and dramatic rather than romantic and triumphant. The narrative resolution that, according to Lisa's fantasy, should be offered by this long awaited moment is thus completely denied. When they next meet, and even as they part at the railway station, there is no music. Their moment, it seems, has passed, and Lisa's fantasy temporarily founders.

Lisa and Stefan's Reunion

It is by some chance that Lisa and Stefan are reunited many years later when their paths cross at the opera house. Lisa's flight from the building on the premise of a headache, however, still has the air of her earlier machinations, as it is this that entices Stefan to follow her under the obvious impression that this respectable woman may be open to the idea of a casual extramarital affair. Their reunion offers Lisa a second opportunity for believing that Stefan may be ready to recognize her, a chance for which she is willing to give up everything that she has achieved in her life so far. Accordingly, her increasingly obvious obsession with attaining his recognition is reflected in the intensification of the musical patterns associated with her desire. As she finally accepts, however, his hopeless *lack* of recognition, the musical weight of the score descends upon her, combining all those signals that have long predicted her downfall.

Lisa has by this time had almost ten years of harsh reality to inform her perception of life, including having no contact with Stefan and struggling to raise their son alone. At some stage, she has married—undoubtedly primarily out of

---

47 It is interesting to note the marked similarity of this scene to the painting of Liszt at the piano by Joseph Dannhauser. In this painting, Liszt is surrounded by friends, including Madame D'Agoult, who sits exactly as Lisa does, on the floor at the end of the keyboard, gazing at Liszt as he stares to the heavens in sublime contemplation. Donald Jay Grout in fact suggests that this painting 'exemplifies the Romantic attitude towards the artist', Grout (1980), *A History of Western Music*, third edition with Claude V. Palisca, London, Toronto and Melbourne: J. M. Dent & Sons Ltd, p. 581.

convenience—but at least now lives extremely comfortably with her solicitous, if somewhat formal, husband Baron Johann Stauffer (Marcel Journet). Given all of this, it seems depressingly, while at the same time strangely affirmatively, fatalistic that her desire for her ideal destiny still prevails over all musical and narrative warnings. Although her affections and her fantasy music are now transferred to her relationship with the rather more compliantly adoring figure of her son, Stefan Junior (Leo B. Pessin), his status as a mere temporary replacement for his father is clear. Following in his father's footsteps, he shows great musical promise at school, but his fate can nevertheless be effectively disregarded as soon as Lisa detects the prospect of a reunion with Stefan Senior. Significantly, even if Lisa is now in a position to realize, as we do, the ominous significance of the diegetic music that returns once again to warn her off her proposed course of action, she chooses to ignore it. And this warning is not only recalled in the accompaniment of her re-acquaintance with the now rather dilapidated lothario by the strains of Mozart's opera. It is also contained in the subsequent non- or meta-diegetic recollection of the melody of the diegetic street singers' song that heralded the beginning of their earlier, ultimately disastrous evening together—the first in the catalogue of diegetic pieces that denied the realization of Lisa's romantic fantasy.

As the story moves towards its ultimate point of no return, the musical–narrative dynamic between Lisa's romantic fantasy and the film's 'voice' of reality is thrown into ever-sharpening relief. Lisa's actions therefore appear, despite her own oblivious emotional trajectory, increasingly irrational, futile and destructive. As she searches for Stefan, eventually finding herself outside his apartment and seeing that his light is on, the now non-diegetic instrumental version of the street singers' music is replaced by her fantasy music. The *anticipation* motif plays complete, but the *resolution* motif halts halfway through before leading into a complete statement of the whole theme an octave higher. The higher pitch of the repetition combines with its interruption of the first statement of the theme to intensify the sense of excited expectation (Example 3.2f). Emphasizing her eternally optimistic faith in destiny over and above the memory of her previous disappointment with Stefan, this final approach recalls her earlier flight back from her family at the railway station. The possible negative connotations of this rhyme are overridden, however, by the different effect of the musical intensification. The previous rising frantic tension is replaced with a sense of her excited joy at believing that all misunderstanding is now in the past. This time Stefan is at home and this time, she believes, he knows who she is and is equally desperate for their long-overdue reunion.

Thanks to the undermining of the resolution of the second statement of the theme, however, this heady optimism is immediately tempered—for the audience at least. The melody ends suddenly on a sustained note in the strings, which is held under Lisa's dialogue with a flower-seller in the street. At the same time, the 'realism' of non-string instrumentation is recalled in a repeated descending flute figure, subsequently constricted to a descending semitone in the darker-sounding clarinet. This music strikes an ethereal and ominous tone, ending with a repeated wide descending interval in the strings. Reflecting the movement of the narrative for better or worse towards some kind of resolution, this descending musical pattern begins to counter the usually prevalent *anticipation* motif. Lisa meanwhile misses the final opportunity offered by the film to realize the pitfalls of confusing fantasy and reality. Like her childhood friend, the flower-seller is placed in Lisa's very path. He disturbs her magnetized movement towards Stefan's apartment with a pointed reminder of the reality of sexual relationships—offering her the same type of flowers that Stefan bought for her during their fateful evening together. Instead of being shocked from her reverie by the irony of the coincidence, however, the final descending string interval lends a dark and negative inflection to her choice to buy those same flowers and take them as a reciprocal romantic 'souvenir' to Stefan.

Her continuing faith in the imminent resolution of her fantasy is then represented by the overturning of this musical–narrative warning by a full rendition of the main theme. As in the earlier episode during their horse and trap ride (see Example 3.2e), this continues through the whole melody of the Liszt piece, but this time returns it to something closer to the original rhythm (Example 3.2g). This extended theme returns her once again to the adolescent state of her complete fantasy, and signifies that she believes once again that it is about to be realized. Just as that evening of romance ended with the denial of her fantasy, however, so now the sudden ending of the theme on an unresolved chord at the exact point that she rings the bell of the main door of the apartment building undercuts her still optimistic trajectory. It seems, moreover, to predict not only her own dire fate, but also Stefan's future at the hands of her cuckolded husband, thanks to its move into a chromatic variation of the extended resolution pattern as the camera reveals him in furious observation of his wife. Unaware of this, she climbs the stairs to Stefan's apartment, with the rhythmic compounding of the *anticipation* motif echoing the gradually constricted musical pattern of her earlier pre-Linz ascent. The removal of rests or sustained notes between the three statements of the motif means that the first and second statements overlap, and are followed immediately by the third—suggesting the further increase in intensity of her excited anticipation. The final repetition continues into the *resolution* motif, but eschews actual resolution by stopping midway through its descent. A variation on the extended resolution pattern (see Example 3.2d) then begins but is also stopped before completion on a sustained, unresolved chord as Lisa rings the apartment doorbell (Example 3.2h). The suspension of this line recalls the musical point at which Lisa knocked the music off the shelf as she stole around Stefan's apartment as a child. As Stefan's servant John discovered her then, so he now answers the door and, where she previously ran out on seeing him, he now admits her entrance. Now, the predominance of the *anticipation* motif, eventually compressed into a rising sequential scale pattern, emphasizes her near-hysterical, 'last chance' anticipation. Resolution is still stymied, however, by the appearance of a solo violin line as she gazes at the piano. Different to that of her childhood episode, this solo line seems to suggest more immediately the idea of resolution by only comprising a variation of the extended resolution pattern (see Example 3.2d). Harmonic resolution is delayed, however, until the full rendition of the *anticipation* and *resolution* motifs that heralds Stefan's arrival.

The score now suggests Lisa's imaginary return to her illicit, fantasizing visit to the apartment many years before. Since Stefan's speech is initially more or less conducive to her fantasy, if a little vague, the music begins by following the same gradually fragmenting pattern of the *anticipation* and *resolution* motifs. The dialogue moves unstoppably, however, towards the words that finally begin to alert Lisa to reality, when Stefan asks John to fetch 'the usual things' for a supper during an evening that she believed was a unique moment of fate. At this point, the music can only reveal once more the ultimate hopelessness of her situation. As the second repetition of the two motifs ends with an octave descent of the supporting pedal note, the mood darkens until dissonant and unresolved chords register Lisa's shocked response to Stefan's clumsily unwitting self-revelation.

Following this, Lisa's descent into despair is inevitable, but her hope never quite fades until one last comment by Stefan confirms beyond any doubt that he has no idea of her actual identity. After he lifts her veil with the otherwise promising words, 'I knew last night, didn't you?', and kisses her, the score places rising anticipatory figures over a gradually descending bassline. Lisa's awareness of the already tentative nature of her fantasy is then reflected in the skeletal, rhythmically hesitant and irregular string variation of the *anticipation* and *resolution* motifs as she tries in vain to tell him about their son. Her speech is interrupted by Stefan and her music is fragmented, making this effort to talk seem like her last attempt to rescue the situation before its irretrievable collapse. Stefan goes to fetch champagne and changes the topic of conversation back to himself. As the camera returns to a close-up of Lisa's face as he talks, the strings are joined by a solo flute which plays a descending, dotted rhythm chromatic pattern with a light, frivolous tone. Alongside her own string instrumentation, this recalls the 'comment' of the earlier woodwind and brass passages, thereby contrasting Stefan's buoyant, self-congratulatory mood with the increasingly desperate futility of Lisa's emotional dedication. Recalling the cadenza pattern of bar 37 of the Liszt Concert Study, where Stefan's hands first stumbled and Lisa's fantasy later became secretly complete (see Example 3.1a), as well as the descending pattern of the *resolution* motif, this predominantly descending passage finally fulfils the promise of the restricted extract of music and all of the score's previous warnings. Her fantasy is therefore brought to an end, rather than a resolution (Example 3.1b).

The descending chromatic pattern continues, although in an altered rhythm, as Stefan's question about Lisa's travel experience means that she can no longer deny his complete ignorance of her identity. Ten years ago it was a key topic of conversation during their evening together, and he joked that he knew little about her except that she had 'travelled a great deal'. Now, in a cruel rhyme of his joke, he asks innocently: 'Do you travel a great deal?' As she reels from this blow and struggles to continue responding to Stefan's prattle, the music reflects her confused emotional state through a pointed fusion of selected material from the past. As the camera focuses in close-up on her distressed face, the solo cello—a 'darker' and more tragic version of her earlier light and improvisatory solo violin—plays a 4-note figure. This recalls both the pivotal notes between the *anticipation* and *resolution* motifs, thereby evoking her transitional state, and a minor version of the beginning of the café waltz music that cheated her out of her ideal romance so long ago. The final matching of the fantasy music of Lisa's imagination to the reality of her lifetime with Stefan then comes as she leaves the apartment. Firstly, the descending chromatic scale and the *anticipation* and *resolution* motifs pursue her as she flees down the stairs. Then, a full orchestral statement of the extended resolution pattern appears in response to the crude proposition of a drunken soldier on the street—finally appearing to alert Lisa to the real nature of her lifelong relationship with Stefan.

'...if only you could have recognized what was always yours...could have found what was never lost...if only'

The truly astonishing nature of Lisa's dedication only becomes clear in the final moments of the film. Here we learn that even after such a bitter defeat, she remains fixated on her original conception of Stefan. If she cannot achieve her fantasy in the real world, then her only recourse is to evoke its impossibility as a tragedy. She blames it on Stefan's inability to recognize destiny as clearly as she always could, and so effectively absolves herself of any responsibility, even for the death of their son. As she is seen writing the last part of her letter, ending her life with the classic woman's film sentiment of 'if only', the original Liszt piece returns at the non-diegetic level. As she expresses her still unchanged love for Stefan, the same fusion of piano and strings that accompanied her earlier pre-Linz waiting scene suggests her continuing adolescent confusion of fantasy and reality. Accordingly, as John reveals her name to the still mystified Stefan, he completes the film's succession of 'voices of reality'. He names her not by her current married surname, Stauffer, nor her previous family surname, Kastner, but as Lisa Berndl, her eternal and inescapable childhood incarnation. As the non-diegetic piano relinquishes its solo line to the violin, however, it becomes clear that Stefan has nevertheless relinquished his own independence from Lisa, and has been absorbed into her idea of the romance of their mutual destiny. As Lisa's voice has told their story, Stefan's independent relationship to music has been gradually lost, until at their final meeting he admits that he no longer plays, and does not even have the key to, his own (locked) piano. Just as Stefan turned the musical–emotional tables on Lisa in order to seduce her, she has now 'used' his own music to subject him to her rather more unusual will, and to force him to adopt her view of the emotional significance of his own musical performance. Stefan remembers her through a series of images that she has evoked of their past liaisons, and the accompanying café waltz melody transforms momentarily into the melody of the Liszt theme. As he plunges his grief-stricken face into his hands, the delicacy of the waltz's resolution is destroyed by a sudden loud and dissonant chord.

While Lisa, like Charlotte in *Now, Voyager*, has moved between different modes of self-silencing and self-expression, the effect on her and those around her is quite different. She is first silenced by her own shyness and then by her romantic idealism. She controls her own voice in order to allow Stefan to speak the words that she longs to hear. She waits in vain, however, and her controlled silence having failed, she channels her voice through the indirect medium of her letter. Her emotionally driven choice of self-silencing and control of her own words therefore renders her a positive danger to all around her. Had she articulated her feelings at the outset, there would undoubtedly be no fateful letter. In fact, the Lisa who claims that she has 'no will but [Stefan's]' has actually created the end of Stefan's story—and his life—before her storytelling even starts. The muse has, despite herself, become the siren, and Stefan must ultimately heed her call. Although he is clearly not normally a moral man, and he could still avoid the duel even though the letter has cost him valuable escape time, he chooses to submit to almost certain death at the hands of Lisa's wronged husband. Rather than dismiss her story as nonsense, he is seduced by both the vision of romantic destiny, which matches his own alleged lifetime search for his equally mythical 'goddess', and his central role in its potential realization. In submitting to death, he accepts the responsibility that Lisa sets before him and allows her to give their lives a shared tragic significance. Stefan and Lisa each fulfil their romantic fantasies, in death if not in life, and any last vestige of reality against which to set this excessively emotional conclusion is as remote as Linz.

Conclusion

Narrativizing the woman's related understanding of music and emotion highlights the processes of her emotional construction. The diegetic music gives the female listener a representation for her emotions. It also, however, frames our understanding of those emotions in a particular way. In this context, the historical ideas of female musicality and the relationship of music, the emotions and femininity outlined in Chapter 1, prove informative as a broad framework. In particular, the emotional positioning of women can be conceptualized according to their passivity or activity in relation to the creation and performance of music. The woman positioned as a female listener may not clearly be one of Kathryn Kalinak's 'types', as discussed in Chapter 1, but her representation is still delineated to some degree by her reaction to or influence on the man. Whether or not she can actually speak in the face of her emotions and the music that represents them, the music that she has been 'given' by him both enables and represses her self-expression. The ultimate renunciation or destruction of the female listener then usually signals the difficulty—if not the impossibility—of living life successfully according to her understanding of the music and the musician. Her mode of romanticism is too idealistic and too prone to ignoring the manifestations of reality that obscure her vision. While the ultimate and inevitable force of this reality strikes her hard, however, it also renders her cinematic representation safe.

As a result of her tendency to over-romanticize, the female listener also demonstrates how the control of the male musician can be so powerful as to extend far beyond his actual knowledge, intention or presence. Once she becomes associated with his music at the non-diegetic level, all her emotional responses relate back to him in some way, so that the influence of his music within the text partially negates her own emotional voice, and at the very least renders her dependent upon his thoughts or idea/image of her for her own representation. The actual presence of a musician within the text therefore thematicizes the issue raised in Chapter 2 of complex musical meaning often involving traffic between characters. The designation of the woman as the muse-like influence on the man's diegetic music only compounds the powerless circularity of her dependence upon him. The male musician meanwhile becomes tantamount to an unwitting voice-over narrator, inflecting scenes, characters and trajectories with his emotional/psychological point of view without even realizing it. The strength of the woman's emotional response to this influence comes from her romanticization of the music's meaning in relation to the musician. In more extreme cases, instead of recognizing her feelings as being purely her own, she reinvests them in her perception of the man's emotions. Her feelings for him therefore become confused with his feelings for her, in her mind at least, so that her emotional response to the music may lend him personal qualities that he does not actually possess. If the man proves incapable of living up to the woman's romantic ideal, and yet she refuses to release him from his presumed obligation to her, the extremity of her emotions may even return to destroy him either physically (*Possessed*, *Letter from an Unknown Woman*) or psychologically (*Humoresque*).

Despite the female listener's explicit relationship to music, therefore, she still operates at a significant distance from this music, and most pertinently from the construction of its emotional meaning. It is her distance from music at the diegetic level, first of all, that is blamed for her misrecognition of the musician's real character or feelings. It is a similar distance, however, that is also often represented as responsible for the impossibility of her emotional attachment to any other man. As both Chapter 2 and this chapter demonstrate, without its subsequent transfer to the non-diegetic realm of feminine emotionality, diegetic music, no matter how emotional in itself, often signals a relatively emotionless existence in which the woman can find only limited fulfilment. When music is transferred in this way, however, the woman's distance from the original diegetic performance is actually compounded to place severe limitations on her that both circumscribe her emotional range and deny her individual emotional subjectivity. It is the problem of this continued distance, and the necessity of determining what happens to the woman when it no longer exists, that defines the next stage of the investigation.

Chapter 4

The female musician

'Miss Julia, you're standing on the edge of a precipice.'
Nehemiah (Tom Walls) in *While I Live*

'Are you a big strong muscular girl?' 'No.' 'Thank heavens for that.'
Kit (Stewart Granger) and Lissa (Margaret Lockwood) in *Love Story*

It may be logical to expect that the characterization of the female musician would run counter to the pattern of the female listener, closing completely the melodramatic 'gap' between the woman, her real emotions and her ability to express them, and her musical–emotional representation. The possibility of using her own diegetic music at the non-diegetic level should also negate the difficulties of the emotional limitation of the female listener and allow the woman to take over the narrational function of the score discussed in Chapter 3. In practice, however, this is not the case. To a certain extent, it seems that if an active association with music is not to constitute women as siren-esque *femmes fatales*, their expressivity or creativity must be couched in clearly mitigating or explanatory circumstances. Otherwise, if they cannot be distanced as secondary facilitators of music, recourse may be made to blaming their direct involvement in music for either their dangerous lack or their equally dangerous excess of femininity. Rather than becoming the equivalent of a Romantic male artist, therefore, the female musician only serves to realize the nineteenth-century warnings to women of the perils of elite artistic endeavour. In this context it is hardly surprising that the idea of the serious female classical musician or composer proves to be a problematic characterization.

This chapter therefore raises difficulties that the others do not, primarily because of the sheer paucity of films that attempt this characterization at all, but also due to the need for a more speculative approach that considers a range of possible characterizations rather than clear trends that unite a body of films. This is because, unlike the female listener, the female musician is a divided figure, whose characterization veers in a rather confused fashion between many of the facets of musicality and gender discussed in Chapter 1, and for whom cinema in the 1940s can find no stable identity. Thus the examples cited in this chapter draw on ideas ranging from the de-feminization of female musicians—demonizing them as monstrous examples of everything a woman ought not to be—through the various manifestations of their excessive emotionality or sexuality—predatory sirens or pathetic victims of their own creativity whose only chance for salvation is to prioritize love over music—to their sometime and paradoxical affinity with female listeners. While it seems sadly ironic that this is the subject represented through the least consistent body of films and presenting the least coherent characterization, it is, at the same time, inevitable. The difficulty of characterizing women as serious classical musicians attests, in representational terms at least, to a continuation of the kinds of difficulties with the cultural conception of female musicality discussed in Chapter 1.[1]

Issues in Characterizing Female Musicality and Performance

The Siren

Perhaps the most obvious example of a cinematic take on the archetypal siren is the *femme fatale* of *film noir*. Janey Place suggests that this is one of the few sites where female sexuality becomes actively expressed, but that its equation with intelligence

---

1 Assumptions concerning the natural restrictions of 'femininity' for women attempting original creativity, discussed in Chapter 1, continued to have far-reaching consequences in the twentieth century. Marcia J. Citron, for example, suggests: '[I]n the sense that for women before *c.* 1950 a male past was "the only game in town," a woman had to relate to that tradition.' Illustrating the identity crisis facing female composers at this time, Citron cites a 1903 review of Ethel Smyth's opera *Der Wald*, which stated that 'with respect to strong climaxes and full brass writing "the gifted Englishwoman has successfully emancipated herself from her sex"', Citron (1993), *Gender and the Musical Canon*, Cambridge, New York and Melbourne: Cambridge University Press, pp. 67–8. In the same vein, Sophie Fuller's collection on female composers contains evidence of such gender prejudice in the early part of the twentieth century. These include: a 1907 *Musical Times* review of Ethel Barns's *Concertstück* for Violin and Orchestra in D Minor, which finds that '"[t]hough not strong the work is graceful, and may be termed feminine in the best sense of the word"'; an account of how, during the 1930s, '[s]ome British critics thought that [Elizabeth] Maconchy's work was too modern and intellectual, qualities they found especially disturbing in music written by a woman'; and an account of Julia Smith, who, again in the 1930s, 'was given a composition fellowship at the Juilliard to study with Rubin Goldmark, who was initially reluctant to accept her as a pupil, claiming that all his other women students had eventually given up their careers to look after their families'. See Sophie Fuller (1994), *The Pandora Guide to Women Composers: Britain and the United States 1629–Present*, London and California: Pandora, pp. 45, 199 and 286 respectively. Despite this continued prejudice, however, Fuller also details many successful twentieth-century women composers, an increasing number of whom were gradually beginning to find their way into the British classical music establishment, including as academics, as performers, through broadcasting, and even as film music composers. She notes, for example, that Grace Williams started composing for the Strand Film Company at the instigation of Benjamin Britten in 1936, and that Elisabeth Lutyens scored her first film, *Jungle Mariners*, for the Crown Film Unit in 1944. See Fuller, pp. 340 and 195 respectively. Concert pianists Eileen Joyce and Harriet Cohen also featured on many British feature film soundtracks and concert pianist Myra Hess CBE (Dame Myra Hess from 1941 onwards) was featured in documentaries *Listen to Britain* (1942), *Diary for Timothy*, and the short film *Myra Hess* (1946). Such continuing confusion over female musicianship means that it is hardly surprising that 1940s film had little framework for representing a stable vision of the female musician—most pertinently whose music, rather than her sexuality/emotionality/domesticity, was most central to her identity.

and power is inevitably associated with the downfall of male characters.[2] While the experience of such dangerous sexual aggression may be exciting and sensuous, it must nevertheless be neutralized by the eventual destruction of the woman herself.[3] The clear traces of the operatic double frame that such a characterization and structure exhibit, however, may still be unable to contain completely the force of the woman. Just as Carolyn Abbate and Gretchen A. Wheelock find the operatic female voice resonating beyond the actual character's narrative constriction (see Chapter 1), Place suggests that 'it is not … [the *femme fatale*'s] inevitable demise we remember but rather … [her] strong, dangerous and, above all, exciting sexuality'.[4]

Since Place's examination is largely concerned with narrative structure and visual style, however, she does not examine the striking frequency of the *femme fatale*'s association with music, particularly in the form of diegetic song. Recalling Kathryn Kalinak's ideas on the association of jazz idioms with female sexuality, it hardly seems surprising that the 'spider woman'[5] of *film noir* should spin her destructive web at least partly through the strong sexual connotations of popular song. In this case, rather than being 'regarded' by the non-diegetic score or subject to the comment of mise-en-scène and editing, she actively and self-consciously adopts the powerful position of the performer suggested by Richard Poirier and Edward Said (see Chapter 3 of this book). The singing woman specifies the nature of the performance and its archetypal resonances not only through the style of music and perhaps even the lyrics, but also through the 'direct' mode of musical communication constituted by song.[6] This leaves her unmediated and unencumbered by any musical instrument other than the (dangerous) body itself. When the woman, and particularly the *femme fatale*, sings—as in, for example, *The Glass Key* (1942), *The Big Sleep* (1946), *Gilda* (1946), *The Killers* (1946), *Dead Reckoning* (1947) and *The Lady from Shanghai* (1947)—she actively seeks the male attention to her body that, as I described in Chapter 1, may otherwise plague female singers and performers. Indeed, even when she only facilitates or requests music to convey her message, the lyrics may still explicitly state the physical and seductive nature of her mission—as in, for example, Kitty (Joan Bennett)'s use of *My Melancholy Baby* (Burnett–Norton–Watson) in *Scarlet Street* (1945). The man, in an appropriate response to the ancient lure of

---

2 Janey Place (1996), 'Women in Film Noir', in E. Ann Kaplan (ed.), *Women in Film Noir*, London: BFI, p. 47.

3 Ibid., p. 48.

4 Ibid.

5 Ibid., p. 47.

6 I am borrowing here from the distinction that Susanne K. Langer draws between the 'direct and indirect utterance' of vocal and instrumental music respectively. Langer suggests that the voice 'is the prime avenue of self-expression', so that vocal music constitutes a directly personal utterance to which instrumental music can only aspire. See Langer (1953), *Feeling and Form: A Theory of Art Developed from Philosophy in a New Key*, London: Routledge and Kegan Paul Limited, pp. 141–5. This clearly coincides with ideas of the sexual overdetermination of the woman who expresses herself musically before men, and specifically suggests a very particular relationship between the *femme fatale* and her song. Within my formulation, however, the 'indirect' musical voice becomes not instrumental music, but rather the woman who lacks the ability or opportunity to adopt the direct musical voice.

the Siren, is often helplessly attracted and potentially completely disempowered. Even if one considers that the role of the *femme fatale* in fact reflects primarily the weakness and desire for transgression of the male character, she is still represented as his predator, and treated accordingly.

The Indirect Musical Voice

In terms of patriarchal fears of female sexuality—as the model of the *femme fatale* makes clear—a woman taking control of her own musical voice is an obvious sign of danger. Those films that seek to represent women through an involvement with diegetic music without evoking such condemnatory connotations must therefore find ways of diverting this threat. The siren singer's performance is marked by the directness of its communication of both sexual awareness and self-possession. This places her in absolute opposition to the female listener, whose indirect access to music marks her emotional dependence on the man and, as a result, her relative powerlessness. Perhaps it is possible, therefore, that more subtle degrees of control may create a continuum between these two extremes, giving the woman access to musical expression, but without the stark directness and negative purpose of the siren. Maintaining the 'innocence' of a woman's musical self-expression may be possible either by distancing her from the actual site of musical production and limiting—but not completely denying—her relationship to its meaning, or by removing her from the sight of a diegetic audience. Her direct musical 'voice', being partially mediated, therefore becomes an illusion.

An example of such contrasting types of woman can be seen in the two female musicians vying for the attentions of the male composer in *Hangover Square*. Claudia Gorbman describes how pianist Barbara (Linda Darnell) and singer Netta (Fay Marlowe) act predominantly as musical and sexual reflections of the different sides of composer George Bone (Laird Cregar).[7] Netta is a classic siren singer who seduces the innocent composer emotionally and musically. Showing little more than contempt for his serious music, she 'steals' a melody from his unfinished piano concerto, adds her own lyrics, and shamelessly persuades George to make it into a song for her to perform. She selfishly saps his strength and resolve with the constant promise of her affections and thus precipitates his ultimate self-destruction. Barbara, despite being a musician herself, is removed from having her own musical voice by her greater concern with encouraging George's career. Like Christine in *Deception* and Cathy in *Night Song*, she places her own ability in the service of the man as his respectable muse. Unlike these other women, however, she manages to survive intact as both a respectably 'feminine' woman *and* a performing musician by playing only in private contexts or, when in public, only strictly as a substitute for George, and by focusing her talent as a performer exclusively on promoting *his* musical voice. *Hangover Square* therefore deals with Barbara by offsetting her musicality against her relationship to the composer whose music she plays. She 'imitates' his voice, in effect, seemingly adding nothing with her own interpretation.

---

7 Claudia Gorbman (1987), *Unheard Melodies: Narrative Film Music*, Bloomington: Indiana University Press, London: BFI, p. 152.

Despite actually being a performer, Barbara's position in relation to music is therefore similar in some ways to that of non-performing women in films such as *Laura* (1944) and *Penny Serenade* (1941). The first of these films bases its monothematic score around a tune that is mooted by the male friends of the 'late' Laura (Gene Tierney) as being her favourite. While it may therefore represent her own taste and personality, Royal S. Brown suggests that it actually operates in the service of her construction from various male points of view.[8] Whatever meaning it may connote in terms of Laura's sexuality[9] therefore appears less directly relevant to her than it is to Waldo, Shelby (Vincent Price) and Mark (Dana Andrews). Although Julie (Irene Dunne) in *Penny Serenade* actually takes the position of (unspeaking) narrator through her visual flashbacks, Caryl Flinn points out that the active controlling position that this suggests is somewhat mitigated by their musical catalyst. Julie's courtship, marriage, motherhood, bereavement and marital separation are recalled by her listening to a succession of records from a set entitled *The Story of a Happy Marriage*. While it is Julie who chooses to put the records on the gramophone in order to reminisce, however, the actual expression of her thoughts and feelings is designated to the authors of the songs and the voices of the singers on those records.[10] Although allowed within the diegetic space, therefore, rather than being exiled to the non-diegetic level, Julie's emotional 'voice' is nevertheless simultaneously silenced and represented. Her apparently active relationship to 'her' music actually constitutes one of facilitation and response.

The Classical Musician and the Romantic Model

The problem of characterizing the woman as a serious classical musician therefore stems from the implicit need for her to be musically active and yet—paradoxically, in terms of cultural assumptions—emotionally and sexually self-controlled. The difficulty with realizing this combination results from the fact that the characterization of the female musician refuses to reconsider the gender prejudice of its Romantic model. Rather than overturning this bias and reconfiguring the woman according to the conception of the male artist, her behaviour is dictated instead by the 'inevitability' of her excessive femininity. The female musician film therefore attempts to characterize the impossible paradox of a woman who is easily overwhelmed by the emotional connotations of music, and unable to control her emotionality in a 'proper' and socially acceptable manner, but who is nevertheless a creative and/or performing musician.

Whereas it does not seem to make any real difference whether the male musician is a performer or composer, in the case of the female musician the difference is

---

[8] Royal S. Brown (1994), *Overtones and Undertones: Reading Film Music*, California and London: California University Press, pp. 87–90.

[9] See Kathryn Kalinak (1992), *Settling the Score: Music and the Classical Hollywood Film*, Madison: University of Wisconsin Press, Chapter 7, on the conflicting attitudes to Laura's sexuality held by those involved in the production of the film.

[10] Caryl Flinn (1992), *Strains of Utopia, Gender, Nostalgia and Hollywood Film Music*, Oxford and Princeton: Princeton University Press, p. 145.

significant. In Hollywood in and around the 1940s, in fact, there appear to be no characterizations of a female composer, despite the appearance of women in other creative careers such as designing and writing. The nearest example may be Christine in *Deception* who, according to her lover/husband Karel, used to compose, but has apparently stopped since being taken under the benevolent wing of male composer Alex. She hardly even plays anymore, and her one performance within the film is visually framed between the dual—and duelling—presence of these two men. Alex eventually interrupts her performance, effectively silencing her musical voice for the remainder of the film, after which point she takes on more of the character of the female listener to the male musicians. Such a paucity of suitable characterizations in both Hollywood and British films at this time problematizes the discernment of consistent trends in the specific characterization of the female composer, making it possible only to consider patterns of representation in relation to female musicians in general.

The two types of female musician do, in any case, share many similar issues. The real or imagined vulnerability of the woman is a case in point. Damage to or mutilation of the hands affects female musicians—in this case performers rather than composers—in both *The Seventh Veil* and *The Lamp Still Burns* (1943). Whereas in *The Lamp Still Burns* it constitutes an incidental issue, in *The Seventh Veil* it provides the main catalyst for the whole narrative. In this case, however, it is primarily the *fear* of damage that affects concert pianist Francesca (Ann Todd), and makes her imagine that the injuries she has suffered in a car accident will end her career. She is both suicidal and mute at the outset of the film, and—we see in flashback—has already ended her first concert appearance by fainting on stage as a result of the same fear. She is, nevertheless, able eventually to conquer this to live—we assume—a normal life with the man she loves, Nicholas (James Mason), her former guardian. Where the female composer is concerned, however, such vulnerability is extended to suggest a more punitive attitude, associating the woman with emotional and/or physical collapse, illness and death. One of the most gloriously overwrought instances of this can be found in the British film *While I Live* (1947). After its female composer sleep-walks to unwitting suicide while haunted by a piece that she cannot complete, the film focuses on the legacy of hysterical—and exclusively female—obsession and mental breakdown caused by her death. *Love Story*, on the other hand, condemns its composer heroine with a fatal heart condition in order, partially at least, to explain her difficulty in withstanding the emotional and physical rigours of performing her own music. The inability to compose or perform music without emotional and/or physical breakdown links all these women broadly to the Romantic notion of the 'impossibility' of the serious female musician. The woman is too purely 'feminine' to be able to control herself effectively in the face of music, and the excess offered by her own creativity or performance therefore overwhelms her.

This gendered Romantic inheritance is made particularly clear in the distinct modes of representation employed for the diegetic performances of male and female musicians. This is the only scenario that is bound to be common to films dealing with both genders of musician, as well as being the point at which character meets music in the most direct way. It is therefore inevitable that the attitude that the film displays towards musicality in practice will reflect the broader approach to emotional characterization within the text as a whole. While this can support a straightforwardly gendered construction of the artist, it also serves to make sense of those characterizations—male or female—that attempt a more subtle balance of masculinity and femininity. The most important distinction lies between the musical performance as 'performance', or even work, and as an expression of genuine and private emotion specific to the performer. Such definitions should, of course, be seen purely as a device of film narrative, since it would be both unreasonable and unnecessary to make the case that such a stark distinction exists in real musical life and performance. The discussion that follows is therefore strictly in cinematic terms. This is obviously not, furthermore, a clear distinction, and requires careful definition in this particular context if not to be misunderstood.

In any musical performance, the performer may strive to convey the emotions that they find implied within the text of the music. It therefore seems fair to assume that the performer will experience these feelings at some level in order to be able to communicate them. The distinction that this body of films constructs lies between this level of emotional involvement and the specific personal memories and feelings of the performer relating to distinct diegetic events. The capacity for visual evidence to demonstrate these emotions allows a kind of separation of the emotions of the piece from the emotions of the performer. It may not necessarily be this specific music that causes the emotional reaction of the player, but merely the presence of music and more specifically the very act of performing itself. While in conventional performance there is therefore the possibility of the performer evoking emotional states in a relatively abstract or 'detached' manner, in this circumstance the relationship is reversed. Now, the music becomes abstracted as an agent of whatever emotion the performer is experiencing as a result of other non-musical diegetic circumstances. Whether this shift in emotional focus impacts on the performance itself is left to each individual instance.

While concise terminology in such a case is certainly problematic, it is nevertheless necessary to identify a way in which to differentiate between these two types of filmed performance. It is impossible to define exactly the divide between a performance that conveys emotions that may be implied by the piece and one that evokes particularly personal resonances in the performer. In order, however, to attempt to indicate the different nature of these involvements, I use the terms 'conventional performance' and 'personal performance' respectively. The diegetic context of the performance determines its possible categorization in these terms. It is then left to the particular way in which the performance itself is filmed to demonstrate how the character reacts to that potential, and what we can understand of their emotionality as a result. Importantly, the development of character achieved through these scenes is almost exclusively reserved for the eyes of the film audience. In the particular case of the personal performance, the performer must, usually, continue playing whatever they feel. It is only the film audience that is party to the inner conflict experienced and the resultant struggle to continue, unless this ends in all too visible failure. Only we, therefore, understand the private thoughts and fears that the music brings to the foreground of the performer's thoughts. As far as the diegetic audience is concerned, it is a conventional performance like any other.

At the heart of this distinction is the articulation of the particular dynamic between the musician and their instrument. In a conventional performance, the active relationship of the character to the instrument is central. The instrument generally remains in the frame and there is a focus on shots demonstrating the performer's technical musical prowess, notably through views of their hands on the keyboard or fingerboard. The performer tends to demonstrate attention to the music and their own part in it, with their gaze remaining on the instrument, the musical score or conductor as appropriate. Performances of this type include Stefan's practising of the Liszt Concert Study in D Flat in *Letter from an Unknown Woman*; Francesca's performance of the Rachmaninov Piano Concerto No. 2 in *The Seventh Veil*; Christine's performance of the Beethoven Sonata No. 23 in F Minor (*Appassionata*) and all of Karel's cello performances in *Deception*; and all of Paul's recitals in *Humoresque*. The personal performance, however, removes attention from potentially distracting musical technicalities. The musician is gradually isolated from the physical presence of their instrument through techniques of framing. This both represents and allows their private emotional removal from the public communication of conventional performance. The music may then appear to reflect their facial expressions or physical gestures, creating an intimate effect that suggests the more usual individual and interior representation of non-diegetic music. One defining characteristic of the personal performance is the musician's fixed, apparently unseeing stare into the middle distance. Even with the instrument still visible, this indicates a certain level of detachment from the technicalities of playing and a concentration on otherwise concealed emotions. As the performance progresses, the instrument is typically eradicated from the frame, with the camera focusing on increasingly close shots of the performer's face as their emotion reaches its greatest excess. Although at some level, therefore, we are still aware of the performance event, the source of the music is obscured and the performer has apparently become oblivious to the physical task in which they are actually engaged.

The gender implications of degrees of proximity to music and the emotions that this stylistic distinction embodies are often used in the female musician film to reflect the broader characterization of the woman. *The Great Lie* (1941), *The Seventh Veil* and *Deception*, as well as films featuring isolated performances by characters not otherwise known as musicians such as *Madonna of the Seven Moons* (1944) and *The Wicked Lady* (1945), show women as capable of both performance types. There is, however, a clear alignment of the styles to specific points of characterization. In *The Seventh Veil*, for example, Francesca's gradual hardening of heart is marked in the difference between her first and last concerto performances. During her debut concert—thanks to the careless words of an old friend immediately beforehand—she remembers an early musical failure following a caning on her hands at school. Despite the outward power of the performance, we are painfully aware through visual signals of her extreme difficulty in continuing—a point that is emphasized by her fainting as soon as it ends. By her last public appearance, however, she is able to deliver a commensurate conventional performance, giving nothing private away to either the diegetic or film audience. She has become so much more cynical and self-possessed at the hands of her overbearing guardian that she is able to keep her excitement and strong feelings about what she intends to do immediately after the concert under cool control, even in the face of the most famously emotional music. Moments of personal performance are less common, however, in male musician films, and tend to indicate an unusual and specific vulnerability that may also only be temporary. While this issue will be covered in greater detail in Chapter 5, particularly through the case study of *Dangerous Moonlight*, it is nevertheless worth noting here that in both this film and *Hangover Square*, the male protagonists are, in a sense, threatened with de-masculinization through periods of lack of control over their own emotions or rationality. The personal performance is therefore used as a means of representing their state of mind at a specific point in time. In each case, however, conspicuous care is exercised in contextualizing these moments as either the result of actual illness or clearly temporary vulnerability that is soon overcome. 'Feminine' emotional display is therefore once again equated with an undesirable loss of self-control—more common and predictable, by far, in female performers.

Characterizing the Female Musician

The difficulty of characterizing the female musician, particularly in the face of her own performance, therefore often leads to representations that deny the woman as a musician and/or a 'woman'. *Deception* not only conceals Christine's musical ability and professional status, but also designates her as cold and mercenary towards Alex, dangerously neurotic, duplicitous, and ultimately murderous. In *The Great Lie*, renowned concert pianist Sandra (Mary Astor) is characterized as monstrously selfish and unfeminine, devoid of humility, sympathy and, most heinous of all, the maternal instinct. To ensure that this is absolutely clear, she is pitted against the non-musical Maggie (Bette Davis), who is sympathetic, patient, devoted and, of course, deeply and unselfishly maternal. And although *Intermezzo*'s Anita is initially presented as both musically and personally impressive in her own right, her solo ability is immediately appropriated by the male violinist, who honours her with both musical and social subjugation as his accompanist and mistress. The fictitious female musician therefore shares many qualities with her 'real' biopic counterpart.[11] George Custen observes that female biopics most commonly depict women as 'entertainers', with, perhaps tellingly, 'the paramour' in second place,[12] thus suggesting the possible attraction of examining the trajectory of the 'actual' siren. Throughout all professions, however, he finds:

> [W]here a male famous figure is ruled by the destiny of his talent, a woman is dominated by the alleged biological demands of her gender … The difference between male and female careers, then, is striking: men are defined by their gift, women by their gender, or their gendered use of their gift.[13]

---

[11] See Chapter 3, footnote 14 for an account of contemporaneous attitudes towards the comparative depiction of real and fictitious musicians.

[12] George F. Custen (1992), *Bio/Pics: How Hollywood Constructed Public History*, New Brunswick, NJ: Rutgers University Press, p. 103.

[13] Ibid., p. 106.

The female entertainer—or musician or composer—is therefore often destined either to give up her profession for love and domesticity or to suffer the tragic consequences of trying to maintain her career.[14]

As a result, and as I suggested at the outset of this chapter, selecting a case study through which to examine the characterization of the female musician is no straightforward task. In 1940s Hollywood, *The Great Lie* offers one of the few examples of an autonomous professional female musician whose diegetic performances continue throughout the film. The film makes little attempt, however, to treat her in the same way as a male musician in terms of the effect of her music on the narrative. In the male musician–female listener narrative, even the man who is only a performer—rather than a composer—is allowed to dominate the non-diegetic soundtrack. The different relationship of the female musician to her male listener, however, means that her music tends not to transfer between the diegetic and non-diegetic levels in quite the same way or to the same effect. Sandra, as *The Great Lie*'s female classical musician, is in fact positioned as a temporary disruption to the otherwise happy relationship enjoyed by her male listener, Pete (George Brent), and his sometime fiancée, Maggie. She is thus designated as both romantically and, in non-diegetic terms, even musically subordinate to her non-musician rival in their battle for Pete's affections.

From the outset, Sandra is defined almost exclusively through her status as a musician. At the non-diegetic level, however, any potential that she may have for achieving emotional dominance of the narrative is undermined by the treatment of the main theme deriving from her most prominent diegetically performed piece. Instead of dominating the score—and rendering it monothematic as is often the case in the male musician–female listener film—Sandra's theme assumes no more importance than either of the two other principal themes. She also has comparatively few episodes in the non-diegetic score where her own theme appears to reflect anything of her own emotions. On the contrary, her appearances and conversations are often accompanied by no music at all, diegetic music that continues regardless of circumstances, or themes recalling other characters. Such instances of music therefore become complicit with those characters who are opposed to her. Her own theme is used as a means of reflecting the feelings of other characters towards her, usually only when she is specifically mentioned in the dialogue, and even then it is often usurped by one of the other two themes. In fact her theme is in many ways outnumbered, since it represents Sandra alone, whereas the other two themes unite Pete and Maggie. The non-diegetic score consequently becomes a kind of thematic battleground for the opposing emotions contained in the narrative—a battleground from which Sandra is predictably but forcibly ejected to take up once again her final position as the lonely producer of diegetic music. Pete and Maggie, therefore, enjoy complete musical–emotional independence from Sandra, so that her music lends her very little emotional weight in the way that would be expected with a male musician. It seems, on the contrary, as if the film goes overboard to deny the dangerous capacity of music to overcome other characters and draw them hypnotically to the musician.

14 Ibid., p. 105.

As a consequence, it makes a continual point of how little emotional grip Sandra holds over the other characters.

The origin of this lies in the lack of mobilization of the emotional magnetism of musical performance witnessed in the male musician–female listener film. There is no first performance through which we see Pete being mesmerized by Sandra's talent, and moreover both Pete and Maggie's ignorance of music and Pete's disinterest in Sandra's career are made explicit. The film, in fact, seems wilfully dismissive of any emotional impact arising from her musicality, either on herself or the other characters, choosing instead to view her talent in an overtly professional way. A significant aspect of this is the very specific representation of her performances as completely stripped of genuine 'feminine' emotion of any kind. They are presented instead as acts of strenuous labour, de-feminization—if not a parody of masculinization—and always as indicative of her active choice of work over romance.

The opening credits show female hands at the keyboard playing the Tchaikovsky Piano Concerto No. 1, which will become—like Stefan's Liszt Concert Study in *Letter from an Unknown Woman*—her most frequently played piece. In retrospect, however, once characters and actors are established, it becomes clear that this sequence simultaneously undermines any claim to narrative authority that Sandra's initial centrality may conventionally imply, by the placement of the paired names of Bette Davis and George Brent over the image. It is only in the subsequent scene that we discover that the hands belong to Mary Astor, rather than Bette Davis, thus relegating Sandra, in romantic terms, to third place in the narrative. Sandra is characterized as melodramatically self-absorbed, forceful and demanding. She has been married before and is completely cavalier about her divorce. Although she does love Pete, she is hard and domineering towards him in a way that contrasts starkly with Maggie's tenderness, vulnerability and all-consuming devotion. Much discussion of Sandra revolves around her brilliance as a musician and the demand for her performances. Occasional references to her magnificence or greatness as a woman only seem to distance her all the more from feminine ideals, and her style of dress, while glamorous, tends towards a severe emphasis of her height and the broadness of her shoulders—a style that seems very much in keeping with her short, rigidly sculpted hairstyle. All these characteristics are brought to bear in the way in which her musical performances are shot. On most occasions, she is seen playing extracts from the Concerto, and significantly, these extracts are restricted to the first and last movements, thus focusing on her power and virtuosity while conspicuously avoiding the more romantic lyricism of the second movement. Her performance style, moreover, is then such that the physicality of the piece is emphasized, if not over-emphasized.

This is first demonstrated early in the film after Pete has issued her with an ultimatum, offering her the choice of marrying him or playing a concert in Philadelphia. After he leaves she approaches the piano almost hesitantly, before suddenly grasping and tearing off its cover with some violence. She then opens the heavy lid, removes her rings and opens the keyboard lid, before sitting down to play the powerful opening chords of the Concerto. The physicality of the piano itself is therefore made an issue even before we see her style of playing, as is the necessity for her to remove the feminine trappings of jewellery and demonstrate her physical strength in uncovering and opening up the instrument. This at once equates playing to an act of work, and in turn equates this to an act of defeminization. At first as she plays, the piano remains in shot, with Sandra in profile playing the repeated ascending chord pattern that opens the Concerto. Her eyes remain steadfastly on the keyboard. She is then seen from over the top of the piano, without the piano in shot, leaving only her head and shoulders in medium close-up. This allows us to see her look up momentarily with an only mildly anxious expression, before a fade to the poster for her Philadelphia concert and the appearance on the soundtrack of the orchestra, thus indicating her decision in response to Pete's ultimatum. This concert offers Sandra's most effortful performance. Her face shows aggressive concentration and great effort, rather than easy mastery, and the movement of her arms and shoulders suggests a certain difficulty in performing the piece, since she makes it look so arduous. The fact that she complains afterwards of cold in her shoulder and acknowledges that she didn't play very well, could account for the peculiarly laboured style of performance and the impatient, irritable look on her face as she plays and glowers up at the conductor. It could also, of course, simply be attributable to Mary Astor's style of miming. The fact remains, however, that although this is not a long concert episode, it is her only extended performance sequence in the film and so carries a good deal of weight in terms of how her general musicianship is represented.

That her performance style should be aggressive makes sense in terms of her overall characterization. On the other hand, however, the effortful aspect of her playing makes something of a mockery of her musical mastery. While she is undoubtedly, as everyone in the film says, a great musician, she requires in this particular scene an almost undignified level of strength and concentration in order to achieve this and after the performance, talking to Maggie, she refers to the fact that she is 'sweating like a stoker'. Her 'masculine' ability to control music and emotionality, therefore, becomes somewhat pitiable and parodic. She is taking on a role culturally defined as masculine, but the effort involved makes her appear ridiculous, and certainly demands a high price in terms of her conventional femininity. Although this suggests a certain revulsion at the idea of the female musician, it nevertheless offers an interesting alternative to the more conventional weaknesses of the characterization. By presenting Sandra as largely emotionless in a conventionally female/feminine sense, the film neatly avoids the question of whether a woman is able to support the emotions she releases during a musical performance. She rarely allows herself to lose self-control, and aggressively resists periods of enforced vulnerability, such as grieving—or indeed femaleness, such as pregnancy. This renders her a very negative model of commensurate female professionalism—incapable of being a 'normal' woman, entirely self-centred and with her musical career constituting an alternative to a real emotional life.

An interesting test of this is contained in her performance of the Chopin Waltz Op. 69, No. 1 in A Flat Major. This is first heard as she lies pregnant in the Arizona shack, listening to a gramophone record. Whether or not it is a recording of Sandra playing the piece, it does form an association between the piece and her pregnancy. In the conventional gender terms outlined in Chapter 1, this piece could be seen as more appropriate for a female performer—it is reminiscent of a social dance associated with couples and its style is relatively gentle, tuneful and serene. Sandra is also temporarily disabled from playing, and so her use of the record is indicative of her vulnerable physical condition and her isolation from her own world and musical 'voice'. When she later arrives at Pete and Maggie's home, intending to use her right to her baby as a means of regaining her former lover, it is her playing of this piece that alerts Maggie to her presence. Initially, as Maggie watches her from the hallway, Sandra looks at the keyboard while she plays. After she sees Maggie, however, a shot-reverse shot pattern reveals her direct gaze at her rival—complete with self-confident smile—while continuing to play. She now has the most threatening combination of factors on her side, and the music underlines this. She has the presumed femininity of her maternal status, but has also regained the strength and independence characterized by her musical ability. The piece that she could only listen to before is now under her fingers, and she plays, interestingly, without the aggressive and laborious style of her previous performances. In this case, therefore, the music is the way in which she reminds Maggie of her strength and fortitude as well as her womanhood, and most especially her secret link to Pete (who currently believes the baby to be Maggie's). In the final analysis, however, this music represents in a rather ironic way only Sandra's attempt to perform femininity and maternity to achieve her own ends, since the motivation that lies behind her visit is emotional blackmail, manipulation and the destruction of Pete and Maggie's marriage. When she is unable to regain Pete as part of the bargain, she no longer wants to take her child and leaves him to the couple's care.

The British film *Love Story*, on the other hand, offers what is at the very least a more generous attempt at characterizing an active female musician. Its protagonist, Lissa Campbell, is located firmly as a musician in contemporary wartime Britain, even to the extent that her opening concert is presented as being part of Myra Hess's National Gallery series.[15] Within this strong supporting context, particularly in terms of its reference to high-profile female musicality, the film can take the unusual and brave step of characterizing her as both a composer and a performer—most specifically of her own music. Remarkable also, is her relationship to her male listener, which actually attempts to reverse the gendering of the usual male musician–female listener configuration.

Lissa's characterization may also be informed by her specificity as a female protagonist in a Gainsborough melodrama. Christine Gledhill has discussed how the traditional domestic context of melodrama is characteristically disrupted by war. As a result, 'If women are drawn out of the home, an image of "woman" must be refound which reties female desire to nation'.[16] Gainsborough melodramas typically present

[15] The National Gallery lunchtime concerts were initiated by Myra Hess as a means of maintaining public morale in the face of the Second World War's blackout. The series was hugely popular and ran from 1939 to 1946. Lissa's first appearance is therefore strongly coded in terms of the cultural role of women in wartime.

[16] Christine Gledhill (1996), '"An Abundance of Understatement": Documentary, Melodrama and Romance', in Gledhill and Gillian Swanson (eds), *Nationalising Femininity: Culture, Sexuality and British Cinema in the Second World War*, Manchester and New York: Manchester University Press, p. 219.

women who are 'flamboyant and aggressive'[17] in a space made 'for the release of unsocialised, personal demands of female desire'.[18] Such female 'waywardness' or 'wilfulness' comes in many forms and with many mitigations, one of which Sue Harper sees as musical activity.[19] Such films offer 'an essentially bohemian notion of artistic freedom: that the creative force should be allowed free play regardless of the gender or class of its possessor, and that its repression is fatal'.[20] Citing as examples *Love Story*, *The Seventh Veil*, *Madonna of the Seven Moons* and *I'll Be Your Sweetheart* (1945), Harper deduces of their female musicians that '[t]heir artistic virtuosity gives them the confidence to seek love in the unlikeliest places'.[21] And such confidence does not just impact on the women's sexuality. Harper also suggests the powerful symbolism of the female musician in countering the advocacy 'of submission to male power'.[22] Although music bears a relationship to the woman's emotions and desire, it also allows her some evident independence of thought and *self*-satisfaction. Accordingly, Harper suggests that in *Love Story* and *The Seventh Veil*, the heroines' 'musical performance permits the expression of autonomy and both films should be interpreted as texts which, on one level, celebrate female creativity and energy in the face of insuperable difficulties'.[23] Women, in other words, are shown to be potentially as involved in their own abilities as they are in their feelings towards others—particularly men.

Despite this, however, Lissa's characterization still does not escape the cultural problems and pitfalls associated with female musicianship. Although her composition of the *Cornish Rhapsody* lies at the heart of the story, it has to contend with other themes before becoming dominant at the non-diegetic level and signifies as many emotional difficulties and misunderstandings at this level for her as it does for her male listener. She is characterized in many ways as a combination of the male musician and the female listener, and sometimes takes on more of the characteristics of the latter. By the same token, Kit, as the male non-musician character, also adopts some of the usual features of the male musician and is even given a contending diegetic theme of his own that transfers onto the non-diegetic track—something unknown for a female listener. This allows the film at once to demonstrate and celebrate Lissa's ability to compose and perform music, while simultaneously clearly feeling the need to apologize for and display the real dangers—to the woman at least—of female creativity. The apparent ambition of her characterization is also rather disappointingly countered by its contingency upon the extreme social and political conditions of the time. She is musically and emotionally empowered on a personal level for the specific wartime purpose of re-injecting a patriotic fighting spirit into a flagging

---

[17] Sue Harper (1996), 'The Years of Total War: Propaganda and Entertainment', in Gledhill and Swanson (op. cit.), p. 205.

[18] Gledhill (1996), p. 223.

[19] Harper (1996), pp. 208–9. Harper lists musicianship among a range of mitigations.

[20] Ibid., p. 208.

[21] Ibid.

[22] Harper (1988), 'The Representation of Women in British Feature Films, 1939–45', in Philip M. Taylor (ed.), *Britain and the Cinema in the Second World War*, London: MacMillan Press, p. 186.

[23] Ibid.

nation. The representation of her emotions, her response to her own music, and the strong link between her emotionality and her physical ill-health still works, however, to reinforce a Romantic construction of femaleness. She therefore enjoys a rather complex, paradoxical and perhaps ultimately only temporary musical dominance. There is no doubt, having said this, that she does eventually dominate the emotional life of her male listener, and the effect of her music is certainly extremely powerful in this respect. Her exercise of such power, however, only seems permissible because she does it on behalf of a greater national cause. In this context at least, this suggests that to avoid construction as a siren, there must be a clear alternative and respectable reason for the female possession and expression of a musical voice. And indeed, in order to allow such a duality of musical expression and personal respectability, the representation of Lissa's initial act of composition actually works to some extent *against* the idea of her own active and original creativity.

It is tempting to speculate, in fact, that the sheer complexity of Lissa's characterization may have been the unconscious motivation for a more overt problematization of her identity within the film. Just as names and titles in *Now, Voyager* play a vital role in marking personal and social identity, so *Love Story* divides Lissa's identity and lends confusion to her recognition by other characters through the provision of a professional name, Felicity Crichton. This initially suggests that Lissa has two distinct identities—one professional and one private—that confirm her ability to achieve both professionalism as a musician and social acceptability as a woman. However, rather than maintain a clear distinction between the two, the film muddies the waters and there is, as a result, some difficulty in establishing which the film sees as her 'real' identity. Her removal from her career at the outset suggests that we are indeed to see the woman beneath the musician when we watch her as Lissa. Although Lissa Campbell is her real name, however, her initial withholding of her professional identity from the other principal characters, and in particular the moment in which she reveals it to Kit, operates paradoxically to suggest that 'Felicity Crichton' is actually her 'real' identity. The truth of the matter is, however, that this confusion is indicative of the film's inability to separate the musician from the woman, at least once she has fallen in love and therefore become identified as much by her emotions as by her musicality. Despite her initially professional demeanour, Lissa Campbell invades Felicity Crichton's world, and while this fulfils Gledhill's proposed function of the woman in wartime melodrama, it also plays to the Romantic construction of the creative woman.

Ultimately, however, it is this very complexity of her characterization, the fact that she is unusual in being allowed to both compose and perform her own music, and her explicit relationship to her male listener that single her out for detailed examination. Simply because she presents a generously ambitious but hopelessly problematic and self-contradictory figure, she indeed exposes both the difficulties of characterizing the female musician and a whole variety of strategies through which this characterization is both attempted and excused. In the absence of a 'quintessential' female musician case study example, *Love Story* therefore provides an intriguing alternative—a showcase of some of the issues that preclude the very possibility of locating a typical example of its type.

Love Story and the 'Mobilization' of Music

'Please go on. Or am I stopping the inspiration?'
'On the contrary, you're part of it. Well, in a way.'
Kit and Lissa in *Love Story*

Love Story follows the fate of Lissa Campbell, a famous concert pianist, who is removed by terminal illness from London to Cornwall, in order that she may unwittingly recuperate ex-fighter pilot Kit. The music that she composes there carries the full weight of her own difficult emotional situation, as 'she is inspired to write a piano concerto into which her love for Kit … her feeling of freedom underneath the Cornish skies, the emotion inspired in her by the grandeur of the rocky coast and the sea, the sadness that her life may be ended just as she has found love, are all poured'.[24] Such a powerful connection between the female and the feminine—in Romantic terms—may threaten Lissa with a dangerous loss of self-control and the possibility of physical illness. This is at least partially avoided, however, by the harnessing and purposeful direction of her desire to selfless, altruistic ends. Throughout the film, her romantic success with Kit is inextricably interwoven with her success as a patriotic 'messenger'. Her 'elemental' emotional strength eventually returns the defeated man to an optimistic outlook, allowing him to restart his life in terms of romance, proper self-control and combat—as, in other words, a fully re-masculinized man.

The film draws a distinction between the insincere façade with which Kit tries to protect himself and others from the truth of his impending disability, and Lissa's sense of time ebbing away and a determination to enjoy life while it lasts. Despite her own tragedy, Lissa still has the courage to face the future and the capacity to love. Kit, on the other hand, tries to deny the inevitability of the future by closing himself off from emotion and commitment. The film therefore demonstrates the power of Lissa's emotions in two ways: firstly, they are dangerously overwhelming for her when not requited; and secondly, they are successful both in recuperative and romantic terms when Kit reciprocates her feelings. The strength of her love not only returns his capacity for commitment, but enables his physical cure and return to war. The association of music, emotion and gender in the narrative—and in particular the effect of Lissa and her music on other characters—therefore mobilizes a particular combination of a Romantic ethos and a conventional wartime message, both of which centre on a specific construction of femininity.

In the context of the role that had established Margaret Lockwood's star status at Gainsborough—Hesther in *The Man in Grey* (1943)—Lissa seems a very restrained character. Given the popularity of this earlier film, however, it is difficult to imagine that the audience would not nevertheless have willingly invested Lissa's character with some of Hesther's spirit. Indeed, as Antonia Lant suggests, Lissa's illness allows her to digress from austerity measures, 'to look two hundred percent female'.[25] This suggests an extremely strong, rather than frail, sense of underlying sexuality, which undoubtedly has more to do with Lockwood than Lissa. Lockwood's star image in

---

[24] John Huntley (1947), *British Film Music*, London: Skelton Robinson, pp. 69–70.

[25] Antonia Lant (1991), *Blackout: Reinventing Women for British Wartime Cinema*, Princeton: Princeton University Press, p. 74.

fact places Lissa in an intriguing position with regard to the peaceful and extremely rural surroundings of Cornwall. Lant refers to *Love Story* as containing two opposing types of femininity, with Lissa representing 'frail, sexual beauty' and Judy (Patricia Roc) representing 'vigorous robustness'.[26] As the major star of the film, Lockwood will win the man and must be expected to be the main focus of visual attention. What Sarah Street terms the 'sparkle'[27] and Sue Harper refers to as the 'energy and *hubris*' of her acting style,[28] however, also works against the idea of weakness of any sort. This remains unaffected no matter what lines she speaks or how many times she (rather energetically) faints. It is undoubtedly this quality that allows Lissa to become a strong character through the discovery of her physical weakness. It may also be this that helps to predetermine the audience's acceptance of what her character eventually comes to stand for. This final status stems from the relationship of the two women to their surrounding environment. It is this that immediately distinguishes Lissa as the most important artist in the narrative, despite Judy's equally active involvement in the theatre. Each woman represents a different personal and symbolic relationship to the coastline and the sea. Judy is more practically linked to the wartime strengthening of national identity, while Lissa's Romantic relationship achieves a more allegorical and emotionally patriotic end.

Lissa and the Gendered Environment of Cornwall

Jeffrey Richards points out that British wartime cinema effectively redefined the entirety of the United Kingdom as England. In many cases, he suggests, this was even further specified as rural, rather than urban, England.[29] Lant describes how 'wartime cinema staked out its meanings through an emphasis on boundaries, borders, coastlines, and maps'.[30] Geographical signifiers of the nation thus became a vital means of reinforcing a sense of national identity and security, as did cultural references such as Shakespeare and Chaucer.[31] The particular meaning invested in this creation of rural England needs to be examined in order to understand how *Love Story* constructs the idea of Cornwall. Both Richards and Lant refer to the value of rural England in offering a picture of the nation as 'eternal, timeless, self-renewing and indestructible'.[32] It allows a removal from the real sites of regular bombing raids, emphasizing instead an unchanging geography. As Richards points out, home front films such as *Tawny Pipit* (1944) and *This England* (1941) do not merely propagate a Romantic myth of the 'authentic' and wholesome nature of rural life. They use the rural landscape as a means of allegorizing the wartime ethos of the transcendence of the immediacy of urban destruction and the ever-present and

[26] Ibid., p. 73.

[27] Sarah Street (1997), *British National Cinema*, London and New York: Routledge, p. 59.

[28] Harper (1988), p. 194.

[29] Jeffrey Richards (1988), 'National Identity in British Wartime Cinema', in Taylor (op. cit.) p. 44.

[30] Lant, p. 32.

[31] Richards, p. 43.

[32] Ibid., p. 46. See also Lant, p. 49.

random spectre of death.[33] Both writers also refer to the logical extension of this allegory, which accords transforming and recuperative powers to the countryside. In particular, it often appears as a site where disparate people can be united in a common cause, before being sent away improved in some crucial sense by their contact with nature.[34]

Like many of its fellow home front films, such as *The Demi-Paradise* (1943), *A Canterbury Tale* (1944), *Millions Like Us* (1943), *This Above All* (1942) and *Tawny Pipit*, *Love Story* is noteworthy for its geographical and cultural indicators. Such geographical features can be inland, such as the Pilgrim's Road and the hills overlooking the city in *A Canterbury Tale*, or the tiny village and surrounding hills and fields of *Tawny Pipit*. *Millions Like Us* and *Diary for Timothy* (1945) show the wartime transformation of the British holidaymakers' beaches, while *The Demi-Paradise* represents the coast through the shipyard and dockside. *Love Story*, however, is located on a stretch of coastline apparently largely unaffected by the war. Leaving aside the absence of anything industrial, the sands are also seemingly free of the barbed wire and landmines common to other narratives that reference beaches. The Cornish mine, with the attendant discussion of metals needed for the manufacture of munitions, is the sole representative of wartime industry. It remains, however, remote from the actual coast. It stands away from the cliffs, is hardly ever seen apart from during the rather isolated mining disaster episode, and is characterized as something dark, dangerous and frightening. It also motivates the presence of Tom (Tom Walls), the omniscient and multifunctional Yorkshireman. Tom seems to represent a regional variation on rural Romanticism, and a nod to mobilization that ironically suggests a lack of mining expertise in Cornwall itself. He is also a foil to the otherwise middle-class accents, and a pivotal point between the principal characters and the 'ordinary' local folk. The stereotypical common sense and straight talk of Yorkshire regionality, however, lends a particular significance to Tom's omniscience. He not only 'sees all', but is also quite willing to take action to ensure what he sees as the correct course of events. Among his many roles as a narrative catalyst, he manages—thanks to Huddersfield musicality—to tune the piano in the hotel's Summer House and engineer Kit and Lissa's movements towards each other, so that Lissa can begin to weave her musical–emotional magic.

The concentration of the film on the very edges of the cliffs, and therefore the absolute border of the nation, is largely provided by the two principal women. Lant proposes a pattern to the distribution of space in wartime cinema, which offers the freedom and power of the skies to the male characters, while the women's feet remain firmly planted on the ground.[35] Through this formulation, the women on the ground

---

[33] See Richards, 'National Identity in British Wartime Cinema'. Lant also makes the point that 'The physical existence of the land, and especially its distinctive geological features, confirms the continued political existence of the nation despite the demolition of human constructions', p. 49.

[34] Richards, p. 48.

[35] Lant, pp. 51–2.

become the support for the men in the air.[36] Lissa and Judy may therefore exist at the very edges of the nation, but they nevertheless remain land-bound. Even when Lissa travels overseas on an ENSA tour, she is seen being escorted and transported by male soldiers, with the emphasis remaining on the rigours and exhaustion of touring over land rather than flying. Kit, on the other hand, accords perfectly with Lant's formulation of 'the young, temporarily injured men of home front fictions', who have the potential to regain their apparently lost masculinity and who yearn, in this case with eventual success, for a return to the skies.[37] In *Love Story*, however, the role of the female is more than just to support. She must, rather, actively recuperate and return the man to his desired realm, and in this respect Judy and Lissa are diametrically opposed to one another. Judy wishes above all else to keep Kit on the land, eventually displaying an almost pathological resolve to sacrifice him for her own selfish reasons. Lissa sympathizes with the pain he suffers at the thought of this fate and will do anything, including reluctantly sacrificing her own desire, to save him from it. The different attitudes and roles of the two women are directly related to their relationship to the land and what it signifies. I examine Lissa's relationship to the coast in the detailed analysis of the film below, but Judy's relative position is an important defining factor in Lissa's narrative capabilities.

Judy's activities place the ultimate cultural capital of England at the extremities of its geography. She is managing, directing and acting in a professional production of Shakespeare's *The Tempest* in an amphitheatre cut into the very edge of the Cornish cliffs. The stage area backs onto a sheer drop to the sea, and the audience watch the action with the water in the background. Borrowing a phrase from Lant, she is, in the most literal way possible, 'spreading culture to the edges of the national boundary'.[38] Her project is largely represented, however, as a commercial rather than aesthetic venture. It is defined by references to finances, sponsorship, box-office potential, tourism and, rather tellingly, even the falsification and manipulation of natural sounds. Apart from watching Kit and Lissa swimming, in fact, Judy seems to take relatively little notice of her surroundings and never comments on them. Although she is represented as being sincerely in love with Kit, the manifestation of her love is directly opposed to a desirable wartime attitude. Judy has waited for Kit all her life, and sees his impending blindness as a perfect opportunity to secure him. Particularly in comparison to Lissa, Judy's lack of spiritual connection to the

---

36 Sue Harper also emphasizes this point by underlining the connection between those films that received official MoI support and the representation of predictably supportive women, for example in *The Way to the Stars* (1945), *In Which We Serve* (1942) and *The Way Ahead* (1944); see Harper (1988), pp. 190–91.

37 Lant, p. 52.

38 Ibid., p. 48. The cliff top theatre used in the film is the Minack Theatre in Cornwall (although storms forced the production to move to a studio set of the theatre). It is perhaps of extra significance that this theatre was the brainchild and lifelong project of a woman, Rowena Cade, and that the production for which she originally developed it was *The Tempest*, which was first mounted there in 1932. In the same vein as Myra Hess's National Gallery concerts, therefore, even the theatre itself evokes a very particular idea of British womanhood in relation to the nation, its culture and, in the specific case of the Minack Theatre, its natural environment.

land, and her unpatriotic and selfish attitude towards Kit, seem to become one and the same thing. She represents a female resistance to a correct and respectable moral stance, which must ultimately be overcome through submission to both the inevitable power of the greater star and the tremendous emotional force of patriotism which that star's character represents. The principal difference between Judy's and Lissa's artistry, and hence their national and emotional characterization, therefore comes from the land itself.

Lissa as Composer and Performer

The intended function of the music in this film, according to John Huntley, was to 'become not so much a quiet, pleasant background, as an integral part of the development of the characters themselves'.[39] Hubert Bath's *Cornish Rhapsody* provided the film with the appropriate means to such an end—the integration of the composition, performance and reception of this central 'concerto' into the subject matter of the narrative in fact allows it to impact on the definition of all the principal characters. The film's contradictory attitudes towards musical creativity are demonstrated through the way in which Lissa and Kit are each introduced in relation to music, their subsequent interaction with both diegetic and non-diegetic music, and the framing and editing of performance sequences. This analysis is therefore broadly divided into two sections. This first section deals with Lissa's diegetic relationship to composition and performance, primarily through her fictitious creation of the *Cornish Rhapsody*. This allows an examination of the most important question of this chapter, which is the way in which a film may attempt a characterization of the female musician that allows her to be both powerfully creative and emotional and yet still 'feminine' and 'respectable'. The second section then looks at issues arising from the transfer of her music to the non-diegetic level. This includes a consideration of the man's related theme and musical role and the way in which the dynamic interaction of both their musics reflects their shared emotional trajectory.

As is conventional in films featuring musicians as characters, the opening titles of *Love Story* are underscored with the music that will become the main piece associated with the musician. The subsequent introduction of the music within the diegesis usually comes relatively early in the film, often with a focus on the technicalities of playing through shots of the musician's hands. In its quest to create a very particular configuration of music, national identity, patriotism, emotion and gender, however, this film begins by overturning this convention to establish an entirely distinct set of representational parameters. It is not unusual that Lissa does not appear as a performer during the opening titles. In fact, if she were to appear in the same way as Sandra does in *The Great Lie*, her subsequent characterization might be problematized. The opening titles actually show the landscape of Cornwall, which will provide the main backdrop for the film as well as a significant inspiration for the music's diegetic composition. The music is restricted to a purely orchestral arrangement with no piano, so that Lissa's performance is not yet even an issue. This allows the film to begin to prioritize the place of inspiration over technical musical

---

[39] Huntley (1947a), p. 69.

prowess—thus already associating music with imagination and rural Romanticism rather than performance.

The potential problems of the gender of the musician are further avoided in the subsequent episodes that present, respectively, Lissa's first performance and the initial composition of her piece. Lissa's intended final concert, which opens the film, follows the codes of the conventional performance. She is identified very clearly as a renowned professional musician, sufficiently famous to be performing to a packed London venue. Inside the concert hall she is seen in long shot, framed by the two sides of the concert audience, and with the piano in full view. She is therefore rendered as only one element of the whole concert experience despite being the actual performer. The camera moves towards her, reaching the front row of the audience just as she finishes playing. We do not see her facial expression while she plays, and in any case we know nothing about her at this point that would contextualize anything personal. Our first experience of Lissa as a musician is therefore a distanced one, which bears little relevance to the opening titles. We do not see her in close-up, there are no shots of her hands on the keyboard, and she is not playing the piece that opened the film. This performance therefore delays the connection between Lissa and her own music, as well as our knowledge of her as a character. While denying many of the conventions of the musician film, however, this introduction also opens up the space which will allow her later and much more crucial musical creativity.

The opening concert creates an important link between Lissa's public face as a musician, her place within an urban environment, the conventional style of performance, and the playing of existing concert repertoire. She is introduced by a concert poster and is playing Chopin's *Étude* Op. 10, No. 12 in C minor. She is presented with the piano always in full shot, which emphasizes the physical presence of her performance rather than any personal emotional aspects. Like the particular extracts of the Tchaikovsky Piano Concerto No. 1 played by Sandra in *The Great Lie*, this piece is also passionate in a rather forthright way, and therefore eschews the more sentimental style of the conventional love theme usually associated with the female character. The avoidance of a closer view of Lissa as she plays, however, somehow also denies the idea that she can be understood purely in terms of her professional musicianship. Despite the conventional style of performance, which in the context of other films often connotes the characterization of the musician through their music, it is significant that we have been denied the usual disembodied hands-on-keyboard shot. We therefore see Lissa as a performer, but without a heightened emphasis on technical virtuosity. The distance makes the performance seem strangely neutral in meaning, suggesting that it is not through this format—the public concert of established repertoire—that we will really come to understand her. Even if Lissa is a musician, there is more to her than just her professional musicality.

At the same time, while some kind of deeper complexity may be signalled, particularly given that the musician is played by Margaret Lockwood, it must nevertheless remain uncertain at this point whether this greater depth can be realized through music. In films such as *While I Live*, *The Great Lie* and *Deception*, this does, after all, prove a difficult prospect. This doubt is furthered by the announcement immediately after the performance that Lissa is giving up her music to take on war work. Taking an exemplary wartime stand and demonstrating the necessity of women entering the male work domain, she exhibits her view of the world as outward and dutiful rather than inward. Her musical career does not blind her to real life and its obligations, or make her wilfully self-centred like *The Great Lie*'s Sandra. The rather drastic force of fate that follows, however, renders her unable to follow through these socially responsible and practical intentions. As a result, she can become justifiably representative of something more transcendent and symbolic.

The distance from personal expression suggested by this first performance is continued by the fact that it is actually her manager Ray (Walter Hudd) who makes the announcement regarding her 'retirement' from the concert platform, with Lissa shown as unable to stop him. She does not speak to the audience in her own defence, choosing instead just to exit the stage as they applaud Ray's sentiments of resistance to her will. Her power and voice within the text seem to be even further diminished in the following scenes. She prattles inanely while being examined by the doctor, only to be refused information about her medical condition and denied entry to the WAAFs. Her diegetic silence is protracted once again after she has visited her own doctor, before she finally reveals the news to Ray that, thanks to a heart problem resulting from childhood scarlet fever, she does not have long to live. It is at this point that Lissa's lack of control over her own life and music is summed up. In her first fully eloquent speech, she silences Ray and tells him about her years as a musician, referring to the endless time that he made her spend practising that prevented her from experiencing life. Like Francesca in *The Seventh Veil*, Olwen (Audrey Fildes) in *While I Live*, and perhaps to some extent Christine in *Deception*, Lissa's life as a professional musician has been signified by work, repression by a Svengali figure and a distance from all other aspects of life. Now she travels away from the urban environment to a rural space where she can experience life at its most raw, natural and eternal. This recalls the source of inspiration shown in the opening titles and prepares for her role as its narrative conduit.

Her personal connection to music remains delayed, however, by the place-setting use of *The Cornish Floral Dance* for the introduction of her time in Cornwall. This piece firmly establishes her new environment in terms of the folk ethic, through one of the traditional cultural codes that Richards might attribute to what he terms the 'Romantic Left'.[40] This new designation for music breaks with the formal London concert. It also prepares the ground for the most important break with the conventional presentation of the musician character. This comes as Lissa closes the gap between herself and the opening titles by beginning to compose the main piece. Through a series of episodes, the music moves from the meta-diegetic of Lissa's imagination, through the diegetic to the non-diegetic level. This proves a crucial reversal of the pattern conventionally relating to the male musician and his female listener, which transfers the initially diegetic piece to the meta-diegetic and non-diegetic levels. Furthermore, the male composer usually first presents his work-in-progress through

---

[40] Richards, p. 44. The 'Romantic Left' encompasses 'folk music, the village community, rural crafts and honest peasantry' as opposed to the 'Romantic Right' and its association of rurality with 'the country house and the country church, the squire and the parson, and a deferential, hierarchical society'. The latter, of course, is also fully in place, in its own way, in *Love Story*.

diegetic playing, with no representation of its place in his imagination before this point. It is this reconfiguration of music and character that allows Lissa to be identified as a musician in an entirely different way from her appearance in the first concert sequence. This not only manipulates the conventional associations of each level of the text, but also establishes a particular pattern of editing and framing that will transfigure future performances.

After her arrival in Cornwall, Lissa hires a donkey trap to see the scenery. At the edge of the cliffs overlooking the sea, she meets Kit. While finding him interesting, she resists his overly charming advances and breaks away from him, running up to a higher part of the cliff. She stands right at the cliff edge and gazes far out to sea in a moment prolonged by a reverse shot of Kit watching her. It is at this point that her composition begins. As she hears the waves crashing on the rocks below, she looks offscreen right (Figure 4.1a) and hears orchestral strings merging with the diegetic sound simultaneously with a shot, from her point of view, of the waves. Next she looks offscreen left in response to the sound of seagulls (Figure 4.2a), which is then replaced by an imitative figure in the flutes. Both of these musical figures are clearly imitative and linked to concrete diegetic elements demonstrated by Lissa's gaze, her point-of-view shots and the diegetic sound effects. The third element of the composition, however, comes in response to no such specific diegetic stimulus. Lissa stares apparently unseeing into the middle distance. Not only is her gaze rather vague, but there is also no reverse shot of what she sees. She then begins to conduct with her finger the music that she 'hears' (Figure 4.3a). As she 'composes' this melody, she is completely self-absorbed, and is obviously annoyed when Kit interrupts her, saying that he has made her lose the theme.

This third theme is the most important key to understanding Lissa's allegorical role as part of the film's philosophy of women, musical creativity and nature. In contrast to the first two motifs, this theme is not imitative of any specific source, but seems to come purely in response to the general surroundings. But the direction of her gaze and the way the music comes to her is important. The first two motifs have set the precedent of Lissa looking at the element that is inspiring her composition. For the main theme, she adopts a far-reaching, unseeing gaze across the sea and sky—a gaze, as it were, into eternity. The music that appears seems more like a voice in her head over which she has no control, so that she merely monitors it as it progresses of its own volition. She therefore seems not to compose it so much as *hear* it. It is almost as if the music is coming to her from the elements, rather than her creating it in response to her contemplation of them. The act of composition is therefore somewhat undermined in its representation, ceasing to be the result of active creativity or imagination, and becoming instead a comparatively passive act of listening to nature and hearing its voice.

Figure 4.1a ***Love Story*****. Lissa (Margaret Lockwood) looks down at the waves and hears music**

Figure 4.1b ***Love Story*****. Lissa translates the music of the waves at the piano**

Figure 4.2a ***Love Story*****. Lissa looks up at the seagulls and hears music**

Figure 4.2b ***Love Story*****. Lissa translates the music of the seagulls at the piano**

Figure 4.3a ***Love Story*****. Lissa stares into eternity and hears the voice of the elements in the form of music**

Figure 4.3b ***Love Story*****. Lissa in the personal performance mode, translating the music of the elements at the piano and associating the theme with Kit's voice**

The pattern of this theme—which I will call the main theme in the *Cornish Rhapsody* and Lissa's theme at the non-diegetic and meta-diegetic levels—recalls the repetitive ebb and flow of waves and, by extension, the idea of constancy and regeneration. It comprises four phrases. The first phrase establishes a pattern of constant rising and falling, which is emphasized by the second phrase beginning a semitone higher. The following phrase comprises a rising and falling four-note phrase that is immediately repeated with an elaborating triplet figure around the second note. The theme then ends with a variation on the opening phrase beginning a further semitone higher. This compresses the opening four-note motif into three notes by accenting and extending the length of the first note, before emphasizing the following descending chords with the addition of elaborating notes (Example 4.1).

Example 4.1 Hubert Bath, *Cornish Rhapsody*. Bars 6–21; melody only. The main theme of the Rhapsody and Lissa's theme at the non-diegetic and meta-diegetic levels

This pattern seems to suggest a constant yearning towards resolution that is eschewed in favour of further repetitions of the basic ascending and descending pattern. The poignancy of this striving seems increased as the first note of each statement of the opening phrase is raised by a semitone. There is also a constant pull between major and minor tonality and a frequent accenting of either non-harmonic or rhythmically weak notes. In particular, the melody line tends to begin its phrases on the second beat of the bar. Throwing the melody off the beat in this way gives it a sense of being almost 'too late' while also desperately 'pushing' forward. The theme seems to encapsulate Lissa's sadness at the ebbing away of time, her hope in recapturing what life there is left to her, and her capacity for self-regeneration, strength and resolve in emotional adversity. At the same time, it resonates with Richards's idea of the rural landscape, and in this case the sea in particular, as perpetual and unchanging. It therefore, as K.J. Donnelly suggests, 'appears to represent the association of female desire with elemental natural forces'.[41] Like *The Dream of Olwen* in *While I Live*, Lissa's music comes from the wild, in both cases Cornish, environment and in turn seems to be part of it.[42] This crucial link grants Lissa's feelings and love a timeless and universal quality, which is perhaps the only way that they could be

41 K.J. Donnelly (1997), 'Wicked Sounds and Magic Melodies: Music in 1940s Gainsborough Melodrama', in Pam Cook (ed.), *Gainsborough Pictures*, London and Washington: Cassell, p. 165.

42 *The Dream of Olwen*, written by Charles Williams, is the piece 'composed' by Olwen, the female musician character of *While I Live*.

made to transcend the immediate horrors and tragedies of war. Through composing and performing the piece, Lissa becomes the voice of the land and sea—the conduit through which its message can be carried to Kit—so that her personal strength and optimism in the face of tragedy can be transferred to him. Following the formulations of Richards and Lant, she becomes a voice for the eternal spirit of the nation. In her role as catalyst for Kit's recovery, therefore, she stands as a goddess-like symbol of the recuperative powers of female love for war-damaged men. The contrast of this to Kit's music, which appears later, is striking.

The use of the meta-diegetic level for the first appearance of the theme is unusual. It allows the music to appear in Lissa's imagination simultaneously with our first hearing of it, and seems to suggest the Romantic idea of composition as a kind of divine inspiration. Even given the fact that the rather passive and effortless representation of her initial composition works against the Romantic vision of the contemplation of nature, we may nevertheless be able to consider Lissa as a woman who combines a 'feminine' proximity to nature with the 'masculine' strength required to channel and contain its powerful voice. There is no doubt, as her later determination and self-sacrifice shows, that Lissa is far stronger and self-possessed emotionally than almost any other character in the film. While the performance of her own music should not, therefore, present her with any problems, the film contrives to avoid the possible difficulties of this scenario by calling on the physical weakness of her heart to provide an additional reason for her later emotional breakdowns. As a kind of actualization of Romantic philosophy, her illness means that her body is literally incapable of supporting the strength of her emotions. The fact that it is Kit, as a man, who interrupts the initial flow of sensibility from the skies to her ears predicts both the problem with the consummation of their relationship and the necessary eventual balance for her creativity. Despite her successful completion of the composition, it is ultimately not Lissa who provides the necessary masculine control of the music, but Kit, by his acceptance of the message that it carries. Without this acceptance and support, Lissa is so overwhelmed by the emotion contained in the music that she can barely survive her own performances and indeed on one occasion faints mid-piece. Kit therefore holds the key to Lissa's successful emotional trajectory in personal, patriotic and cultural terms. It seems a little cruel, as a result, that the timing of the success of her recuperative 'mission' means that she never gets to perform the *Rhapsody* in a contented frame of mind.

Lissa's inability to exercise control over her own emotions and music is visualized during the various composition and performance sequences of the piece, which continually recall the shot construction of the original cliff top episode. The first of these occurs as Lissa transfers her music to the diegetic level through realizing her musical thoughts at the piano that Tom has thoughtfully tuned for her in the hotel's Summer House. At this stage, the piece undergoes a certain amount of alteration that recollects the process of musical gendering apparent in Chapter 3's analysis of *Letter from an Unknown Woman*. Most importantly, the significance of Lissa's theme (Example 4.1) is refined in order to link it more strongly to Kit, before it is appropriately singled out to become the main theme of the composition. As she reconstructs the imitative wave and seagull figures of the composition, the shot pattern of the cliff top episode is repeated, although the actual direction of her gaze is altered (Figures 4.1b and 4.2b). The redefinition of Lissa's theme comes after she has played the seagull motif. Lissa remains looking offscreen, with the piano in the shot, and 're-hears' both the non-diegetic solo violin statement of the theme and Kit's voice, saying: 'What's your name? Mine's Kit. You're going straight into my box of special memories.' She then turns to face over the top of the piano with the editing following her movement. She is now seen in a shot almost identical to her moment of 'heard' composition (see Figure 4.3a), with the piano excluded from the frame and her gaze reaching once again into the middle distance as she transfers the melody to the piano (Figure 4.3b).

The effect of this particular pattern of editing is to separate the first two motifs from the main theme. The first two motifs are still linked to her new environment in a very concrete way by imitating real noises. Accordingly, the act of creation comes to the fore, with the piano in sight and an emphasis on Lissa's hands at the keyboard. For the main theme, however, she is divorced from her immediate surroundings and placed in the same abstracted image as on the cliff top. The framing therefore allows a focus on her emotions while she plays, rather than her actual playing. Perhaps because of the restrained physical style of Margaret Lockwood's miming at the piano, it would be easy to forget what she is actually doing and see this as a straightforward extended shot showing the emotions that this theme represents. The music that she plays effectively becomes non-diegetic, reinforcing the (too) close link between the female composer's music and her own imagination and emotions. This is a uniquely 'self-centred' moment by the standards of any male or female composer film, whereby the musician is simultaneously feeling her own emotions, giving them representation through her own composition, and providing the only diegetic response to this music. Kit's intervention in the composition process at this point, although still unwitting, works in a similar way to his interruption of Lissa's original inspiration. This seems predicted by the disruption of her composition and a repeat of her earlier disturbed facial expression as she plays what she considers 'wrong' harmony. Her creativity is thus halted just before Kit's first appearance in a series of cutaway shots that show his gradual progress towards the Summer House. The resultant punctuation of the piece allows a shift in its musical focus, eliding the wave and seagull motifs in favour of constant and increasingly elaborate repetitions of the main theme. The theme already associated with Kit therefore becomes the musical means by which the film draws him towards Lissa. After a full chordal version finally heralds his discovery of her crucial secret identity, the theme takes its appropriately meaningful place on the non-diegetic track.

Kit's discovery of Lissa at the piano therefore creates a gendered variation on the conventional form of a male musician–female listener scene. He is effectively drawn to Lissa by her music, even though he is apparently deaf to it—despite its volume—until he appears in the Summer House doorway behind her. At this point, he is literally stopped in his tracks by what he finds. He moves silently through the room to take a seat behind her. Like the male musician with his female admirer at a distance, Lissa does not even notice he is there until he applauds after she stops playing. In their subsequent conversation Lissa tells him that the main theme represents 'some of the emotions [she] felt at the time' of their first meeting. In response to his question about what sort of emotions these are, she replies, significantly: 'If I could express them in words, I wouldn't have to write music.' From being a profession by which she could not be adequately defined, and which she intended to leave behind, albeit for very specific reasons, music has now become her explicitly personal emotional voice. This voice, if she did but know it, speaks for the whole nation. Her music represents a spirit that is both part of, and something other than, herself, as well as having an emotional object in Kit, and his role in making the music necessary is registered when Lissa continues to explain her composition:

> Kit: 'Please go on. Or am I stopping the inspiration?'
> Lissa: 'On the contrary, you're part of it. Well, in a way.'

Kit's compromised status as a muse for Lissa's music is important. He is only a partial muse, and of course at the crucial point of composition shown in Figure 4.3b he is also a disembodied muse. The fact that he only 'appears' to Lissa through her memory of his voice means that we avoid actually having to *see* him through Lissa's inspired eyes. Rather than seeing him as she sees/imagines him—and therefore also risking his possible feminization as the object of her gaze—we see *her* face in response to this memory. This continues the emphasis on Lissa's extremely close involvement with the music while nevertheless giving it an exterior motivation. At the same time, it signals a distance between Kit and music that proves essential as a contextualization for the later appearance of his own theme. Despite the similarities between this scene and many comparable male musician–female listener scenes, therefore, Lissa is still very different from a male composer. Even though she admits that Kit is part of the inspiration behind the piece, she keeps the emotions behind the music secret. Music is not a means of seduction for this female composer, but something much more personal—and genuine. The emotions it contains cannot be summed up as a relatively quantifiable response to another person, but really do express what her words cannot.

Lissa is now demonstrably capable of both the conventional and personal styles of performance, and the dynamic between these possibilities becomes the point of her subsequent performances. In particular, as the story involves her in a situation of increasing emotional complexity, each performance becomes imbued with the tension of whether she can survive until the end of the piece. This occurs explicitly during the next diegetic performance, which shows her back at the cliff edge—this time as a replacement for Judy's theatre performance—playing the *Cornish Rhapsody* in front of an audience for the first time. The emotional context for this performance is fully understood only by herself and the film audience, and is set with the news that Kit is simultaneously undergoing his potentially life-threatening eye operation. Although she might have chosen to play any piece, Lissa nevertheless puts herself to the test by playing the music that was—at least partly—inspired by Kit. She must then sustain the performance in the knowledge that he may be dying as a result of her own actions in persuading him to undergo such dangerous surgery.

Initially, her performance follows the original cliff top and Summer House pattern shown in Figures 4.1a, 4.2a, 4.1b and 4.2b, and even goes so far as to duplicate absolutely the shot construction of Figures 4.1b and 4.2b. Lissa looks offscreen over the edge of the cliffs as she plays the waves motif, and then turns to look offscreen towards the sky while playing the seagull motif. As the main theme begins, she is seen from over the top of the piano, framed by its body, lid and lid stand. This shot then takes its place in a series, alternating with the audience's point of view and views from the cliff side of the piano. Throughout all these shots, Lissa's performance as a musical event is emphasized by the retention of the piano in the frame. This pattern is only broken as the end of the fourth phrase of the main theme is reached, when Lissa is seen in medium close-up without the piano. Immediately following this, the scene cuts to Tom and Judy backstage as Lissa begins a variation on the main theme with a quiet, non-diegetic orchestral accompaniment. Since neither the volume nor the sound quality of the music changes in response to this edit, the whole score seems to become momentarily non-diegetic despite our knowledge of the continued diegetic source of the piano. The dialogue between Tom and Judy allows Tom to draw attention away from Judy's distress to Lissa's, by him asking her the explicit question: 'Remember Lissa out there playing. What do you suppose she's thinking?' The immediate cut back to Lissa marks a move to a new pattern in the editing and framing. This answers Tom's question by replacing the conventional performance style with a representation of Lissa's increasingly uncontrollable personal emotions.

As the visual style of the performance changes, so does the tone of the music. It shifts from the sentimental style of the main theme to a non-melodic, sequentially rising pattern with no orchestral accompaniment. As the pitch of the music rises, there is an increasing predominance of shots that show only Lissa's face, obliterating the piano from the frame altogether. Her gaze moves away from the piano keyboard and adopts the stare into the middle distance familiar from previous shots connecting music and her emotions. This time, however, her expression reveals a growing distress that seems to build from the earlier moments of discontent when her music was disrupted by Kit's interruption on the cliff top and her own use of the wrong harmony in the Summer House. From a repeat of the earlier view framing her within the piano's body and lid, we cut to a closer shot without the piano, and then to an extreme close-up of her face as she reaches the highest point of the rising musical pattern (Figure 4.4a). An immediate cut to a longer shot of both her and the piano in profile and the audience in the background then coincides with her physical collapse and the resultant dissonant crash of the keyboard.

Figure 4.4a ***Love Story*****. The move to the personal performance mode reflects Lissa's distress during the cliff top concert**

Figure 4.4b ***Love Story*****. The end of Lissa's performance of the *Cornish Rhapsody* in the Albert Hall concert, revealing her distress through the personal performance mode**

Repositioning Lissa at this precise moment as part of a whole performance event seems to emphasize the incompatibility of her interior and exterior worlds. Her private failure becomes a salutary public humiliation. This marks a very particular height of emotional excess, made possible only by the most direct conflation of the woman and her music. Judy, despite her love for Kit and her distress at his dangerous operation, is given no more elaborate expression of her emotions than a brief scene of crying and a refusal to take the stage as scheduled. The course of Lissa's emotions, on the other hand, becomes the motivating factor for the editing of her performance scene. This brings the visuals and the diegetic music into violently direct correlation, and makes her complete physical and mental collapse appear the only possible conclusion to the scene. Judy's feminine excess can be calmed and controlled by the quietly masculine Tom. Lissa's emotions, on the other hand, can only be made more excessive by her being compelled to play and hear music that marks the very absence of the male. In the end, her emotions and her music together prove to be more than she can bear.

The final concert features an entire performance of the *Cornish Rhapsody* in the Royal Albert Hall in London. This performance constitutes both the epitome of Lissa's professional career and, as Ray suggests, a final chance to 'make [her] playing tell them all [she] want[s] to say'. Her conversation with Tom immediately before the concert reveals her continuing distress over losing Kit, particularly since she has heard of his impending marriage to Judy and learns that he has given Tom no message for her. Since this renders the emotional context of this performance very similar to that of the earlier open-air theatre performance, the question naturally arises as to whether she will survive playing the whole piece. In formal terms, it may be supposed that a successful performance is necessary both to balance the earlier failure and to allow Lissa a triumphant end to her career. The film is no doubt on her side in this respect, furthermore, since the demands of the educational 'project' of film music,[43] the conventional format of the composer/musician film and the extra-textual status of the *Cornish Rhapsody* as an 'answer' to the *Warsaw Concerto*, all dictate the necessity of a full performance of this specially composed 'tabloid' concerto.[44]

Throughout the majority of this performance, accordingly, and particularly until the final moments, the editing is governed primarily by the structure and rhythm of the music. As is the case with the main concert sequences of many musician films, it becomes something more like documentary footage, incorporating multiple audience and orchestral point-of-view shots and isolating various instrumental groups as they become prominent within the piece. There are occasional shots of Lissa from across the top of the piano, either framed by its body and lid or with it removed from the

---

[43] See Chapter 3, footnote 1.

[44] Donnelly suggests that the popularity of the so-called '"tabloid concertos"' in 1940s film was partly inspired by the unprecedented success of the *Warsaw Concerto* written at the beginning of the decade for *Dangerous Moonlight* (see Chapter 5 of this book); see Donnelly, p. 164. Conceived according to Huntley as a 'second *Warsaw Concerto*' (Huntley 1947a, p. 69), the *Cornish Rhapsody* was hailed alongside its predecessor as having created 'an entirely new standard of screen music', Louis Levy in Donnelly, p. 164.

shot. While these shots recall Lissa's emotional investment in the music, they show her initially at least to be absorbed in her performance rather than demonstrating any notably personal response. This emphasis is completely reversed, however, when she reaches the point in the piece that heralded her earlier collapse. As in the earlier performance, this shift is conveyed by a change in the visual style, with a dramatic increase in the pace of editing and the use of extremely jarring camera angles. Lissa is seen at the piano from an extreme low angle, followed by a head-on shot of the trombones, before an extreme high angle shot of Lissa appears to necessitate that Lockwood tip her head slightly backwards in order to make her character's face visible. There is the greatest concentration at this point of shots that focus on Lissa's face to the exclusion of the piano, and a repeat of her distressed expression as she plays. Although she ends the piece successfully as far as the diegetic audience is concerned, in its final moments we can see only her face, staring fixedly over the top of the piano in obvious, but still private, distress (Figure 4.4b).

The Non-diegetic Score and Kit's Theme

At the non-diegetic level, Lissa's theme—the main theme of the Rhapsody—seems to work in a relatively conventional way. It represents her 'feminine' emotions and functions as the love theme to her romance with Kit. At the same time, however, it still embodies the eternal elements of national identity from which Kit has become alienated. Its transfer to the non-diegetic level therefore allows the next stage of the recuperation process after he realizes the implied emotional content of Lissa's composition. The conflation of their romantic love with his physical and moral regeneration becomes inextricably linked to patriotism and his return to the air. As with the diegetic performances of the piece, however, the disruption of Lissa's theme represents the stymieing of her 'corrective' emotions by his initial stubborn non-cooperation and, accordingly, her music is not allowed to dominate the score in the way that Stefan's does in *Letter from an Unknown Woman*. Although Kit initially seems to return Lissa's feelings, his fear of his impending blindness leads to an 'incorrect' resistance to wartime regeneration. Rather than give in to the feelings that her music represents, he therefore introduces music of his own that represents a denial of not only his emotions for Lissa but also his emotions in general. By pretending to be completely emotionally independent, he hopes to avoid facing reality. The interaction of Lissa's and Kit's themes as the film progresses therefore becomes equally important in understanding the extent to which the musician–listener configuration can be redistributed across the characters when it is the woman who is the musician.

The transfer of Lissa's music to the non-diegetic level confirms the focus on the main theme suggested by her process of composition in the Summer House. As in *Letter from an Unknown Woman*, however, this movement is also marked by a change in instrumentation. Lissa's non-diegetic theme does not remain a piano piece, but is orchestrated for string and woodwind instruments. As the couple kiss for the first time by the wishing well, the strings become more prominent. A solo violin line is then extracted specifically in conjunction with a shot of Lissa's face and her speaking of Kit's name. This recalls a particular connection between Lissa and music by evoking her original moment of meta-diegetic composition. The suggestion of the solo violin as representative of her deepest emotional voice—an association which, as I discussed in Chapters 2 and 3 respectively, occurs in both *Now, Voyager* and *Letter from an Unknown Woman*—therefore seems to distance this moment from her professional musical activity. Whereas the piano is cast as her public means of expression, with the version of her music for piano and orchestra constituting the publicly respectable and extra-textually marketable translation of her feelings, the solo violin enters the non-diegetic and meta-diegetic score as a contrasting representation of her private emotional state known only to her and the film audience. Thus, even when Kit tells Judy that he will make sure Lissa does not get hurt, the use of the solo violin foregrounds the idea of her emotions rather than his.

Once removed from its diegetic source, the theme also becomes more flexible to its romantic motivation. Up to and during the couple's first kiss, for example, the increasing intensity of the moment is reflected in its rising volume and ascending sequential pattern. While this may reflect the characters' mutual feelings, however, the music nevertheless suggests that the kiss is neither a triumphant moment in itself nor the unproblematic beginning of a new relationship. In a similar way to the long-awaited embrace in *Letter from an Unknown Woman*, Kit and Lissa's kiss ends accompanied by unresolved harmony and, in this particular case, a solo violin melody line that diminishes into nothing. It therefore places doubt over the success of the moment, suggesting that their situation is far from resolved. Unlike in *Letter from an Unknown Woman*, however, both Kit's refusal of involvement and Lissa's upset response are immediately clear to each of the characters. The subsequent introduction of Kit's theme, discussed below, then directly contradicts the ethos of Lissa's theme by providing a logical development of the distance he is trying to create from Lissa's musical–emotional influence. In a move that is perhaps marked by being *too* masculine in terms of the conscious exercise of control, this theme represents Kit's attempt to construct a defence against any real emotional involvement or expression. The ostensible musical–emotional voice that this gives him is therefore actually used in the service of his desire for protection from emotion. As in numerous films that characterize musicians and their listeners, this raises the issue of emotional (in)dependence, and how the particular allocation of the musical–emotional voices of the characters indicates their gendered narrative positioning.

The power of Lissa's musicality to entrance her male listener and eventually seal his fate in loving her is demonstrated early in the film, and the growing strength of her emotional hold over him is indicated by the role of her music in accompanying their relationship. Her obvious allure and her own emotional involvement are, however, perceived as a threat. No matter how innocent and unwitting her siren song, it must be countered by a self-conscious musical assertion of independence that defends against submission to the feelings she inspires. Lissa's theme is therefore delayed in recuperating Kit by its motivation of this countertheme. Kit is in fact the only character who takes full diegetic control of the appearance of his own music. He introduces it purposefully into the conversation as a way of representing his pretended emotions, placing it in direct opposition to the unexpected way in which Lissa's theme comes to her. Lissa's theme offers the possibility of both a non-diegetic and diegetic emotional voice, inner strength and a constructive depth of emotion. Kit's theme, on the other hand, attempts to control and silence both his own and her diegetic voices. He uses it as a shorthand way of preventing dialogue about his lack of involvement in the war, and Lissa is compelled always to obey his diegetic musical command. It demonstrates, in both narrative and musical terms, a superficial attempt to force an emotional independence from Lissa and the world in general that he clearly does not really feel.

Kit's theme first appears as the couple ride away in the donkey trap from their disastrous first kiss, and he explains his affected philosophy on life. He likens himself to the Miller of Dee and, in another reference to the folk cultural appeal of Richards's Romantic Left, encapsulates this through the fictitious character's song (Example 4.2).

Example 4.2 ***The Miller of Dee*** **(traditional song)**

Although the lyrics are only used in the first appearance of the theme, they nevertheless establish the meaning that Kit wants his music to retain for all subsequent appearances. The tune, which he sings unaccompanied, is light and jaunty. The compound time signature and use of dotted rhythms lend it the feel of a folk dance. At the same time, however, the conventional implication of sadness connoted by its minor modality detracts slightly from this apparent sense of levity and happiness. Kit's philosophy therefore seems a little superficial. He may wish to appear happy in his independent and carefree state, but there are darker feelings underlying this façade. He is trying to pin down the dangerously intangible qualities of music through his choice of a clear, concise song form with self-descriptive lyrics. The capacity of the minor modality to undermine the tone of the melody line, however, is tellingly developed in the following episode when the couple make a bargain to have a completely uncommitted relationship and seal the beginning of this agreement with a kiss. The instrumental version of Kit's theme that accompanies this scene reflects this avowed lack of mutual commitment. Although it reaches a resolving cadence, however, it is still in the minor mode and, according to the conventions of musical connotation, this cannot present their arrangement in anything other than a negative light. Furthermore, although the purely woodwind orchestration suggests the song's basis in folk music, it also presents a telling opposition to Lissa's earlier heartfelt string scoring. They may have resolved on a feasible way forward together, but the music undermines what is now a shared pretence.

As Lissa and Kit's relationship progresses, the two themes effectively stand in opposition to each other. Kit's theme—whether diegetic or non-diegetic—always suggests his resistance to seriousness, emotional commitment or personal discussion. Lissa's theme, meanwhile, alternates between emphasizing her personal feelings and the national spirit. As the couple row a small boat towards the cave under the cliffs, for example, Lissa apologizes for talking seriously about the war when Kit sings his song to remind her of their bargain. As they subsequently reach the shore, however, Lissa's theme accompanies the cheerful documentary-style montage of the fishermen at work. After Kit has refused Tom's offer of important mine work, Lissa's protests are once again stymied by his song. The timely appearance of wounded servicemen during their subsequent trap ride then seems to take the place of her music's message and at last renders her unable to continue with their pretence. Kit's resistance to her emotional truth, however, dictates that their resultant separation is underscored by another instrumental version of his song. Only when Lissa subsequently discovers the truth about Kit's combat injury and impending blindness can her music truly supersede his. After his theme underlies his confession and embarrassed expression of grief, Lissa's theme floods over their embrace and declaration of love. After this point, only his actual mention of the song, or the renewed denial of his real feelings that enables his later engagement to Judy, can cause the return of *The Miller of Dee*.

The power of Lissa's music and emotions is therefore represented as benign and romantic. It remains, however, *her* music. When she confesses to Judy about her own terminal illness and is later forced to leave Kit, the theme therefore becomes more representative of the prevention of the proper realization of her own emotions. Judy refuses a compromise that would allow Lissa to spend the last few months of her life with Kit. As Judy's intransigence becomes absolutely clear, the theme is interrupted and then ends mid-phrase as Lissa is left alone to dissolve into tears. As she subsequently pretends to Kit that she no longer cares about him, the return of the solo violin with her theme emphasizes the continuation of her original emotions despite her words to the contrary. Now, therefore, it is not Kit who disrupts the emotional purpose of the music, but Lissa herself. Like Charlotte in *Now, Voyager*, she is taking a strong and active control of her own emotions and voice for what she believes is a higher purpose. There can be no doubt in this case, however, that the concealment of her emotions is wrong for her, Kit and, ultimately, even Judy. As she leaves Kit's hospital room and is replaced in the frame by her rather regretful-looking rival, her theme is played in a minor key with a melodramatic use of rubato, accented notes and full orchestration.

Kit, on the other hand, is never represented through Lissa's music in her absence, and the strength of his obvious and conscious romantic fixation on her is represented instead through the music with which he tries to defend himself against her influence. No matter how hard he tries, however, he is unable to resist her. Lissa is effectively blackmailed into leaving Kit so that Judy can draw him into the relationship she always wanted. Although they become engaged, the timely diegetic appearance of Lissa's playing and voice on the radio reminds both Kit and Judy of where his feelings really lie. Judy's only magnanimous action in the film is, as a result of this, to engineer their reunion. When the couple are reunited following Lissa's final concert, and particularly as the film draws to a close, the romantic power of Lissa's theme is once again evident. The purpose that it has suggested throughout the film of enabling the transcendence of the everyday wartime fear of death and loss can finally be realized. The couple's embrace therefore encapsulates a courageous and eternal stand against adversity, and the subsequent consummation of their relationship in marriage represents the ultimate selflessness necessary in war. The film's closing shot shows us Lissa, complete with conspicuous wedding ring, returned to her soul sister environment of Cornwall and waving to Kit as, returned to the socially responsible and respectably masculine role of fighter pilot, he flies overhead into battle. The heroic self-sacrifice of their willing resignation to what may be permanent separation is appropriately heralded by a full orchestral, triumphant statement of Lissa's theme, concluding with an emphatic cadence in a triumphantly positive major key.

Conclusion

In many ways, *Love Story* structures a gendered divide through its music in much the same way as a male musician–female listener film, except that the basic configuration is reversed. As I discussed in Chapter 3, in those films that consider the position of the female listener, such as *Possessed, Interlude* and *Dangerous Moonlight*—as well as *Letter from an Unknown Woman* by default—the man gives a certain amount of concrete meaning to the music through his words and/or actions during its performance. As a result, the music is brought under some kind of control, perhaps to fulfil the function of seducing or charming the female listener or to convey the absolute depth of the musician's emotions. The woman can then become emotionally represented through the music of the man, which becomes flexible to her particular moods and situations. This imbuing of the music with concrete meaning becomes part of the downfall of the woman, although she does also give the music back its capacity for less tangible and more genuinely excessive emotion.

In Kit's case, however, the intended function of the music is extremely self-conscious. It is meant to deny emotion and, by extension, national identity, rather than to simulate or indicate its presence. Lissa, instead of coming under the spell of Kit's charisma and music, adopts his pretended philosophy of non-commitment because she wants to enjoy her last few months of life and believes that this will be harmless. She therefore consciously *tries* to become emotionally defined by him. Kit uses diegetic reference to his song in order to prevent her overstepping the agreed boundaries of their 'no-questions-asked' relationship and she usually, if sometimes grudgingly, obeys his musical command. Ultimately, however, in true melodramatic fashion, neither Lissa nor the film can be defined by insincere or denied emotions and Kit's attempt to take control of both his own and Lissa's emotional trajectories fails when she finds herself unable to continue with the façade. Her emotions are strong and sincere, and if it is her female lack of masculine control that prevents her from concealing them to order, this is actually presented, in this particular context at least, as a good thing. In a similar way to Charlotte in *Now, Voyager* and Lisa in *Letter from an Unknown Woman*, the very integrity of the emotions represented by Lissa's music means that they cannot be easily denied or undermined. Her musical–emotional voice therefore proves to be the more significant and certainly the stronger of the two, so that it can eventually overpower Kit's resistance. The combination of her national symbolism, her physical illness and her self-sacrifice in the face of Judy's intransigence, however, allows her this eventual dominance without jeopardizing her essential femininity.

Love Story therefore raises many questions about the construction of the female musician, the female listener and the male listener. Although Kit has a tangible reason for not wanting to get involved with Lissa, the narrative nevertheless rehearses the scenario of the defenceless man fighting to resist the siren-esque draw of the female musician. It is only when we see him witness her playing the piano for the first time that we can be sure of the greater depth of his feelings and his anger at the challenge she poses to his emotional independence. But Lissa is not an intentional siren. She is not writing and performing music in an attempt to attract or impress Kit, but to express genuine emotion sanctioned by her personal and patriotic spirit as well as her ill-health. Her characterization is therefore dualistic. Whereas she does attract a man by her performance, she is not in full control of the power contained in her own musical message. Unlike the typical male musician, moreover, her performance is not duplicitous—unwittingly or otherwise—and she does not construct its intended meaning for, or significance to, Kit. Rather like a female listener, she is also overpowered and even physically endangered by the emotions implied by her own music, chiefly because, due to the completely genuine nature of these emotions, she has no distance from the music. Apart from her evident difficulties with its diegetic performance, this allows it to operate at the non-diegetic level as if she was indeed the female listener—it is still she, primarily, who *suffers* from such a close association with music. Her diegetic musicality, however, is allowed by the inner strength aligned to patriotic dedication and, perhaps most importantly, her absolute selflessness. This enables both her innocence of her musical–emotional power and her ultimately feminine victory. Despite her active narrative agency she therefore remains, unlike the would-be *femme fatale* Judy, a sympathetic and attractive character.

Kit, by contrast, attempts to use music in the manner of a male musician rather than a male listener. He not only tries to convey an emotional picture of himself and his relationship to Lissa through his choice of music, but then attempts to mould her in this false image. His more genuine position as a muse to Lissa, however, means that no matter how hard he may try to the contrary, it must be he who answers to her musical voice. Her music enjoys the more omniscient narrative position of 'knowing' what Kit really wants and forcing him to realize this himself. As we know, for example, from poor Elliot's fate in *Now, Voyager* and perhaps also Stefan's final resignation in *Letter from an Unknown Woman*, the integrity of non-diegetic music tends to overcome those whose relationship to music is in any way detached. Neither Kit nor Lissa are, therefore, solely designated as the musician or the listener in their characterizations. Although all the usual qualities of both characters are present, they are redistributed between the man and woman in order that more conventional gender attributes can be taken into account. Being a musician is therefore not a threat to Lissa's femininity, and being her muse does not compromise Kit's masculinity, but in fact returns him to it in its fullest sense.

Love Story therefore offers an extremely informative example of the problems of characterizing the female musician. As I outlined early in this chapter, the figure of the *femme fatale* suggests that one of the most prevalent models for the active female musician may still be, to some degree, the Siren. The idea of the woman self-consciously and/or self-confidently giving a voice to her emotions or sexuality through music therefore remains problematic. In Chapter 2, I suggested that the woman's relationship to both emotion and music can be rendered respectable and even safe, in narrative terms, by the creation of a certain distance from her actual words and actions. In Chapter 3, narrative safety was assured by the musical denial of the woman's independent emotional voice. The characterization of a woman who closes the musical–emotional 'gap' that sustains the narratives discussed in previous chapters and who enjoys a close and active relationship to music as a reflection of her own personality, but is nevertheless not intended to be 'dangerous' to men, society or herself, is therefore problematic.

This is the point, after all, at which films must finally confront the cultural codes of music and gender in their most exposed form—and the point at which, sadly, we find that the confrontation fails to produce a satisfactory solution. Instead, confusion and cultural distress continue to surround the representation of the classical musical woman, and as a result, female musicality of this type often comes with some kind of mitigation. The woman may, for example, be subject to the kind of physical and/or psychological damage or destruction predicted in the nineteenth century, or, if she is represented as strong in these respects, her very femininity may be placed in question. The particular social role that *Love Story* gives its heroine, however, allows her the capacity for original creativity and acceptable femininity by turning her musicality to a muse-like purpose. Lissa may be a musician and composer, and may also be concerned with her own future, but her most important function within the narrative is to empower and inspire Kit through reminding him of his true personal and national identity.

The diegetic performances in *Love Story* also, however, open up further questions for consideration. Their mobilization of the distinction between the conventional and personal performance styles suggests a very particular relationship between Lissa and her music. As she becomes visually separated from the piano, it is clear that the narrative focus shifts from her conventional professional musicality to the personal emotions that she experiences while she plays. Especially when considered alongside Kit's equally variable relationship to music, this implies the possibility of a more fluid deployment of conventional and personal modes of performance—or even styles of non-diegetic musical–emotional representation—in order to highlight crucially different nuances of the same personality. This in turn reopens the question of the gender of the performer or character in relation to music. The characterization of the female musician is clearly uniquely problematic, and cultural prejudice, of course, favours the equally controlled depiction of masculinity. Nevertheless, given the Romantic evocation of the potential for the male creator's feminine interiority, there is no formal reason why such fluidity of musical styles and their emotional connotations could not be extended to the female musician's male counterpart. The relatively contained and controlled male musicians of Chapter 3's female listener-focused narratives may not, therefore, offer a sufficiently complete picture of male musicality after all.

Chapter 5

The male musician

'There are so many things I would like to say, but I can't.'
Captain Hasek (Michael Redgrave) in *The Captive Heart* (1946)

'Careless talk costs lives.'
Ministry of Information propaganda slogan

Considering the number of films depicting such figures, the actual character of the male musician is surprisingly elusive. As I suggested in Chapter 3, films that feature male musicians often make the female listener and/or muse the real object of their investigation, and while this woman's psychology or emotions become the central focus of the film, the man may remain comparatively enigmatic. His character and particularly his music act more as catalysts for her behaviour than anything else. Because of this, it remains possible for the narrative to portray the gendered relationship as a Romantic configuration, which throws the weight of emotional excess and loss of control onto the woman. The films therefore sit comfortably within the body of women's films, concentrating on female psychology and emotional issues. The further one delves into the musical–emotional characterization of female characters, however, the clearer it becomes that this investigation cannot be effectively completed without a more comprehensive examination of male characterization and music. Not only is this because it becomes increasingly obvious that the association of male characters and music—as with female characters—is much more complex than may at first be apparent, but also because the fuller picture of gender–music relationships emerges as dependent upon a sense of balance and interrelation. That is to say, the musical–emotional characterization of women only works as it does in relation to the musical–emotional characterization of men, and vice versa. It is, as a result, impossible to fully understand either in isolation. The heretofore missing half of gendered musical–emotional characterization is therefore the subject of this final chapter.

The most effective way to begin to redress the balance is clearly to follow the leads of Chapters 3 and 4, by focusing on the characterization of the male musician himself. Focusing on the personality of the male musician, however, raises certain problems and issues. If the Romantic formula were to remain consistent, such films would have to find a way of allowing music to reveal the inner femininity, sensibility and perhaps even the emotional vulnerability of the man, as well as his overriding controlling masculinity. The difficulty of such a complex characterization, particularly at the crucially emotional point of musical performance, is hinted at by the fact that male musician narratives often avoid this basic problem by showing the musician/composer as otherwise emotionally or psychologically disturbed. Such is the case, for example, in *A Bill of Divorcement* (1932), *Hangover Square*, *Deception* and, to some degree, *Dangerous Moonlight*. In many ways, in fact, their mentality may be as fragile in this context as that of their female listeners, or indeed their counterpart female musicians. The use of the personal performance style in diegetic concert or performance sequences certainly distinguishes musicians such as George in *Hangover Square* and, in certain contexts, Stefan in *Dangerous Moonlight* from their male counterparts in the female listener films. Like so many female musicians and listeners, these men are ultimately unable to find an unproblematic place in society, or even in life. Hilary (John Barrymore) in *A Bill of Divorcement* is confined to a life of mental illness with only the company of his daughter and his music, while George in *Hangover Square* and Alex in *Deception* must both die. *Dangerous Moonlight*, however, attempts to find a way of reconciling the man and his music.[1] The idealized Romantic model is redefined through drawing on the conventions of wartime narratives, the codes of the woman's film, and a certain conception of masculine identity. The resulting characterization enables the distinct address of both female and male cinema audiences, as well as fulfilling a particular wartime function.

Before considering how these films approach this characterization, however, it is necessary to examine and question the basic assumption that music belongs mainly with female characters. In order to do this, I begin with a brief survey of the ways in which male characters in and around the 1940s are represented in relation to a more conventionally 'female' style of music. From this, the possibility emerges of constructing and testing masculinity in relation to carefully contextualized 'glimpses' of the (musical–emotional) femininity that lies beneath its social façade. This prepares for the case study of *Dangerous Moonlight*, a film that witnesses both the bravery and resilience of men in combat and the potential conflict between love of country and romantic love. It therefore places its male composer/musician in circumstances that test both his masculine strength and his feminine depth of emotion to the full.

Music, Men and Masculinity in Film

In 1940s films, male characters are usually only explicitly represented through music in very particular narrative situations. No doubt because of the different gender implications of the revelation of interiority, there appears to be more at stake in the individualized representation of a man with his own theme than there is in the equivalent treatment of a woman. This is indicated by the various narrative justifications for male characters who enjoy, or suffer, an unusual proximity to

---

[1] It is interesting to note that all the male musicians listed here are in fact composers. Whereas it does not seem to matter in the male musician–female listener narrative whether the man is a composer or a performer, the majority of films that focus at least to some reasonable degree on the male musician himself tend to favour composers. While the representation of the female composer of Chapter 4 is inherently problematic because of a lack of viable models, however, the characterization of the emotionally disturbed male composer finds a predecessor in the Romantic idea of the tortured genius.

music—ranging from men specifically associated with a non-diegetic theme, through those who obviously hear music or experience it in a particular way inside their own heads, to male musicians and composers. In the Western and the combat film, for example, the otherwise ultra-masculine demands made upon the characters by their circumstances seem to enable a surprisingly liberal, if not overly effusive, association of emotion and music. In *film noir*, on the other hand, the transfer of music from the female to the male character tends to signal the man's emotional entrapment by the *femme fatale*. In psychological dramas, the distortion of music at any narrative level can be used to make an issue of the link between the character's relationship to music and his mental state, with the music itself sometimes even becoming the agent of chaos in that character's life.

Some qualification must also be made about the specific type of music and emotion under examination. It is certainly true that in any kind of film involving characteristically male physical action during this period—a wartime combat scene, for example, a chase or a fight—it is possible that music will be used. It would be wrong to suggest that this music did not represent some kind of emotional aspect to the situation, that such emotion may not be felt by some or all of the characters involved, and that this may not be communicated and equally felt by the film audience. More pertinent to an interrogation of the Romantic application of music to men, however, are those occasions when the sentimental or painful feelings of male characters are accompanied by a typically 'feminine'/female, lyrical style of music. Whereas this may represent heartfelt emotional depth, it may also indicate an interiority that is anything but powerful, autonomous or pleasurable. In these cases, however, an important distinction is made that still seems to distinguish male emotions from those of women. Rather than being constituted within the music itself, this often appears to be evoked in the particular relationship of the character to the music.

The sense of interiority usually associated with the female character comes from her specific connection with a theme that can vary to her emotional states with some degree of intimacy, and the frequent combination of statements of this theme with extended, often close-up, shots of her face. It seems that the increasingly familiar and developing music, in a concentrated convergence with her facial expression, allows us to believe that we understand the woman's thoughts and emotions to an intimate degree. In the emotional representation of men, however, this particular configuration is usually avoided. Men are rarely associated with such intimate themes or shot in close-up to their accompaniment. Although, therefore, *isolated* emotional moments may be recorded through the combination of a close-up and sentimental music, its lack of thematic relevance seems to register the emotion at a rather more general level than tends to be the case with female characters. As a result, it may be possible to extrapolate a gendered distinction with regard to the supposed audience response to these characters. It is of course likely that any emotional response will also be based to some extent on the gender of particular audience members. However, it nevertheless seems possible that, in *very* general terms, we are asked to witness and sympathize with male emotion, whereas our drawing into the woman's musical–emotional trajectory offers the sense of *experiencing* female emotion.

This pattern is broken, however, in certain circumstances. Films that deal with male psychological problems provide some of the most prevalent instances of the musical representation of male emotions. These films offer an interesting comparison to their female counterparts in terms of narrative structure and motivation. They also raise important questions about music's role in indicating the real nature of the threat of excessive feminine emotion. Mary Ann Doane points out that films that deal with the psychological problems of men define the mental conditions of their characters in very different ways to those of female patients. The woman patient typically suffers from a condition that 'implicat[es her] entire being' in her illness, marking it as the result of the very 'essence' of her character.[2] As I discussed in Chapter 2, in the most extreme instances the woman can be brought to the point of mutism, amnesia or even catatonia by her condition. In such cases, she requires the help of a male authority figure, typically a doctor or psychiatrist, to effect her—sometimes enforced—cure. Once she is given back her voice through this medical process, she can embark on what Doane terms the '"talking cure"'—which provides the structure of the film[3]—and, as she speaks, the doctor can in turn interpret her memories. This gives other diegetic characters and the film audience both clear diagnostic reasons for her behaviour and an eventual cure, and enables her return to an acceptable female position in a society that was badly in need of reinforcement in times of wartime upheaval.[4] Male patients, however, are presented in rather different terms. Rather than being a product of their very selves, Doane contends that men's psychological problems are severely 'restricted and localized by linking the illness directly to a war trauma'.[5] At the root of such trauma—not unlike the original childhood incident affecting the women patients of films such as *The Locket*, *The Seventh Veil* and *Lady in the Dark*—lies a war-related episode or problem which must be discovered and faced to free the man from his torment. Films such as *This Above All* and *Mine Own Executioner* (1947) structure their narratives around this discovery and the man's response to it. *The Blue Dahlia* (1946) confuses the effects of Buzz (William Bendix)'s war injury with his memory of more recent events, and *The Small Back Room* (1949) suggests Sammy (David Farrar)'s physical and psychological war injury as the reason for his alcoholism.

Contrary to Doane's suggestion, however, it is certainly true that, even during the 1940s and certainly into the 1950s, male characters and psychological illness do co-exist without this historically localized motivation. *Spellbound* (1945) uses the same talking cure structure as the women's films, but bypasses the war in order to return John (Gregory Peck) to a childhood-based guilt complex over his brother's death. *Secret Beyond the Door* (1948) puts Mark (Michael Redgrave) through a similarly Freudian examination to connect his obsession with recreating rooms in which famous murders of women took place, and his drive towards the murder of his second wife, to his misunderstanding of an upsetting childhood incident with

---

2 Mary Ann Doane (1988), *The Desire to Desire: The Woman's Film of the 1940s*, Basingstoke and London: Macmillan, p. 39.

3 Ibid., p. 47.

4 Ibid., p. 46; Jeanine Basinger (1993), *A Woman's View: How Hollywood Spoke to Women, 1930–1960*, London: Chatto & Windus.

5 Doane (1988), p. 46.

his mother. *Strangers on a Train* (1951) seems, although never explicitly, to link Bruno (Robert Walker)'s murderous psychosis with his difficult relationship with his father, and *Laura*, like the later *Vertigo* (1958), suggests the possibility of male psychological disturbance as the result of romantic obsession with an apparently dead woman who is later 'reincarnated'. Despite the seeming extremity of this latter situation, the male protagonists of both *Laura* and *Vertigo* are, in formal terms, not far removed from women such as Louise in *Possessed*, Lisa in *Letter from an Unknown Woman*, and Helen (Joan Crawford) in *Humoresque*. In a rather cruel twist, however, it seems that the possibility of unrequited love being suffered by a man is only possible if the object of his affection is (apparently) dead. Even then, in both films, the 'reincarnated' woman does eventually return the man's love. Indeed, particularly as the aftermath of the Second World War subsides, an increasing number of films emerge that locate the problems of masculine psychology in different sources. Childhood trauma or unhappiness, or problematic relationships with parents, motivate amnesia, extreme emotional or psychological disturbance, or even psychosis. Such is the case, for example, with the young male protagonists of films such as *Rebel Without a Cause* (1955), *East of Eden* (1955), *The Cobweb* (1955), *Tea and Sympathy* (1956), *The Young Stranger* (1957) and *Home from the Hill* (1960), as well as those in psychological horror films such as *Peeping Tom* (1959) and *Psycho* (1960).

As a counterbalance to the lush symphonic scores of the 1940s women's films, it is interesting to note the extent to which the style of composition tends to differ in films about male psychology. Notwithstanding that film music is a constantly developing artform and that different composers, of course, tend towards different styles, it does seem that particular stylistic devices suggest an important difference in the prevalent cinematic attitude to male characters' conditions. Where women such as Charlotte in *Now, Voyager* are concerned, the music may surge and overtake the dialogue and wash over huge expanses of hysterical diegetic silence. It will rarely, however, leave the safe overall 'control' of the tonal system or the pleasurable familiarity of the symphonic sound. The use of chromaticism tends to remain within the—albeit generous—boundaries of the late Romantic idiom, without too much evidence of the developments into atonalism that had long since happened in classical concert music. This is certainly not to suggest, of course, that musical dissonance and techniques of distortion are never used in relation to women, but that such methods are restricted to only the most extreme moments of disturbance. Music that is less melodic, more dissonant or somehow distorted is relatively common, however, in both contemporaneous and later films dealing with male trauma, whether war-related or as a result of medical conditions or addictions. The very particular sound of the theremin, for example, is used in *Spellbound*, *The Lost Weekend* (1945) and *The Small Back Room*. Through its wavering movement between notes, it seems to evoke a sense of each male protagonist's own tenuous relationship to control. Electronic distortion signals the psychological disturbance or removal from reality of Buzz in *The Blue Dahlia*, Bruno in *Strangers on a Train* and Mark in *Laura*. *Vertigo* contrasts its lushly melodic love theme with the dissonant habañera music of Scotty (James Stewart)'s nightmare arising from his fatal 'addiction' to Madaleine (Kim Novak), and George's piano concerto in *Hangover Square*, which eventually signals the final onset of his psychosis, is placed in equally stark stylistic contrast to the music hall songs that he draws out of it for Netta.[6]

The troubled male adolescents of the 1950s are often represented through music that moves still further away from melody and tonality towards dissonance and even atonalism. In the case of *East of Eden*, in fact, it is the young man's eventual settling into a romantic relationship with a caring woman that returns the score to tonality. In this context, tonal music seems to be recodified as 'normal' and desirable (female) emotion, with dissonance and atonalism representing a level of tortured (male) emotion in excess of this. In comparison with women's films, this suggests that women's psychological problems are being conceptualized in some sense as more containable and less threatening after all, being perhaps inevitable given women's characters in general. Men with problems, however, are a different matter. If men are representative of social order, their illness is synonymous with social chaos. The fear that this poses is therefore mirrored in the disruption of the music's tonal system. This recalls Jacques Attali's contention that the structure and process of music demonstrates the possibility of the organization of society out of the potential chaos of noise.[7] More specifically, it may draw on Edward Said's related suggestion that atonalism constitutes 'a negation, a blotting-out of the society that gave rise to it'.[8] In between these contentions, as it were, lies Susan McClary's equation of chromaticism with a brand of femininity that threatens the borders of the synonymous systems of society and tonality.[9] The significance of the chromaticism or particular rhythms of her operatic 'madwomen's' arias lies principally in their contrast, and return, to a diatonic, rhythmically regular standard. Atonalism, however, eschews any reference to or dependence on the tonal system. The musical system suggested by McClary and others such as Catherine Clément and Kathryn Kalinak therefore specifically reflects the—usually successful—attempt at the narrative containment and neutralization of female characters. Their difficulty in escaping definition through ostensibly masculine musical systems stands in stark contrast to the sense of chaotic panic elicited by the rootless dissonance and atonalism of those boys who cannot or will not conform.

Films that deal with the testing of male power, strength and control such as Westerns and combat films, on the other hand, often make positive use of music's capacity to reveal the inner vulnerability of men. Although this tendency operates in varying degrees between films, I would nevertheless identify it as a 'glimpse' of femininity that ultimately defines the necessary resilience of masculinity. Since there is, after all, no power in control if there is actually nothing to control, for a man to be proven masculine there must be evidence that there are alternative aspects to his

---

6 Interestingly, these contrasts find a telling parallel in *The Two Mrs Carrolls* (1945), where the psychotic disturbance of Geoffrey (Humphrey Bogart) can be similarly traced through the different styles of painting he employs for portraits of his wives.

7 Jacques Attali (1985), *Noise: The Political Economy of Music*, trans. B. Massumi, Minneapolis: University of Minnesota Press.

8 Edward Said (1991), *Musical Elaborations*, New York: Columbia University Press, p. 48.

9 Susan McClary (1991), *Feminine Endings: Music, Gender and Sexuality*, Minneapolis and London: University of Minnesota Press, Chapter 4.

personality that he holds in restraint. Expressing this through non-diegetic music, however, and often reserving the man's expression at his moment of revelation solely for the camera, enables the character to retain his otherwise masculine identity within the diegesis by emphasizing the absolute privacy of the moment. Other characters do not need to appreciate what the film audience has seen. Perhaps inevitably, it seems that the more conventionally masculine the pursuits of the male characters, the more safely these momentary feminine aspects can be revealed. In the context of male suffering in particular, a greater sympathy seems possible towards such revelations, since the way in which the character subsequently deals with those feelings demonstrates his complex personal sacrifice as well as his higher sense of cultural and social duty. A 'real man', therefore, has room for emotions. This can only make him appear more sympathetically human rather than weak, because his ability to be masculine when necessary is not in doubt. It is only when the balance of masculine and feminine attributes weighs in the opposite direction that the man begins to become codified as 'feminine'. Such films therefore play out the dynamic of the masculine construction. They measure the strength of the man by his control over his own interiority, evidenced by his ability to allow its occasional display.

This recalls the representation of manhood examined by Jane Tompkins in the Western. Tompkins suggests of the Western hero that '[h]is pain is part of our pleasure' in viewing (or reading), with the detailed depiction of physicality and suffering 'guarantee[ing] that the sensations are real'.[10] Tompkins frequently returns to ideas of the suppression of feeling and interiority in the genre, the typical taciturnity of the hero, and the outlet for obviously subjugated emotions 'through physical action—usually fighting'.[11] She fails to note, however, the role that music takes in marking the equivalently genuine nature of these concealed sensibilities. The presence of music in films such as *Red River* (1948) and *The Searchers* (1956), for example, constantly attests to the vulnerable reality of the emotional life beneath the rough exterior of the men and their ultra-masculine lifestyle. Despite Tompkins's emphasis on the male–male relationships of the Western, and even her noting of the men's singing in the novel of *The Virginian*,[12] therefore, she misses the significance of the very specific non-diegetic use of male-voice choirs in certain scores, especially when they are singing songs about men. This points to a generic drive to make the experience of emotion an acceptable part of masculinity, even though it is simultaneously generalized by avoiding the explicit linking of music to only one character. Men's non-diegetic singing voices seem to fill in for their diegetic taciturnity, allowing emotion by equating it with the mutuality and universality of male understanding. As will be seen later in the examination of the war film, only men can really understand the struggle to be masculine.

More personalized connections between male characters and music are found, perhaps not surprisingly, in those genres that pit a single man against his often hostile surroundings. This is notable in the detective thriller and *film noir*, with the

---

[10] Jane Tompkins (1992), *West of Everything: The Inner Life of Westerns*, New York and Oxford: Oxford University Press, p. 3.

[11] Ibid., p. 39.

[12] Ibid., p. 64.

latter in particular demonstrating the delicate balance of the masculine/feminine dynamic through its entrapment and disempowerment of the man in the musical–emotional influence of the *femme fatale*. As long as the overall control of the man seems unquestionable, moments approaching the typically female combination of theme and close-up are clearly permissible. A further mitigation of this may lie in the frequent linking of musical themes to a male–female relationship, with the nature of that relationship defining the influence of the glimpse of femininity on the man's characterization and narrative position. Dave Bannion (Glenn Ford) in *The Big Heat* (1953), for example, can be seen in an emotional, musically accompanied close-up as he leaves the house where he lived with his (now murdered) wife and their daughter. The music is not his own theme as such, but was associated with his relationship with these two specific females, a distinction underlined by the notable lack of music during his association with Debbie (Gloria Grahame). The love that Bannion shared with his wife justifies the intensity of this moment, while its very isolation ensures that he can regain control despite his continuing pain and channel his emotion into the more conventionally masculine response of a ruthless quest for justice. In this man's world there is clearly a time for sentimentality and a time for action.

As the masculine grip on power slips, however, so the music of the female character becomes more prevalent. As I discussed in Chapter 4, it is certainly no coincidence that detective thrillers and *films noirs* often present women as the diegetic source of music. Even if the woman does not actually sing or perform, an explicit control over or association with diegetic music can signal a similarly powerful function—for example in *Laura*, *Casablanca* (1942) and *Out of the Past*. The transfer of the music from the diegetic to non-diegetic level in this context seems almost an antidote to the conscious or unconscious appropriation of the man's music undertaken by the female listener. As the *noir* hero is pursued by the musically signified female influence, he risks increasing weakness and compromise. Only by resisting this latter-day siren song can he emerge intact in his masculinity, in the way of Rick (Humphrey Bogart) in *Casablanca* and Rip (Humphrey Bogart) in *Dead Reckoning*. Otherwise, he may succumb to the tragic slavishness of Jeff (Robert Mitchum) in *Out of the Past* or, ultimately, become the completely feminized Chris (Edward G. Robinson) in *Scarlet Street*. Chris not only displays his unusual imagination through painting, but is also surrounded and destroyed by the literal enticement of Kitty's apparently favourite song, ['Come to me'] *My Melancholy Baby*.

Of all the genres presenting both masculinity and femininity under pressure, however, the wartime combat and home front films respectively are among the most extreme. In these genres, the battle to control the appalling emotional situations also being faced in reality takes on a very real propagandist aspect, so that the location of an ideal balance between emotionalism and control becomes a crucial motivating factor. In most wartime films, whether focusing on combat or the home front, speech on certain issues is proscribed. Rather than the possibility of emotional verbal expression being completely denied, however, it tends to be channelled in specific propagandist directions. Regardless of gender, any character may be excessively emotional, complete with soaring non-diegetic music, on the subject of patriotism. Stefan's relatively understated allegiance to Poland in *Dangerous Moonlight*, for example, rather wanes in the face of Pru (Joan Fontaine)'s rabble-rousing tribute to the virtues of England in *This Above All*. It is preferable, however, that personal grief should not give rise to such outbursts. Scenes of emotional devastation are therefore made infinitely more moving by their unbearably staunch containment. The restraint of characters such as Toddy (Rosamund John) in *The Way to the Stars*, Dai (Mervyn Johns) in *The Captive Heart*, Celia in *Millions Like Us* and Walter (Bernard Miles) in *In Which We Serve* in fact seems particularly definitive of British cinema at this time.

Like most other male characters, of course, the man in combat is unable to speak about much of what he feels. Acknowledging hidden emotions, however, is of the utmost importance in this context. By showing traces of 'femininity', men forced into the ultra-masculine combat role demonstrate the sacrifice of putting their own personalities on hold for greater patriotic purposes. They also maintain a continued sense of humanity in resisting transformation into cold-blooded, Nazi-esque murderers. When the issue of masculinity is at a premium, therefore, glimpses of the vulnerability of characters are crucial. They define the even greater possible resilience of masculine strength against the reassuring humanity beneath. While this is inseparable from issues of national and historical behaviour, the combat film nevertheless puts particular strain on the more universal concern with the stability of 'masculinity' that is evident in other genres. It is out of this extreme pressure that the British Second World War film in particular produces what might be termed the 'art' of self-restraint. This specific historical and social circumstance therefore offers a counter-definition to the Romantic idea of the gendered basis of artistic expression. For wartime men such as David (Michael Redgrave) in *The Way to the Stars*, Stefan in *Dangerous Moonlight*, and even to some extent Clive (Tyrone Power) in *This Above All* (a US production but set in England), artistic expression may be a way to cope with and bypass the enforced *inability* to speak. Rather than the Romantic model promoting the male as superior in his natural control, this re-presents the masculine construction as externally imposed and problematic, not least for the men who have to live it. Caution must be exercised, however, when considering the possible ramifications of such a re-presentation. While it may appear to suggest that men exist under similar general cultural or social constraints to women, it is also important to acknowledge that the active balance of control and emotionality actually results in very different gender connotations. The war's representation of masculinity under such extreme pressure from the demands of femininity renders these films an especially rich point at which to examine this strained interplay of gender.

Dangerous Moonlight: Men and the Art of Self-restraint

> 'Now listen young woman, I don't like talking about these things but you asked for it.'
> Stefan to Carol in *Dangerous Moonlight*

Dangerous Moonlight presents the male musician in an unusually wide variety of emotional and performance contexts. Not only does this mean that his interaction with music becomes a central part of the film's subject matter, but also that the different aspects of his personality come largely to be associated with distinct pieces of music. As his interiority is represented in this way, he transcends communication through speech, and depending on whether this transcendence is facilitated in a purposeful and self-conscious way or achieved at a less controlled level, it fulfils very specific functions. This representation is also indivisible from that of his female listener/muse. Most importantly, their central conflict over issues of patriotism and personal loyalty is presented as synonymous with their mutual (mis)understanding of musical meaning.

The film focuses on this conflict, strongly opposing the romantic love between man and woman to the patriotic love of a man for his country. The film remains equivocal, however, as to which is ultimately stronger or more important. This disappointing, although perhaps unintentional, ambiguity may be made more acceptable by the distancing effect created by the non-British nationalities of the principal characters.[13] What Marcia Landy sees as the film's move 'to internationalize the issue of the war'[14] may therefore also allow a more extreme polarization of the film's melodramatic conflicts, which perhaps leads the film to ask more questions than it can answer. Landy suggests that the film 'uses music as one means by which to mediate the [gendered] conflict through affective identification'.[15] It is certainly true that one of the most prevalent motifs of the narrative is the musically motivated crossing of physical and emotional divides. What Landy does not address, however, is the way in which such apparent mediation bypasses, rather than solves, the basic emotional opposition of the narrative. In fact, even the meaning accumulated within the music itself, and the associated characterization of the musician, deny the score the possibility of such an uncomplicated role. On the contrary, the almost equal focus of the narrative on both the male musician and his female muse/listener, enables a full, if unresolved, investigation of the complex meanings and potential misunderstandings of the musician–listener musical transfer. Music is revealed as a deceptively divisive element, so that the film's apparent insistence that the melodramatic conflicts embodied within the characters can be neutralized simply by their mutual attraction is undermined. Even when the couple appear reconciled, an uncomfortable lack of resolution is maintained through either the meaning of the music itself or its overt inability to gloss over narrative problems.[16]

---

[13] Stefan's best friend Mike (Derrick de Marney) is actually Irish, but is clearly set up as opposed to the English in any situation other than a world war. This, together with his status as a 'freelance' soldier, therefore separates him completely from the conventional British soldier.

[14] Marcia Landy (1991), *British Genres: Cinema and Society, 1930–1960*, Princeton and Oxford: Princeton University Press, p. 157.

[15] Ibid.

[16] The main difficulty with making a close case study of *Dangerous Moonlight* arises from the very reason that makes it an interesting film to examine in the first place. It mobilizes many classic issues of the British Second World War combat and home front genres, the international love story, the male musician–female listener narrative, and the talking cure psychological drama. Its hybrid status, however, results in a story which not only seems to contain more than its fair share of implausible and/or contrived situations, but also leaves some of its most important issues bewilderingly unresolved. While there is much about the film that is appealing and useful for study, therefore, it can hardly be denied that, hanging together

The representation of Stefan's emotionalism, particularly in terms of music, is clearly divided between his romance with Carol and his patriotism for Poland—which finds a kind of personification in his friendship with Mike. In his relationship with Carol, the film effects a transfer of the emotional signification of Stefan's music in a similar way to films such as *Letter from an Unknown Woman* and *Possessed*. His response to his own music is replaced by Carol's, so that while she is given a musical subjectivity of sorts, her emotional representation must always reference Stefan and his interpretation of what the music means. Carol is also objectified by the music, however, so that she effectively appears to be held permanently in Stefan's gaze. While the music plays, we therefore see her both as a woman feeling love towards her husband, and as a woman as seen through her husband's loving eyes. Perhaps even more than Lisa in *Letter from an Unknown Woman* or Louise in *Possessed*, Carol is inescapably surrounded by Stefan's music. It seems simultaneously to draw her to him and yet to distance her through objectification. Its use in her accompaniment will therefore always be more complicated than the way in which Stefan Brand's or David's music operates in relation, respectively, to Lisa or Louise. Carol's already compromised position in relation to the love theme is further compounded, however, when she learns that her husband also attaches patriotic significance to it, which denies her presupposed autonomous claim to his affections. She then learns that he also expresses his purely patriotic emotions through playing a particular Chopin piece, and thereby finds herself in a position where Stefan can use his final concert to demonstrate his ability to distance himself emotionally from her solely through musical performance. Only where patriotism and Mike are concerned is Stefan apparently unable to exercise such manipulation. Whereas his emotions for Carol seem somewhat tempered by romantic convention, albeit spiced by what he himself calls his 'continental charm', his feelings for Poland and Mike are almost beyond his own understanding.

Gendered Issues of Silence and Vocality in War

Dangerous Moonlight mobilizes the structure of Doane's talking cure narrative, rather paradoxically, to tell a story that emphasizes the virtue and potentially greater expressivity of *not* talking. With Stefan as the patient, the actual verbal silence of the cure—taking place as it does through an unnarrated flashback—frames the story, thus both allowing and validating his self-restraint. This recalls Kaja Silverman's problematizing of the incongruity of male subjectivity and the embodied voice-over as a means of narration. She suggests:

> Hollywood dictates that the closer a voice is to the 'inside' of the narrative, the more remote it is from the 'outside,' i.e., from that space fictionally inscribed by the disembodied voice-over, but which is in fact synonymous with the cinematic apparatus. In other words,

---

fairly loosely in places, and with important character decisions and actions going completely unexplained, its ultimate raison d'être seems somewhat unclear. I will therefore consider the gendered roles of music, silence and dialogue in their own narrative contexts, resisting the temptation to pull all these threads together by claiming to have found one coherent meaning throughout the text as a whole.

> it equates diegetic interiority with discursive impotence and lack of control, thereby rendering that situation culturally unacceptable for the 'normal' male subject.[17]

In support of this, Silverman points to the fact that 'the embodied male voice is likely to speak "over" the image track only because of drastic circumstances, when it is (or recently has been) *in extremis*' [emphasis in original].[18] This certainly justifies the use of such narration in the case of, for example, war-traumatized men or the anti-heroes of *film noir*. There is, however, surely an important difference between spoken and 'thought' modes of narration—that is to say, between a voice-over that is actually spoken out loud within the diegetic space, and an interior monologue or a flashback that is motivated by non-verbalized memory alone. The most pertinent distinction in relation to female voice-over narration, or by extension that of the 'weakened' male narrators suggested above, is that being forced to speak out within the diegetic space, in whatever form, for the ears of other characters, gives the narrated story more of a quality of 'public property', thereby removing complete interpretive control of that story from the narrator and opening a space for its critical reception by other characters. A sense of diegetic 'privacy', however, can be seen in operation with male—or indeed female—narrators who, while appearing within their own story, tell that story to the film audience alone. The exclusive use of interior monologue or non-verbalized thoughts can therefore lend the narrator a paradoxical freedom or independence within the narrative, and may allow them to escape the full force of diegetic examination or judgement for their stories.

Dangerous Moonlight's gendered divide also singles out the female act of talking within the flashback as indicative of the destructive indulgence of expressing self-interested emotions, as opposed to more private and/or interiorized methods of expression. The latter are represented as more meaningful, comparatively selfless, mature and dignified, easier to sympathize with and, in this context, exclusively male. Drawing on the national experience of suffering, the repression of words signifies both those things that should not be said and those that do not require saying in order to be understood. The psychoanalytical—and in wartime perhaps luxurious—question of the negativity of emotional self-repression cannot surface, understandably, until peace has returned. Accordingly, the verbally unrestrained woman is upheld as socially and indeed personally undesirable. To gaze at her physically may still be a source of pleasure, but to contemplate the character beneath the surface is not so satisfying.

At the opening of the film, Stefan bears many of the marks of the heroine of Doane's medical discourse (see Chapter 2 of this book). He is suffering from amnesia and is in an almost catatonic state—unable to speak and unresponsive to the voices of others. He is able to move, at least enough to be able to play at the piano keyboard, if not actually to produce anything other than noise. He is already in hospital, under the care of a resident doctor, who has also called in a specialist to help with the case, and the watchful eye of his wife Carol. It is at this point, however, that his similarity

---

17 Kaja Silverman (1988), *The Acoustic Mirror: The Female Voice in Psychoanalysis and Cinema*, Bloomington and Indianapolis: Indiana University Press, pp. 53–4.

18 Ibid., p. 52.

to a female patient ends and the crucial signs of difference in his medical discourse begin to become apparent. Stefan is initially seen with Carol, who is encouraging him to respond to her sung snippets of what is later found to be his own composition. Stefan has been given a very large hospital room to himself, and Carol is able to instruct the nurse not to put up the blackout screens. From the conversation of the nurses, we also find that Stefan has been allowed to disturb the hospital with his playing for some time. The nurses remove some of the usual mystery around the mute patient by making it clear that his trauma is war-related, rendering him masculine not only in Doane's terms but also, thanks to the more specific knowledge of his status as a fighter pilot, in Marcia Landy's (see Chapter 4 of this book). The feminizing potential of his musicality is thereby countered by confirming his restriction to the land as accidental and temporary, his chosen location being the male domain of the skies. Together with the more detailed subsequent conversation of the doctors, this enables Stefan to become partly known, in factual terms, without having to speak on his own behalf.

It is the tolerance of Stefan's silence that initially distinguishes him from the conventional male or female psychological patient. There is no need for Stefan to reveal the basic details of his identity, since he comes to the hospital as a known celebrity—a fact that obviously gives him a certain status within the institution. It is unclear whether the nurses actually know who he is, but we are left in no doubt that the more learned and sensitive doctors fully understand his cultural and, therefore, national importance. Both know his work, and one already owns a recording of the *Warsaw Concerto*, Stefan's own composition that his wife is currently humming to him. Stefan's treatment is likened to giving traumatized children their old toys to play with. While the comparison may seem trivializing of his musical talent, it actually puts him in control of his own recuperation. He has been allowed to play at the piano for three days, but has still remained resistant to treatment. The doctors nevertheless decide to give him more time to himself. Unlike a conventional patient, this emphasizes the importance of self-healing in Stefan's case. His music is recognized as something that can make him well again, rather than potentially furthering his traumatized state, and this marks him as clearly different from most if not all of the female musicians, and listeners, discussed in previous chapters. In *Love Story*, Lissa's music causes her the greatest trauma of all. Francesca in *The Seventh Veil* collapses as a result of her memories throughout one performance and encounters a persistent mental block when playing a piece that recalls a particularly violent episode with her guardian. Olwen in *While I Live* is driven to accidentally suicidal distraction by her own process of composition, and even non-musician women such as Helen in *Humoresque* and Louise in *Possessed* are disturbed and/or destroyed by the presence of music rather than cured by it. If Stefan, on the other hand, can recall what his music signifies, he will be able to understand his own condition and therefore cure himself. Importantly, this makes the clear assumption that he will be able to cope with whatever secrets the music contains.[19] The female character, therefore, whether musician or listener, must be cured of whatever music does to her or suffer the consequences. The male musician, on the other hand, can potentially be cured through the understanding of his inner self that his own music brings—a contention which, interestingly, suggests that the female listener, in her 'over-romantic' interpretation of the musician as understandable purely through his music, may be right after all. The doctors correctly sense that Stefan does not need them. All he requires is the right environment in which to 'find' himself.

In discussion of his cure, therefore, more concern is expressed over his inability to produce music than to speak. This thematicizes the dynamic between self-expression and meaning through speech and music found in melodramas and women's films that I discussed in Chapter 2. As such, there seems to be a surprising degree of similarity between Stefan's relationship to his music and Charlotte's—albeit unknowing—interaction with non-diegetic music in *Now, Voyager*. This not only suggests that music constitutes the route to Stefan's true voice, but also makes him iconic of all damaged artists in wartime. He will express his feelings through playing the piano and keep his exact thoughts to himself. This combination of silence and music both demonstrates and bypasses accepted codes of masculine control. Unable to express emotion in an everyday way without risking a 'feminizing' loss of control, the male character may channel his feelings through some kind of conduit. Music, poetry, painting or literary quotations represent, in an acceptable form, what he is culturally disabled from simply saying or doing. The male understanding that this performance must be upheld means that Stefan's behaviour is respected in turn by his doctors, the men of the RAF Polish squadron, and his RAF Commanding Officer (John Laurie). The latter consoles Stefan after Mike's death with the line: 'We British don't say much, but we feel things the same as most people.' The statement clearly contrasts British—in the Commanding Officer's specific case, Scottish—reserve with Stefan's recent display of Polish emotionalism. The film also, although not explicitly, draws a gender contrast along the same lines. Within the context of the film, there is neither an example of a female who restrains herself from speech nor, for that matter, any woman who is even British. It is specifically the men in this film, most literally in Stefan's case, who make an artform out of self-restraint.

The tolerance of verbal silence and the resistance towards forcing speech remove much of the potential threat to Stefan's masculinity posed by the process of psychoanalysis. The methods of the doctors are extremely non-invasive and their respect for their patient is obvious. This is not some anonymous woman who merely

---

[19] This is perhaps a dangerous assumption given the suicidal consequences of George's final 'self-realization' in the closing moments of *Hangover Square*. After his arrest, his performance of his own piano concerto is punctuated with increasingly frequent point-of-view shots, detailing not only his physically distorted sight of the concert hall around him but also his rapidly returning memory, which confronts him with a chronological catalogue of his past misdeeds. George, however, is revealed from the outset as a psychotic murderer and is therefore made somewhat peculiar in this discussion because of his primary significance as something else besides a composer and musician.

provides an interesting example of a particular illness, but a symbol of national importance, as the dialogue of the doctors indicates:

> Hospital Doctor (J.H. Roberts): 'If we could get him better, I should feel that we'd done something for the world. Something for… well you know what I mean.'
> Visiting Specialist (Cecil Parker): 'Well if you feel like that too, we'll get him better alright, even if it takes a miracle or an act of God. I just don't like the idea of another great artist finishing up in a home.'

Stefan's cure is part of the war effort, as well as signifying something for world culture. Accordingly, the doctors are more concerned with seeing him cured than with prying into his private thoughts. It is interesting to note how less central the idea of a cure is for Lissa in *Love Story*. She is a comparable international figure, has a vital role to play in maintaining the morale of both the troops and the home front audience, and is, of course, British. Her illness, however, seems merely to be accepted, with no suggestion of eminent surgeons risking cutting-edge techniques to save *her* for posterity. As Stefan finally begins to play his concerto, the doctors leave their room to watch him from a concealed distance. Even at this stage, they choose not to interfere with his cure, but merely wonder at his mental processes:

> Visiting Specialist: 'Perhaps that music will bring back a lot of things.'
> Hospital Doctor: 'I hope so.'
> Visiting Specialist [over a medium long shot of Stefan playing, with a focus on his face]: 'I'd like to know what he's thinking about now.'

This dialogue and their extended admiring gaze motivate a tracking movement towards Stefan. This gradually removes him from his immediate environment and begins the flashback that will constitute almost the entire remainder of the narrative. Since Stefan still does not speak, as far as the doctors and Carol are concerned the entire length of the film must consist of Stefan playing his concerto in a hospital room. The story that we see occurs only in Stefan's memory, despite the inclusion of scenes that he could not actually have witnessed. This allows Stefan to become a 'known' character, without the objectifying diegetic indignity of medical diagnosis so common to female—and sometimes even male—psychological dramas. He is, as a result, both known and unknown, revelatory and secretive, vulnerable and in control, feminine and masculine.

This framework therefore indicates the dual gendering of Stefan's character. He is, like Kit in *Love Story*, Landy's 'ultimate war hero' fighter pilot,[20] but he is also a concert pianist. He is patriotic, but constructed as exotically Polish rather than British. He is emotional, but self-contained and controlled. In Doane's terms, he may almost be the perfect male hero of a love story,[21] if it were not for his other love. Embodying within himself the polarities of the film's melodramatic conflict,

---

20 Landy, p. 157.

21 See Doane on the way in which 'men in the love story frequently … "act like women" insofar as they are attentive to detail, minute incidents, and the complexities of intersubjective relations'. She goes on to suggest that male love story protagonists 'are what women would want them to be, and what they want them to be is like themselves', Doane (1988), p. 116.

his heart is divided between the land and the air, with his dilemma being largely caused by his American wife's very 'un-British' resistance to his patriotism, which she selfishly sees as tantamount to a romantic rival. The conflict between these two characters—the woman on the home front and the very human, vulnerable fighting man—gives rise to the nearest thing to a coherent message within the film, even if its ultimate consequences are rather opaque.

Alongside depictions in wartime films of women who, through what was considered sexual promiscuity, appear to threaten national morality and the wellbeing of the fighting man, Carol is representative of another type of woman perhaps just as dangerous. Whether through a wilful refusal to accept the reality of the national situation, or through unthinking naïveté, women who fail to give full emotional support to fighting men are often represented as a source of acute individual pain and communal disruption. Miss Winterton (Joyce Carey) in *The Way to the Stars* gives a more specifically destructive slant to the backbiting older women in *Love Story* when she complains about the airmen enjoying themselves in the bar, refusing to acknowledge how much they deserve their fun. In a cruel extension of this, reminiscent of the interrupted final parting of Laura and Alec (Trevor Howard) in *Brief Encounter*, she barges in on what will turn out to be the last goodbye of David and Toddy, denying them this important moment for the sake of a petty complaint. The naïve expectation that the behaviour of their male lovers will not be changed by the war clouds the judgement of both Iris (Renée Asherson) in the same film and Caroline (Jane Barrett) in *The Captive Heart*. Iris fails to detect the real reason why Peter (John Mills) cannot continue his relationship with her after David's death, and Caroline, unable to comprehend the emotional vulnerability of Steven (Derek Bond)'s situation in the prison camp, blames him for believing Beryl (Meriel Forbes)'s poisonous and self-interested letter claiming Caroline's infidelity. In each case, however, the inevitability of an eventual happy reunion is assured by the basing of the women's reactions on sincerely hurt feelings rather than malice. A less pleasant conclusion comes from Carol's selfish refusal to accept Stefan's patriotic drive to fight. Her intransigence forces him to leave her and undergo the pain of trying to forget her in England. It is his resultant closed state of mind, however, that leads to his disastrously fatal row with Mike.

The emotional vulnerability of the fighting man is clearly revealed in narratives dealing with injured men during or after the war, such as Kit in *Love Story*, Adam (Kieron Moore) in *Mine Own Executioner*, and Sammy in *The Small Back Room*, or those in captivity such as Steven and David (Gordon Jackson) in *The Captive Heart*. The man actively involved in combat, however, can also be badly affected by his own vulnerability, notably if his concentration is divided between his duty and emotional or superstitious concerns. David in *The Way to the Stars*, for example, almost seems to have died as a direct result of being without his lucky talisman cigarette lighter, and in *Dangerous Moonlight*, the Commanding Officer actually emphasizes this point after Mike has failed to survive combat under the influence of his row with Stefan about Carol. This then appears, in combination with Stefan reading Carol's letter to Mike, to lead directly to Stefan's over-emotional suicide dive during his own subsequent dogfight. Combining both themes, this film seems to state quite clearly that Carol, as representative of the unsupportive woman, can effectively be as lethal in the skies as an enemy fighter plane. The man, revealed as deeply sensitive beneath his strong masculine façade, cannot survive without the full emotional and moral backing of the home front.

The unsympathetic light in which *Dangerous Moonlight* views Carol, and indeed in which all the films mentioned above see their demonized females, is only part of this film's broader project in representing wartime masculinity. From the embarrassed but mutually understood exchanges of the doctors, through the affectionate banter and forgiving relationship between Stefan and Mike, to the silent regimental sympathy for Stefan's grief after Mike's death, the film constantly claims the sensitivity of men. Despite their wartime roles and the pressures put upon them to act like men, they still have emotions. Within the context of this particular film, however, only men seem fully able to understand this. Only men can really perceive the mental torture of other men having to leave the people they love to defend the country they love. The male-only spaces of the film are therefore rife with expressions of camaraderie—revelations of emotion that would be impossible in the presence of women. It is certainly not unusual for war films like *The Way to the Stars* and *The Captive Heart*, or indeed films dealing with post-war trauma such as *The Best Years of Our Lives* (1946), *The Blue Dahlia* and *The Men* (1950) to openly represent close friendship and strong sympathy between men, as well as their pain at the loss of comrades. The particular expression of this emotion through music and performance, however, makes a much greater issue of self-control and the lack of *need* for speech in certain circumstances, while also adding a more obviously vulnerable depth to male characterization. Carol, as the sole representative of women in *Dangerous Moonlight*, appears by contrast hard-hearted, selfish and extremely vocal about her feelings. Apparently independently minded and wilful, she refuses to understand Stefan's point of view and fails to perceive the subtleties of enforced models of masculinity. She constantly runs to her father—who, torn between paternal love and his own masculinity, is equally sympathetic to everyone's point of view—for verification of her childishness. Through Stefan's refusal to force Carol into submission, however, the film espouses the inappropriateness of wasting time on such romantic individuality in wartime. Carol's final move towards conciliation is of her own accord, and her presence in the hospital may therefore indeed offer the 'oblique commentary on American neutrality' suggested by Landy.[22]

Music, Romance, Patriotism and Love

Both Stefan's relationship to music and his emotional control in Carol's presence are apparent from their very first meeting during an air raid in Warsaw. In the way of a typical female listener, Carol is repeatedly drawn across space towards Stefan by his music—a pattern first seen when she hears the sound of his playing coming from a bombed-out house. Stefan reveals his masculine duality during their first few moments together. He counters his brief willingness to admit fear about the war with a firm establishment of personal power over Carol through his playing, his charming manner—which includes equating her voice with music—and his obvious

[22] Landy, p. 157.

pleasure in remaining secretive about his musical renown. The limit of his capacity for emotional expression is revealed, however, when Carol challenges him about not actually being in combat at this precise moment in time. He leaves the piano, standing in medium long shot with his back to the room while he tells her of the depleted state of the Polish air force. Rather than witnessing his own facial expression while he speaks so emotionally, we see Carol's response to his words. Even when he turns to speak directly to her, his face is half obscured by shadow. The closest shot, although still only a medium close-up, comes after this as he speaks his final sarcastic line: 'They'll pay you well.' The correlation of Stefan's face, his music and his emotions is therefore marked as problematic, particularly in front of a woman. To be able to express himself fully in words, he must stop playing the piano and turn away from his female listener.

Despite their otherwise flirtatious conversation, there is no real emotional bond between the couple until Stefan's music draws Carol towards him in the manner discussed in Chapter 3, equating the crossing of physical space with the closing of an emotional distance. Stefan stops playing the piano as he reaches the point where he claims his composition currently ends. He then stares fixedly at Carol, and through the following series of reverse-shots the camera tracks slowly towards each of their staring faces. Apparently discomforted by this intensity, Carol breaks the mutual gaze. Stefan protests, however, saying that she has given him 'something lovely'. He plays the music she has inspired, which is the melody that will become the most lyrical theme of his concerto as well as the love theme of the film. As he plays, she walks slowly towards him as if being drawn in, hypnotized, by his unblinking gaze. When she reaches his side, he trails off from playing without ending the melody. Immediately, a bomb falls so close-by that they both dive for cover under the piano—a move that ends with their embrace. The lack of resolution of the love theme's first diegetic appearance, however, suggests that the couple's involvement will not end simply with the emotions discovered during this romantic moment. The very specific interruption of their mutual gaze by the explosion makes it apparent that the war will come between them.

Stefan has already claimed that he has just had the idea for the beginning of this music, which later becomes part of the aptly named *Warsaw Concerto*, presumably in response to the immediate situation of the air raid. Even though the love theme is inspired by a person, therefore, the fact that it becomes part of the same concerto makes its meaning more complex. In a later episode, Stefan describes this music as an account of him and Carol in Warsaw and New York. In his musical imagination, their relationship is always associated with a place, and by extension with the international political situation. It is for this reason that he claims he cannot finish the piece—because he does not know where they will be in the future. The theme, and perhaps the whole concerto, therefore suggests the possibility of the indivisibility of romantic love and love of country. The couple are not just Stefan and Carol, but Stefan and Carol in Warsaw. Since this connection only exists for Stefan, however—at least until he makes it clear to Carol during their honeymoon—each character reads the significance of the theme in a quite different way. Once again the typical female listener, Carol fails to understand the real meaning of Stefan's music, believing that it represents an all-consuming love for her. Stefan, on the other hand, understands the music as representing two loves which for him must be allowed to survive together. This division in understanding is central to their very different views of the place of their romance next to wartime events, and although the containment of this double meaning within the same piece of music seems to point to an attempt by the film to demonstrate that the two kinds of emotion can co-exist, this is, sadly, the very message that *Dangerous Moonlight* seems unable fully to convey.

The disjuncture in personal and musical understanding is emphasized in the move to the following scene, which locates Stefan back at his Polish airbase. The interrupted love theme is now replaced by a mechanically reproduced and repeated phrase from Chopin's *Polonaise* in A Major Op. 40, No. 1, which, the Bomber Commander (Frederick Valk) reminds the men, represents the continued stand of Poland against Germany. This reflects the opening title sequence's direct juxtaposition of the concerto's love theme with the Polish national anthem. It also foreshadows Stefan's later reference to being 'like a man who is riding two horses' as his visual memories of war-torn Poland interrupt the non-diegetic love theme during the montage of his American concert tour. Continuing the idea of the qualified place of romantic emotion in music that Stefan's relationship to his own composition suggests, the Chopin *Polonaise* carries a clear association with patriotism and community rather than romantic individualism. The difficulties of the love–war dichotomy therefore find expression in a specifically musical way that parallels the similar message of *The Way to the Stars*. This film states the problem in no uncertain terms during the wedding reception of David and Toddy. Tiny (Basil Radford), giving his Best Man's speech, turns to Toddy with the words: 'And to the bride, I would say only this.' At this point the air raid whistle sounds, the non-diegetic music—which is reserved in this film primarily for male–female relationships—stops, and the reception must be disbanded. A clearer message to war brides, one could not hope to find.

Dangerous Moonlight emphasizes this crucial opposition through the different styles of the *Warsaw Concerto*'s love theme and the *Polonaise*, particularly in its original piano version heard later in the film. The simplicity of the Concerto's love theme emerges like an oasis of romantic calm in its otherwise rather turbulent dramaticism. Its rhythmically simple melody line is accompanied by endlessly fluid, rising and falling arpeggiated chords in quavers and triplet quavers. The theme conveys a sense of simple yearning that seems to come from its particular dynamic of ascent and descent and its constant delaying of harmonic resolution through the use of seventh chords. The overall downward direction of the first half of the theme is contrasted with its own short ascending motifs—which end by turns with ascending and descending intervals. The second half of the theme constricts the melodic intervals and seems to fight the previous overall descent of the melody line. It ends its first two bars on the same melodic note, firstly as a seventh note requiring resolution and secondly as a fully resolved tonic note. It then delays final harmonic resolution through an appoggiatura chord (Example 5.1). The theme therefore seems to be pensive and wistful but nevertheless, perhaps, quietly determined in its resistance to defeat. It creates tensions and resolves them in a way that appears sad and yet somehow optimistic. As a result, it seems to encapsulate the emotional dilemma of Stefan and Carol's relationship. By contrast, the movement of the *Polonaise* is unremittingly ascending, with a militaristic sense of determination and aggressively

Example 5.1 Richard Addinsell, *Warsaw Concerto*, pages 13–15; piano only. The love theme that binds together Stefan, Carol and Warsaw

Example 5.2 Fryderyk Chopin, *Polonaise* in A Major, Op. 40, No. 1; bars 1–4

forceful energy. The fluid legato of the Concerto's love theme is replaced by brisk staccato quavers, semiquavers and triplet semiquavers. Its moderate tempo and gentle rubato is replaced by the loud 'allegro con brio' of the *Polonaise* (Example 5.2).

The next time Stefan and Carol meet, at a press conference in New York, Stefan does not recognize her. Even after her repetition of the significant line from their first meeting, '[i]t's not safe to be out alone when the moon is so bright', there is no music to reflect his realization of her identity. The love theme does not reappear until their date the next evening, when it seems clear, however, that it now reflects listener/muse Carol's emotional response to the situation rather than Stefan's. Firstly, and most tangibly, the juxtaposition of the music with their dialogue and the particular way in which the scene is shot seems to link the music explicitly with Carol's emotional refusal of reality. We will also find later, however, that Stefan has forgotten the theme, and remembers it only during their subsequent honeymoon. There is no evidence of whether Carol remembers the melody either, and I certainly do not wish to suggest that the music is actually meant to be heard in the heads of either of the characters. This does raise the question, however, of whether music that Stefan composed but has forgotten could really be used to reflect his emotions, even at the non-diegetic level.

The theme makes two appearances during Carol and Stefan's date, the second and most notable of which occurs after Stefan is flippant about the possibility of future meetings. The subsequent appearance of the theme accompanies a focus on Carol's distressed face as she expresses her fear that they may not see each other again. As she speaks, the camera tracks round to bring Stefan back into the shot, and as he appears, the love theme gives way to non-thematic music. This non-thematic music continues as they kiss and Stefan tells Carol how he feels about her. During this dialogue, the camera remains focused on Stefan's face, making Carol's expression invisible to the viewer (Figure 5.1). Stefan is therefore expressing his emotions at close range, but without the accompaniment of the music that he wrote as his first response to Carol. After he proposes, the love theme reappears for Carol's positive response. They kiss, and as Stefan asks how soon they can get married, Carol laughs about him being in such a hurry. They embrace again, turning slightly so that the focus moves to Carol's face rather than Stefan's for his final line: 'We have to be, there's a war on.' The love theme, being stated in the solo cello, now follows Carol's reaction intimately, continuing slowly for a few notes while her expression freezes momentarily, before she fixes into a worried, unhappy expression just as the cello line is disrupted to end incomplete on a note alien to the usual melody, and with the harmony unresolved (Figure 5.2; Example 5.3). Stefan speaks this line cheerfully, still laughing from his successful proposal. Since we are unable to see his face, his tone of voice must act as evidence that he does not share Carol's jarring change of emotion.

Figure 5.1 ***Dangerous Moonlight.*** **Carol (Sally Gray) and Stefan (Anton Walbrook). Stefan's expression of emotion to non-thematic music**

Figure 5.2 ***Dangerous Moonlight.*** **Carol's unhappiness linked to the disruption of the love theme**

Stefan: "We have to be, there's a war on."

Example 5.3 Richard Addinsell, *Dangerous Moonlight*. The love theme disrupted

The music's intricate reflection of Carol's response puts the score out of step with Stefan, so that his own music seems to represent less his feelings and response to Carol, and more her reaction to him. Like Lisa in *Letter from an Unknown Woman*, Carol has been given a musical expression for her emotions by Stefan. Although this is obviously not comparable in terms of the conscious appropriation of the man's music, it is true that it is Carol, rather than Stefan himself, who dwells most on the significance of Stefan's musical talents. Later in the film, in a rather implausible scene, she impresses upon him the importance of his creativity and the way in which this places him apart from other people. This seems to have escaped Stefan's attention despite his international renown. Although this is clearly part of her attempt to prevent him from rejoining the airforce, it may also suggest that it is his musical ability that has made her fall so deeply in love with him. After all, as she herself admits, she knows little else about him when they marry, and her priority on the day that she has apparently set out to induce him to propose has been to have a grand piano delivered to her family's rather palatial 'shack' in the country, ready for their arrival as newlyweds later that evening.

When Stefan and Carol arrive at the shack, Stefan deposits his wife rather unceremoniously on a sofa and makes straight for the piano. Even at this stage, however, he plays established classical repertoire rather than his own music. It is not until later in their honeymoon, and in the middle of the night, that he remembers the love theme. Carol wakes, hears him playing the piano, and is once again drawn across space to his side—this time by the melody that she inspired in him. Leaving the bedroom, she appears in the landing doorway as if seen from Stefan's point of view, although we have not yet seen Stefan and can only assume this from subsequent shots and the memory of the location of the piano. She hesitates in the doorway as the melody draws to its close, waiting, as if choreographed, for the final note before she steps forward. As she walks along the landing and hesitates at the top of the stairs, held in long shot as she watches Stefan playing, she is accompanied by a series of trill figures that lead into the next statement of the melody. This also underlies the first of her point-of-view shots of Stefan, who watches her as she begins to walk down the stairs, towards a waiting area of key light. At the exact moment that she steps into this light, the music settles on a chord that reintroduces the love theme, so that it goes on to accompany her slow, now highly lit descent. As we watch Carol watching Stefan as she continues this descent, the camera tracks towards her so that we are removed from Stefan's point of view to a much better vantage point from which to see her adoring expression (Figure 5.3). The reverse shot of Stefan, however, marked by the final chord of the first statement of the melody, still reflects Carol's actual position in relation to him and does not offer a similarly intimate view of his face (Figure 5.4).

Figure 5.3 ***Dangerous Moonlight*. The idealized view of Carol**

Figure 5.4 ***Dangerous Moonlight*. The distanced view of Stefan**

Figure 5.5 *Dangerous Moonlight.* Stefan in the personal performance mode, immune to Carol's displeasure

As she takes her place at his side and they begin to talk, Stefan stares blankly ahead, rather than looking at Carol, as he plays and speaks. Stefan's unseeing gaze offers a variation on the stare into the middle distance of the personal performance mode. It not only suggests this as a moment of interiority that induces him to be rather brutally honest, but also means that he remains absolutely unaware of the effect of his words on Carol. It is therefore the negative aspect of such self-absorption that is emphasized by the stare in this case. The first full statement of the theme ends as Carol reaches Stefan's side, and a second begins using fuller chords as he pays her romantic compliments. He tells her that this music is hers because, he says: 'You gave it to me. I'll never play it again without thinking of you. Without you deep in my heart.' She asks him how it will end, to which he replies: 'Happily, I hope.' At this point, the melody draws to a close and the music, while still from the Concerto, makes use of different material. His explanation of this comment, that he cannot finish the piece without knowing where they will be in the future, upsets Carol. Although he does not seem to realize that she has responded in this way, she frowns, pulls away from him and tries to change the subject (Figure 5.5). Despite the fact that the theme does reach a resolution at this important point in the dialogue, therefore, it is clear that this does not reflect a similar sense of comfort in their relationship. On the contrary, it is at this point that Carol begins to realize Stefan's alternative understanding of the music, which is so germane to their—at least temporary—incompatibility.

This marks an important turning point in the music–narrative relationship. The film seems to remain insistent that the use of the theme, at least at the non-diegetic level, continues to unite the couple in love despite all the obstacles of reality. The narrative–emotional disjuncture between the characters, however, is now clearly contained within the music itself. As a result, its use in the subsequent 'star and following star' dialogue, for example, seems rather ironically to emphasize their separation as much as their togetherness. The shot structure and dialogue of this whole episode, rhyming very obviously with the opening sequence of the couple's story, also only add to the theme's already complex layering of meaning. Although the melody represents both Carol's feelings for Stefan and his emotions towards her, there is a marked difference in how these are represented and the result of this for each character. Stefan has written the music but states that Carol gave the melody to him, so that the theme represents Carol's muse-like influence on Stefan. The shot structure of the performance sequence, however, does not emphasize Stefan's response to his wife. We are denied any really detailed shots of his face as he looks at her, being given instead a very intimate portrait of Carol, both in terms of Stefan's view of her and her secret responses to his words. The music's representation of how Stefan feels about Carol is therefore displaced onto an encouragement to us to see Carol as he sees her—hence the extended staircase sequence and the 'idealized' version of Stefan's point of view as the camera moves closer to Carol and she is held in the glowing key light. At the same time, of course, any suggestion that the music reflects Carol's feelings for Stefan must be tempered by the knowledge that the music actually originated with him.

By the time Stefan and Carol reach their final conflict, therefore, both the love theme and the Chopin *Polonaise* have accumulated a complex combination of meanings. Both individually and in relation to each other, they can now give full meaning to Stefan's profession to Mike during his concert tour that the musical notes he writes 'can say more than [he] ever can in words'. As Carol is about to discover, Stefan's ability to say more in music will give him the final word, as it were, on their ongoing dispute. He has decided, unbeknown to her, to cancel his American touring commitments and travel to England to join the RAF Polish squadron. As Carol enters their hotel room, she is visibly disturbed to find Stefan playing the *Polonaise*. While she complains that it reminds her of the last days in Warsaw, Stefan argues that this is exactly why he plays it. As if to suggest that his primary emotions are no longer concerned with Carol, he ignores her objections by starting to play the piece again. When he stops to tell her his plans, she retaliates with a divorce threat. He storms in silence from the room, and the couple do not see each other again until he walks out onto the concert platform for his final performance later that evening. As he acknowledges the applause of the audience before the concert begins, he looks up at Carol with a defiant expression. The performance of the *Warsaw Concerto*, shot in the familiar documentary style typical in films of this type (see Chapter 4) then finds him locked into the conventional performance mode. He exhibits total concentration, looking at either the keyboard or the conductor and displaying very little emotion.

Figure 5.6 ***Dangerous Moonlight.*** **Stefan directs the patriotic significance of the Chopin *Polonaise* at Carol**

Figure 5.7 ***Dangerous Moonlight.*** **Carol is defeated by Stefan's musical statement**

As he reaches the love theme, however, the camera moves to focus on Carol's response, showing her face in medium close-up profile. As she looks lovingly at Stefan in a highly lit, soft focus, extended shot, the camera tracks closer to her and the duality of the music is once again recalled. We see what Carol feels for Stefan. We are also, however, bound to remember what he at least used to feel for her, and to see her as he sees, or used to see, her—particularly since during their honeymoon he told her that he would never again play this melody without thinking of her. The reverse shot of Stefan at the piano, however, from the general direction of Carol's point of view, shows that he keeps his eyes steadfastly on the keyboard as he plays the theme. He clearly refuses to make the visual link with Carol that she expects, which would acknowledge his continued understanding of the theme's intimate emotional meaning. To break this musical link is to sever their most private and romantic connection, and Carol's reaction shot testifies to her understanding of this. She looks crestfallen, glancing towards her father to check if he has witnessed what is, in effect, a public rejection. This exertion of musical–emotional power is, however, by no means Stefan's final statement to Carol. He returns to the stage to play an encore, introducing the Chopin *Polonaise* with the words: 'I play one more piece… the last music to come out of free Warsaw, the music that told the world that Poland was still alive. And tonight it still is.' He then stares pointedly and aggressively up at Carol as he sits down at the piano. A series of reverse shots while he plays shows the couple locked into an angry exchange of glares very different to their usually enraptured gaze, which ends with Carol leaving the concert hall (Figures 5.6 and 5.7).[23]

Stefan's decision to target Carol in this way overturns the entire history of their communication through music. He uses the privately understood meanings of the two pieces in order to silence her once and for all. He eschews the romantic intimacy of their love theme in favour of its conflicting alternative meaning, attacking her with the strength of his patriotism by transferring the idea of the gaze to the *Polonaise*. After such a musical statement there is no further need, or indeed space, for words. Carol is placed at a distance from both the man and the means of expression, which renders her completely helpless and vulnerable. This position is further emphasized during her following taxi ride, where she finds herself effectively pursued by Stefan's message through the live radio broadcast of his performance. The gaze that once held her in love now turns on her and drives her away in contempt. The poignancy of the loss of the mutual gaze in conjunction with the love theme is then underlined by the subsequent non-diegetic statements of the theme. The version that first of all accompanies her at her father's house indicates the continuation of her emotions for Stefan, with the omission of the piano from the orchestration suddenly appearing significant in emphasizing their separation. The theme's next appearance comes at the shack, when Carol finally seems to give up hope of finding Stefan to resolve their argument. Now, the music's greater non-diegetic connection to her emotions is confirmed by Stefan's actual physical absence from the narrative. Although it is non-

[23] It is interesting to note how this sequence works as an extension of the performer's privacy in the personal performance mode. In this case, even though Stefan's expressions are violent and clearly aimed at Carol, no one else in the audience appears to be aware of them.

diegetic, the love theme nevertheless appears to draw her for the third time across space to its previous diegetic source. She walks down the same stairs on which Stefan watched her as he played their theme at the piano during their honeymoon. Now however, Carol's expression is one of growing distress rather than romantic fixation. The point-of-view shot of her, which previously belonged to Stefan, now has no source except the piano itself and the empty piano stool. Accordingly, as at her father's house, the melody appears in the flute and solo violin rather than the piano. In the absence of Stefan, we witness Carol's complete hopelessness as a woman removed from the man she loves but still identified—as if it could never be any other way—through his (musical) vision of her. Like so many of her fellow female listeners she seeks solace in the iconic piano, sitting where Stefan once played and crying onto the keyboard.

Since the rest of the film's lengthy flashback concerns Stefan's time in England, the love theme makes no further reappearance until his return to the present at the very end of the film. It is through this diversion into his friendship with Mike and specifically Mike's death, however, that Stefan's deepest vulnerability is revealed. Apparently unable to discuss his loss with the other men, it is a diegetic musical performance, intended to be private, which testifies to the deep emotions underlying his verbal silence. It is not his own composition that allows this glimpse of femininity, however, but music that has been given to him by Mike. The melody that Stefan plays and that later appears on the non-diegetic track represents Mike's earlier diegetic musical self-characterization. This is as tied to national identity and personality as the Chopin *Polonaise* is for Stefan. In playing it at the piano, Stefan appropriates it for his own use in remembering Mike in the same wordless way as he expressed his various feelings to Carol. In an unconventional move for a male musician, his emotions are therefore finding expression through borrowed music. Stefan's appropriation of Mike's music places him in a position reminiscent of the female listener. He is relating to the object of his affection through the man's own music, so that he is bound to repeat this music in order to express his emotions towards him. The effect of this musical appropriation and communication, at least during its diegetic performance is, however, quite different in this case, as is the reaction of his diegetic audience. Unlike the female listener, Stefan can also evidently experience and express emotions that are independent of his feelings for Mike. His overwhelming grief therefore remains only one of his various emotions, and Mike only one of his emotional referents. His appropriation of Mike's music does, however, place him at the mercy of the non-diegetic score.

For the majority of the narrative, Stefan and Mike enjoy a close relationship that is completely unaccompanied by non-diegetic music. Evidence of their mutual affection comes instead from the familiarity and humour of their banter, their shared past, and the transcendent quality of their friendship. Their eventual musical link is created gradually through Mike's humming of his favourite Irish song *The Rose of*

Tralee. Rather than lingering on its original pensive quality, he changes the rhythm of the melody and never sings the words. It therefore sounds more like a jaunty and cheerful ditty than the romantic love song that it actually is.[24] Although he calls it 'the finest song to come out of Ireland', therefore, he must alter it to suit the carefree personality he exudes despite his deeper level of emotionalism. What lies beneath the surface in this case is his loyalty to England, his professed love for Carol, and his barely contained anger at the breakdown of his friends' marriage. His death is indicated by the direct transference of his last hummed version of the song as he flies into battle into a much slower, more sombre piano version in the Officers' Mess later in the day. The initial focus is on a group of airmen discussing Mike's apparently inexplicable action in battle that has led to his death. One of the men notices the music and we are reminded that it was Mike's tune. The airmen turn and walk slowly towards the music, being drawn to Stefan as Carol was, until he is seen at the piano in the back of the shot, caught in the collective gaze of the silent men. He is then seen in medium close-up, locked into the mode of the personal performance. He stares into the middle distance as he plays, completely oblivious to his audience. A slow track towards him removes the piano from the frame, leaving only his face paralyzed with grief, his eyes brimming with tears. Again we see the men watching, but Stefan has still not noticed their presence. As he plays on, however, he suddenly becomes aware of his comrades, looks surprised and embarrassed, and stops playing. The men continue to watch him in silence as he walks between them out of the room.

The emotional power of this scene derives at least partly from the extended combination of the close-up of Stefan's tearful face, his obvious, disempowered unawareness of being watched in what he believes to be a private moment, and his accompaniment by sentimental music. Furthermore, this music is specifically a love song, which he has returned to something nearer its original musical state. He is the producer of this music and is therefore setting its mood to suit himself. The usual sense of control over the emotions associated with the male performer, however, is countered by his very evident loss of self-consciousness in the face of the feelings underlying the performance. The 'performance' is being stripped away, laying bare the personal significance of the music. At least on this occasion, therefore, Stefan shares Francesca's experience of the Grieg Piano Concerto in *The Seventh Veil*, Lissa's of her *Cornish Rhapsody* in *Love Story*, and even Lisa's of the Liszt Concert Study in *Letter from an Unknown Woman*. This is the second time within the flashback that Stefan has adopted the personal style of performance. The first time—in the shack during his honeymoon—demonstrated his self-absorbed lack of awareness of Carol's emotions and his ability to exercise a degree of control over the emotions implied by the performance. In this second case, however, his focus seems to be entirely on the personal emotional significance of the music he is playing. Any former sense of distance is collapsed, making him as much the listener as the performer. Like the female musician overcome by the emotions invoked by her own

[24] The version of *The Rose of Tralee* (Glover–Spencer) that I am using as a reference point for the song's original form is the piano and voice arrangement by Horatio Nicholls, published in 1939. This offers a relatively steady rhythm, and indicates that the song should be played/sung: 'Slowly (with feeling).'

Figure 5.8 ***Dangerous Moonlight.*** **Stefan in a 'feminine' state of excessive emotion**

playing, Stefan is now stunned into a fixed, unblinking silence reminiscent of his traumatized expression as he first began his flashback to the bombing of Warsaw.

What distinguishes Stefan's moment of personal performance from the examples of *The Seventh Veil* and *Love Story*, however, is the recognition of the diegetic audience. Only the film audience comprehends the full extent of the torture that Francesca and Lissa undergo during their performances. Even though Tom raises the question of Lissa's suffering during her cliff-top concert, there is no corresponding diegetic point-of-view shot. Contrary to this, *Dangerous Moonlight* places almost as much emphasis on the sympathy of the diegetic audience as it does on the pain of the performer. While the female listener can so easily misrecognize the emotional capacity of the male musician or misread the feelings communicated through the music, these male listeners appear to realize the exact meaning of the performance. This comprehension, in true wartime style, is demonstrated not through effusive words and dramatic actions, but absolute silence and contemplative stasis. What is usually solely a moment of intense personal interiority therefore becomes extended to symbolize the universality of male suffering in wartime. Each man recognizes and respects the depth of emotion that can underlie masculinity. The necessary art of self-restraint, therefore, bonds them together beyond the understanding of all but the most sympathetic women. Accordingly, it is not the love theme that accompanies Stefan's subsequent reading of Carol's letter to Mike, and his realization of his own responsibility for what has happened to his friend. Instead, his reaction to seeing his wife's writing and learning that she will soon arrive in England is accompanied by a non-diegetic, sentimental, string orchestral version of Mike's song. Rather than the letter freeing him from his grief to remember how he feels about Carol, this transfer of Mike's music to the non-diegetic level reflects the knowledge that Stefan would undoubtedly prefer not to have. By their separation, he and Carol have brought about his best friend's death. With the tenuous sense of control that diegetic performance gave him now removed, he reaches the ultimately feminine position, combining his closely-shot, soft-focus, crying face with painful music that is beyond his diegetic control (Figure 5.8).

Stefan's return to the present is perhaps the most enigmatic of all the film's scenes. It is only through injury that he has been removed from combat and we might assume that he would wish to continue fighting once he has recovered. His response to the news of Carol's imminent arrival in England was also by no means positive, and Carol's letter to Mike was certainly not clear about whether she had come to Stefan's way of thinking. With so many loose ends still waiting to be tied up, it therefore comes as something of a surprise that this final scene does nothing to resolve these narrative tensions. Instead, it chooses simply to gloss over them with the romantic and almost wordless reunion of the couple. Not even the music or the structure of the scene give any real clue to how things will resolve, since both only repeat the film's motivic scene of drawing the couple together in the way that has proven so woefully temporary in the past. Stefan is pulled violently from his reverie through the recollection of his aeroplane crash. He begins to play the love theme, but stops halfway through. As he slumps at the keyboard it appears that his 'therapy' has come to nothing. The camera follows Carol's distressed response as she walks away in silence unable, consequently, to see that he has woken from his trance. By the time she hears him whisper her name she is on the other side of the room, and the large space between them echoes their earlier scenes of physical and emotional distance. Returning their relationship to the very beginning of the film, he indicates his recognition of Carol not through playing their love theme, but through those fateful words: 'It's not safe to be out alone when the moon is so bright.' The only difference this time is that it is Stefan who crosses the space to Carol for their final kiss to the non-diegetic accompaniment of the love theme.

Considering the difficulty of their personal reconciliation and the complexity of meaning with which the film invests its various pieces of music, it seems almost inevitable that resolution will be impossible. The capitulation of either character is highly unlikely, and the music that is supposed to unite them despite everything is so imbued with their mutual misunderstanding that it can no longer convincingly suggest an all-conquering love. What excuses or at least qualifies this failing, however, at least for the purposes of this study, is the film's demonstration of the sheer complexity of music, which is unfortunately more than it actually seems able to handle. Perhaps, in fact, by relying too much on music's expressive capacity, it becomes a kind of showcase, which while not strong in terms of a coherent narrative, pays dividends in terms of examining the representation of music, vocality and different kinds of emotion in relation to masculinity. It therefore both offers a vital point of comparison for the consideration of different uses of silence in gendered characterization, and suggests an important distinction between gendered associations with music across all genres, which may begin to go beyond the assertion that music is chiefly representative of female emotionality.

Conclusion

This book began by considering the apparently established association of women and music in both film and film music theory, and has ended with a consideration of how music is used to represent men and their emotions. Indeed, the analysis of *Dangerous Moonlight* bears out the contention that whether at the level of an overall schema or a single film, music must be considered in terms of both genders—even if that entails an interrogation of why some characters enjoy no musical representation at all. The necessity for such a balanced approach has its origins in the historical debates of Chapter 1, where I discussed the way in which the relationship between women and music is more specifically a product of constructing female characters according to a particular concept of femininity. The emotional characteristics labelled 'feminine' since Romanticism are not, however, in themselves connected to the female body. On the contrary, Romantic thinking supported the belief that men were perfectly capable of encompassing feminine sensibilities—the ability to express a 'feminine' experience of the world was, in fact, essential to the higher reaches of Romantic male creativity. As the nineteenth-century conception of gender suggests, therefore, and as this final chapter in particular demonstrates in terms of 1940s cinema, the issue of each gender's musical–emotional construction must itself centre on the balance of assumed biological and culturally determined attributes.

While acceptable maleness becomes as much of a balanced construction as acceptable femaleness, however, the results of their dynamics of emotional expression and repression/control are not the same. According to nineteenth-century thought, a man's ability to control and express his feminine soul is dependent upon the physically and emotionally 'masculine' qualities of strength, rigour and virility that are attributed exclusively to the male body. Only these attributes enable the proper control and safe expression of his contemplation of the sublime. The woman's body, however, being purely 'feminine' in its presumed qualities of delicacy and weakness, offers her no such obvious contrast to her feminine soul and, therefore, no protection against its overwhelming power. The root of these assumptions therefore lies in the cultural and social codes that dictate that 'masculine' and 'feminine' gender qualities are each *inherent* to only one sex. Thus, in these terms, while women are seen as essentially or inherently feminine, men are seen as essentially or inherently masculine. Since, therefore, masculinity is associated with mental and physical strength, these are seen to be inherent qualities of men, while the association of the feminine with the emotions means that women are deemed essentially emotional in constitution. These inherent attributes are of course those that society deems desirable and correct, so that if a woman demonstrates too strong, effective or targeted a control of her inherent emotionality or sexuality, she may be considered as invested with an undesirable level of masculinity (i.e. male physical drives). Many warnings and negative models for female behaviour are therefore mobilized to warn women away from the path of too great a degree of emotional or sexual self-possession.

The fact that 1940s cinema in Hollywood and Britain gravitates towards the nineteenth-century style of composition, that this style plays a significant role in the representation of interiority and 'excessive' emotion, and that each national cinema is clearly more at ease with the association of this level of emotion with female characters, indicates the palpable inheritance of the Romantic confusion of sex and gender. This duly brings with it all the associated prejudices against and fears of female self-possession, emotional/sexual independence and agency that were previously invoked to consign women to subordinate roles in society and the home. It is indeed through the associated history of patriarchal society's fear of the female musical–emotional–sexual 'voice' that it is still possible to detect the echoing songs of the Siren and the Muse in 1940s cinema. It also, however, perpetuates by extension equally pervasive ideas of maleness, specifically in terms of the expectation of self-control. While male characters may not be so typically associated with music, its use does have a very particular effect on their gendered construction. As this final chapter has shown, male characters can certainly be represented by the 'feminine' style of music that is more typically associated with female characters and sentimentally emotional situations. In fact, it actually seems that the more conventionally masculine the man, the more acceptable such an association might be—although this is contingent upon restrictions in terms of the amount of musical–emotional representation and its particular presentation. What I termed the 'glimpse' of femininity therefore offers a carefully contextualized and limited interaction between the man and his music. Combined with, depending on the context, either emotional or restrained behaviour, this 'glimpse' serves a dual purpose. It evidences control as an element of the man's characterization, and proves the strength of that control. It also, however, prevents the control itself from being perceived as too extreme and 'inhuman'. Most pertinently, it demonstrates that no matter how strong any revealed emotions may be, they should only be permitted occasional and preferably private display if the man is to remain fully 'masculine'.

Such cultural prejudices are extremely informative in considering music's role in gendered characterization in film. There is certainly nothing new in pointing out that music signifies the emotional implications of the narrative either for a particular character or characters, the film audience, or both. At the broadest level, all characters who appear in a film may be presumed to have what might be deemed 'ordinary' emotions whether or not they are ever represented by non-diegetic music. Any character may also exhibit an openly emotional response to events without the help of musical accompaniment. Pinpointing a particular character through musical–emotional representation does not single them out as being the only emotional figure, or mark their musical moments as their only instances of emotion. Rather, it suggests that their emotions are in some sense 'extraordinary', and of particular importance, within the narrative. As the different context of each of the case study chapters then demonstrates, such musical suggestion of emotion does not exist in isolation. Exactly how we understand and interpret the emotions of a particular character depends to a large extent on how that character interacts with diegetic or non-diegetic music and the emotions with which it is associated.

There is, therefore, hardly a more effective way of foregrounding the emotional *construction* of a character than through the use of music. If there is no non-diegetic music in a film, so that, as I have said, all the characters are merely assumed to be emotional to some implicitly ordinary level, the balance of emotion and control can hardly be a foregrounded issue. As soon as music becomes involved in characterization, however, it raises questions of depth and excess that cannot be avoided. Emotion that may otherwise be displayed through acting, costume, mise-en-scène and dialogue takes on a unique intensity, and—particularly taking into account the potential narrative independence of non-diegetic music discussed in Chapter 1—can be invested with any amount of complexity depending upon the specific connections constructed between characters and music. A witting or unwitting relationship with music, therefore, inevitably places a character in a more dynamic emotional position, so that they are understood more fully according to the balance between their actions and words and their musical–emotional context.

Further to this, however, is a yet deeper level at which the score's role operates, whereby a more complete reading of the gender implications of the music–behaviour–dialogue dynamic arises from its combination with assumptions about what we take to be the pre-determined inherent characteristics of characters according to their gender. The balance of music, vocality and behaviour may signify the role that a character's emotions perform within the narrative. It is their combination with these cultural assumptions, however, that informs the particular way in which we are likely to interpret the represented balance. Having traced the potential influence of Romantic ideas through the series of case studies, I wish to suggest a broad formulation through which this complex musical–emotional gender construction operates. This is based on a balance of what I will call the 'given characteristic' and the 'issue' of each gender, and is purposefully broad, in order to offer a basic and flexible explanation for the way in which music operates in relation to our reading of gender.

The continuing slippage that 'naturally' conflates women and emotion suggests emotion as the 'given characteristic' of the woman. Melodrama and the woman's film of the 1940s do not invent this important generic link, but rather incorporate and maximize on an association that is already culturally pervasive. Since these genres conventionally, therefore, present female characters as *inherently* emotional, the 'issue' of the narrative becomes the way in which these emotions are channelled or brought under control. Such channelling or control may be self- or externally imposed, to the ends of respectable socialization or selfishly evil intent. The balance of the motivating 'given characteristic', the strength of which is indicated by the musical–emotional representation of the woman, and the resultant 'issue', which is to be found in her relationship to this musical–emotional representation, therefore gives rise to a whole variety of narrative patterns which examine the different possibilities and effects of controlling excessive female emotionality. The comparatively restricted close musical accompaniment of male characters, however, suggests the opposite of this formulation. Although men may clearly be emotional in all sorts of ways, their more usual non-diegetic musical 'silence' implies a very masculine level of self-control over 'excessive' sentimental emotions or feelings indicating vulnerability or dependence. The 'given characteristic' of the man is therefore strength of control, so that the 'issue' of his characterization can centre on the question of the nature, depth and veracity of the emotion that he contains. In this context, the role allotted to non-diegetic music is to *prove* the genuine presence and veracity of this emotion.

Revisiting some of the films discussed throughout this book, it is possible to see how each woman, regardless of her specific circumstances and national or historical context, is formulated according to this dynamic. Charlotte's first appearance in *Now, Voyager* is marked by her diegetic silence, so that we come to understand her through a combination of her behaviour both in the face of other characters and in relation to her non-diegetic music. Like Louise in *Possessed* and most of the female subjects of Doane's 'medical' and 'paranoid' narratives,[25] she represents the woman who has become the victim of her own excessive emotions, and who has therefore descended into the kind of physical and psychological disorder predicted in the nineteenth century. The music tells us from the outset that she is currently determined entirely by her emotional repression, and that the effect of this repression is far greater than any of the other characters have thus far supposed. It therefore immediately raises the issue of how what is evidently such excessive emotion can be brought from unhealthy repression to healthy control. As Chapter 2 detailed, the whole narrative then concerns itself with the process of achieving this control—the success of which is determined not by the disappearance of Charlotte's non-diegetic musical–emotional representation, but by her ability to behave 'correctly' *despite* its continuing presence.

The involvement of diegetic music in *Letter from an Unknown Woman*, *Love Story* and *Dangerous Moonlight* highlights the role of music in exploring this issue. Lisa's love for Stefan in *Letter from an Unknown Woman* is clearly marked as excessive, even if she is treated with sympathy, and the narrative demonstrates the danger of such excess. Our access to Lisa's subjective view of events constantly reminds us that, however she may appear to other diegetic characters, she lives in a world of romantic fantasy that can only be put on hold rather than brought under control. From the beginning of the film, in fact, it is clear that she has ultimately failed to exercise self-control, since her letter is given to Stefan after her death, and her death is apparently the result of the story that she is about to tell. Accordingly, the channelled 'voice' of her letter always speaks the errant emotions that she has invested in the diegetic and non-diegetic music that he unwittingly 'gave' her. Despite the distance that the narrative places between her and her own musical–emotional representation, she is therefore unable to resist its call in the way that Charlotte can. She must, as a result, both die herself and cause the death of the man she loves from the very effects of her own emotional excess.

Lissa, in *Love Story*, of course, has no distance between herself and either her own diegetic composition or the non-diegetic music drawn from it. The issue of whether she can control the emotional excess that her non-diegetic music and her diegetic performances evidence is also inextricably linked to the question of whether she has the will to deny her own personal emotions for the sake of the greater national good. Once again, like Charlotte, she must achieve this by proving to herself and the film audience that she can speak and behave in ways contrary to the dictates of her musical–emotional representation. Only when she has indeed proved this, and

---

25 Doane (1988), Chapters 2 and 5 respectively.

thus fulfilled her patriotic mission, can she be allowed to return to speaking its real emotional meaning, although this remains tempered by the threat of her imminent death and the potential death of the man she loves. Carol is faced with very much the same dilemma in *Dangerous Moonlight*, with the issue of whether she can control her emotions being similarly tied to questions of wartime patriotism. Like Lisa in *Letter from an Unknown Woman*, however, her ultimately destructive role is a result of her similar unwillingness even to *try* to exercise self-control. Even worse than Lisa, moreover, Carol is actually made aware of the 'real' emotional significance to Stefan of the music that he has 'given' her, but still actively refuses to accept any meaning other than that which accords with her personal desires. Her uncontrolled emotionality in this case, manifested in her attempts to force Stefan to heed only her interpretation of his music, brings about the death of an innocent bystander, rather than herself or the man she loves.

While there are certainly ways in which a woman can be seen to exercise positive and desirable self-control, therefore, this often carries the implication of *super-human* effort. When Charlotte in *Now, Voyager* prioritizes the welfare of Tina and their precious mother–daughter relationship, she is seen to deny herself romantic love with a painfully forceful physical and mental resistance of Jerry. Lissa, in *Love Story*, is willing to destroy what is left of her life for the sake of the restoration of Kit's sight and masculinity, but the toll that this takes on her health is evident when she performs the music that recalls their time together. Other women, such as the eponymous Stella Dallas (Barbara Stanwyck), Anita in *Intermezzo*, Helen in *Interlude*, Myra in *Waterloo Bridge*, Ray (Irene Dunne) in *Back Street*, Celia in *Millions Like Us* and Toddy in *The Way to the Stars*, make similarly extreme efforts of self-possession for the sake of either personal integrity, selfless love, social propriety or the war effort. Whatever her reasons, the victory of a woman who exercises such control seems tantamount to a victory over the very 'nature' of womanhood. Accordingly, the exceptional strength required for the woman to conquer her own presumed 'given characteristic'—her inherent emotionality—is often registered by the sheer force of the music that represents her real feelings. In the same way as I suggested in connection with the men of this chapter, therefore, the strength of control being exercised by a female character is measured by knowledge of what there is to be controlled. The effect in this case, however, is to demonstrate the overcoming of the 'given characteristic' rather than to evidence its strength. If appropriate to the circumstances of the woman, therefore, by virtue of its 'mute' voice and its independence it can also offer melodramatic victory to those emotions that we may feel are subdued or stymied for all the wrong reasons.

Too much emotional or sexual self-possession or control in a woman is, however, a dangerous matter. The *femme fatale*—undoubtedly the most obvious translation of the Siren onto the screen—evidences the dangers to herself and men of a woman in command of her own excessive feminine sexuality and emotionality. This is signalled by, among many other things, her musical display through song performances or her use of diegetic music, and/or by her own unwitting relationship to the non-diegetic score. Alternatively, as a female musician, the woman in too much control of her emotions may become disturbingly domineering and 'unfeminine' like Sandra in *The Great Lie*, or criminal like Christine in *Deception*. To avoid such condemnation, control or ability in musical creativity or performance seems possible only if mitigated by the extreme cruelty of a Svengali figure, as in *The Seventh Veil*. It may also be allowed if subsequently punished by injury, as in *The Seventh Veil* and *The Lamp Still Burns*. Otherwise, it seems as if the exposure to the excesses of her own femininity offered by musical performance can only monitor the nearness of illness and death, as in *Love Story* and *While I Live*.

Since male characters start from the different cultural 'given characteristic' of control, however, their relationship to music and emotion is bound to be different. Whereas we seem almost conditioned to expect that the woman will be unable to control her emotions—so that we admire her all the more when she does—we seem equally conditioned to presume that the man *will* control his. His limited association with music therefore becomes a means of reinforcing the behaviour that society expects and considers 'natural' to a man. In this light it is interesting to reconsider some of the male characters who featured in Chapters 2, 3 and 4—prior to the closer examination of masculinity and music that has been presented in this final chapter—in order to test how the 'issue' of emotional revelation affects how they are viewed as characters. In each case, possibly because of the greater focus of the films on female rather than male emotions, the musical–emotional representation of the men tends to deny us the 'glimpse' of femininity central to the 'given characteristic'/'issue' construction. In all cases, however, there is a definite point to this denial that relates to the trajectory of the female protagonist.

Elliot, in *Now, Voyager*, is notable for his lack of representation through or engagement with music, and this works within the schema of the film to suggest his ultimate irrelevance in Charlotte's life. No matter how boring and wrong a prospect he may be for Charlotte, however, it cannot be denied that Elliot is presented within the film as the socially 'respectable' choice—an upright and steady man with no dangerous passions threatening to rage out of control. It is his very lack of musical–emotional representation that signifies this stolid respectability, by its suggestion of absolute and easy control. The implication that perhaps this ease means there is nothing much *to* control, however, serves simultaneously to mark him as a somewhat 'un-masculine' man. Jerry, on the other hand, although a desirable lover for Charlotte, is positioned by the non-diegetic score as ultimately subservient to her will. The principal control that he exercises throughout the narrative is in 'doing the right thing' by his wife, although he does tend to view this duty in a rather technical light, so that although he will not actually leave his wife, he will nevertheless not deny himself the opportunity for emotional or sexual infidelity. Despite his emotional role in the narrative, furthermore, he has no music of his own, and all the evidence for his emotions is presented only through his words and actions. While these are persuasive and indeed convincing, the rather easy self-control with which he finally accepts Charlotte's decision does raise the question of whether or not the prospect of losing her could have induced an impassioned 'glimpse' of femininity had he had his own independent theme.

Similarly, it is Stefan's behaviour, no matter how bad it may be, in *Letter from an Unknown Woman*, that the film signals as 'normal' or at least realistic. His detached relationship to his own music and perhaps by extension his own emotions is only broken when Lisa's obsessive pursuit extends to her posthumous letter. It is at this point that he is drawn away from his sordid reality to become absorbed into her rather more attractive fantasy. The implication that he has not so much been exercising emotional control in his life thus far, however, but has rather been so superficial in his approach to life that he has never truly engaged with anything or anyone, detracts slightly from the potential that his final breakdown would usually offer as a 'glimpse' of femininity. It does at least, however, suggest that he is capable of achieving the depth of emotion that Lisa always presumed, and makes sense of his subsequent bravery in repaying his debt to her husband. Kit, in *Love Story*, is perhaps the exception that proves the rule, as he is in fact deeply affected by music. The point here, though, is that the particular brand of emotional 'control' in which he engages is self-consciously false, entirely contrary to the ideal of masculine, self-controlled bravery in wartime, and therefore strongly signalled by the film as wrong. The emotions beneath the façade therefore need to be forcibly reawakened by Lissa and her music so that 'proper' masculinity—the emotional self-control that enables his valour in the skies—can be restored.

There are myriad ways in which a man's emotions can be carefully revealed and confirmed without jeopardizing his 'given characteristic'—the presumed inherent control of masculinity. While the combination of music and controlled behaviour suggests the super-human in women, it becomes a way to positively emphasize and reinforce what we take to be the existing masculine constitution of the man, as is seen in films such as *Dangerous Moonlight*, *The Captive Heart*, *Red River* and *The Searchers*. As this and the male characters described above suggest, therefore, the man's very masculinity is at stake in the nature of his relationship to music. The momentary 'glimpse' of femininity in an otherwise controlled performance confirms his positive masculinity—as is the case in *Dangerous Moonlight* when Stefan momentarily surrenders to the extreme emotion of losing his best friend in combat. If the man loses altogether his controlling position in relation to the signification of the music, however, he loses his emotional self-possession and suffers as a result. The social extremity and undesirability of such a threat is evident in the extreme and distressing causes of the man's potential vulnerability: desperation caused by blindness in *Night Song*, for example, alcoholism in *The Lost Weekend*, or murderous psychosis in *Hangover Square*, to name but a few. Relationships, sentimental emotions and sexual feelings are less often the direct cause of illness or instability in male than in female characters, except, of course, for the supposed victims of the appropriately demonized *femmes fatales* of *film noir*. Even in this case, however, it is the man's own weakness that tends to be the real cause of his own downfall, with the woman acting primarily as the catalyst for or embodiment of his transgressive desires.

Seen as part of the whole dynamic of the film, music therefore becomes completely integral to our understanding of gender construction. The predilection of film for defining women and men according to cultural prejudices of femininity and masculinity respectively, means that non-diegetic music becomes primarily associated with women. Its actual use is more fluid, however, than is often acknowledged. The meaning of the association also changes depending on gender and narrative circumstances, so that representation through diegetic or non-diegetic music can constitute a site of emotional strength or weakness, dependence or independence. The social and political context of 1940s cinema naturally determines its gender representation and issues to a huge extent. It is hardly surprising, for example, that films at this time work towards reinforcing very particular images of the correct behaviour and social roles of both men and women. It is for this very reason, however, that 1940s film music codes are an ideal place to investigate and establish certain 'norms' in the role of musical–emotional representation in gendered characterization. The harder the films work to reinforce socially acceptable gendered modes of behaviour, the more they reveal of their own conventions and processes. By the same token, conventions established at such an important period in social and cinematic history also provide the ideal point from which to examine more recent developments in music and gender construction/representation. It should perhaps follow that changes in social expectations and codes regarding sex and gender, and related changes in cinematic representations of gender, will be reflected in developments in the representational role of film music. It is certainly my intention that this formulation is flexible to the examination of any genre of film in any period of film history—as well as being adaptable in broad conceptual terms to other modes of scoring. In this way, it is hoped that it may be used beyond this 1940s model and so prove instrumental in determining the broader history of film music's role in constructing gendered characterization.

Bibliography

Abbate, Carolyn (1991), *Unsung Voices: Opera and Musical Narrative in the Nineteenth Century*, Princeton and Oxford: Princeton University Press.

Adorno, Theodor, and Hanns Eisler (1994), *Composing for the Films*, second edition, New York: Oxford University Press; London: Athlone Press.

Altman, Rick (ed.) (1992), *Sound Theory/Sound Practice*, New York and London: Routledge.

Aspinall, Sue (1983), 'Women, Realism and Reality in British Films, 1943–53', in James Curran and Vincent Porter (eds), *British Cinema History*, London: Weidenfeld and Nicolson, pp. 272–93.

Atkins, Irene Kahn (1983), *Source Music in Motion Pictures*, Rutherford, Madison and Teaneck: Fairleigh Dickinson University Press; London and Toronto: Associated University Press.

Attali, Jacques (1985), *Noise: The Political Economy of Music*, trans. B. Massumi, Minneapolis: University of Minnesota Press.

Austern, Linda Phyllis (1989), '"Sing Againe Syren": The Female Musician and Sexual Enchantment in Elizabethan Life and Literature', *Renaissance Quarterly*, **42**: 420–48.

—— (1993), 'Alluring the Auditorie to Effeminacie: Music and the Idea of the Feminine in Early Modern England', *Music and Letters*, **74**(3): 343–54.

—— (1994), '"No women are indeed": The boy actor as vocal seductress in late sixteenth- and early seventeenth-century English drama', in Leslie C. Dunn and Nancy A. Jones (eds), *Embodied Voices: Representing Female Vocality in Western Culture*, Cambridge: Cambridge University Press, pp. 83–102.

Baker, M. Joyce (1978), *Images of Women in Film: The War Years, 1941–1945*, Ann Arbor, MI: UMI Research Press.

Basinger, Jeanine (1993), *A Woman's View: How Hollywood Spoke to Women, 1930–1960*, London: Chatto & Windus.

Battersby, Christine (1989), *Gender and Genius: Towards a Feminist Aesthetics*, London: The Women's Press.

Bourget, Jean-Loup (1985), *Le mélodrame hollywoodien* (Paris: Stock).

Branigan, Edward (1992), *Narrative Comprehension and Film*, London: Routledge.

Britton, Andrew (1995), *Katharine Hepburn: Star as Feminist*, London: Studio Vista.

Brooks, Peter (1984), *The Melodramatic Imagination: Balzac, Henry James, Melodrama, and the Mode of Excess*, New York: Columbia University Press.

Brown, Royal S. (1994), *Overtones and Undertones: Reading Film Music*, California and London: California University Press.

Cavell, Stanley (1996), *Contesting Tears: The Hollywood Melodrama of the Unknown Woman*, Chicago: University of Chicago Press.

Chion, Michel (1990), *Audio-Vision: Sound on Screen*, trans. C. Gorbman, Paris: Editions Nathan; New York and Chichester, West Sussex: Columbia University Press.

—— (1999), *The Voice in Cinema*, ed. and trans. C. Gorbman, New York: Columbia University Press.

Citron, Marcia J. (1993), *Gender and the Musical Canon*, Cambridge, New York and Melbourne: Cambridge University Press.

Clément, Catherine (1989), *Opera, or the Undoing of Women*, trans. B. Wing, London: Virago.

Clifford, Hubert (1944), 'British Film Music', *Tempo*, **8**: 14–15.

—— (1945a), 'Music From the Films', *Tempo*, **10**: 10–11.

—— (1945b), 'Music From the Films', *Tempo*, **11**: 13–14.

—— (1945c), 'Music From the Films', *Tempo*, **13**: 11–12.

Cook, Pam (1983), 'Melodrama and the Women's Picture', in Sue Aspinall and Robert Murphy (eds), *BFI Dossier 18: Gainsborough Melodrama*, London: BFI Publishing, pp. 14–28.

Creed, Barbara (1978), 'The Position of Women in Hollywood Melodramas', *Australian Journal of Screen Theory*, **4**: 27–31.

Custen, George F. (1992), *Bio/Pics: How Hollywood Constructed Public History*, New Brunswick, NJ: Rutgers University Press.

Dahlhaus, Carl (1989), *The Idea of Absolute Music*, trans. R. Lustig, Chicago and London: The University of Chicago Press.

Daubney, Kate (2000), *Max Steiner's* Now, Voyager*: A Film Score Guide*, Westport, CT, and London: Greenwood Press.

Doane, Mary Ann (1980a), 'Ideology and the Practice of Sound Editing and Mixing', in Elisabeth Weis and John Belton (eds), *Film Sound: Theory and Practice*, New York and Chichester, West Sussex: Columbia University Press, pp. 54–62.

—— (1980b), 'The Voice in the Cinema: The Articulation of Body and Space', in Elisabeth Weis and John Belton (eds), *Film Sound: Theory and Practice*, New York and Chichester, West Sussex: Columbia University Press, pp. 162–76.

—— (1987), 'The "Woman's Film": Possession and Address', in Christine Gledhill (ed.), *Home is Where the Heart Is: Studies in Melodrama and the Woman's Film*, London: BFI, pp. 283–98.

—— (1988), *The Desire to Desire: The Woman's Film of the 1940s*, first published 1987 Bloomington: Indiana University Press, Basingstoke and London: Macmillan Press.

Donnelly, K.J. (1997), 'Wicked Sounds and Magic Melodies: Music in 1940s Gainsborough Melodrama', in Pam Cook (ed.), *Gainsborough Pictures*, London and Washington: Cassell, pp. 155–69.

Dunn, Leslie C. (1994), 'Ophelia's Songs in *Hamlet*: Music, Madness and the Feminine', in Leslie C. Dunn and Nancy A. Jones (eds), *Embodied Voices: Representing Female Vocality in Western Culture*, Cambridge: Cambridge University Press, pp. 50–64.

Dyer, Richard (1998), *Stars*, second revised edition, London: BFI.

Einstein, Alfred (1947), *Music in the Romantic Era*, New York: W. W. Norton & Company Inc.

Elsaesser, Thomas (1987), 'Tales of Sound and Fury: Observations on the Family Melodrama', in Christine Gledhill (ed.), *Home Is Where the Heart Is: Studies in Melodrama and the Woman's Film*, London: BFI, pp. 43–69.

Fleishman, Avrom (1984), *Narrated Films*, Baltimore: Johns Hopkins University Press.

Flinn, Caryl (1992), *Strains of Utopia: Gender, Nostalgia and Hollywood Film Music*, Oxford and Princeton: Princeton University Press.

Fuller, Sophie (1994), *The Pandora Guide to Women Composers: Britain and the United States 1629–Present*, London and California: Pandora.

Gledhill, Christine (1987), 'The Melodramatic Field: An Investigation', in *Home Is Where the Heart Is: Studies in Melodrama and the Woman's Film*, London: BFI, pp. 5–39.

—— (1995), 'Women Reading Men', in Pat Kirkham and Janet Thumim (eds), *Me Jane: Masculinity, Movies and Women*, London: Lawrence and Wishart Limited, pp. 73–93.

—— (1996), '"An Abundance of Understatement": Documentary, Melodrama and Romance', in Christine Gledhill and Gillian Swanson (eds), *Nationalising Femininity: Culture, Sexuality and British Cinema in the Second World War*, Manchester and New York: Manchester University Press, pp. 213–29.

Goodwin, Sarah Webster (1994), 'Wordsworth and Romantic Voice: The Poet's Song and the Prostitute's Cry', in Leslie C. Dunn and Nancy A. Jones (eds), *Embodied Voices: Representing Female Vocality in Western Culture*, Cambridge: Cambridge University Press, pp. 65–79.

Gorbman, Claudia (1987), *Unheard Melodies: Narrative Film Music*, Bloomington: Indiana University Press; London: BFI.

Grout, Donald Jay (1980), *A History of Western Music*, third edition with Claude V. Palisca, London, Toronto and Melbourne: J. M. Dent & Sons Ltd.

Harper, Sue (1988), 'The Representation of Women in British Feature Films, 1939–45', in Philip M. Taylor (ed.), *Britain and the Cinema in the Second World War*, London: Macmillan Press, pp. 168–202.

—— (1996), 'The Years of Total War: Propaganda and Entertainment', in Christine Gledhill and Gillian Swanson (eds), *Nationalising Femininity: Culture, Sexuality and British Cinema in the Second World War*, Manchester and New York: Manchester University Press, pp. 193–212.

Higson, Andrew, and Ginette Vincendeau (1986), 'Melodrama', *Screen*, **27**(6): 2–5.

Huntley, John (1944), 'Film Music', *Sight and Sound*, **12**(48): 91–3.

—— (1947a), *British Film Music*, London: Skelton Robinson.

—— (1947b), 'Film Music', *Penguin Film Review*, **2**: 21–4.

—— (1947c), 'Film Music', *Penguin Film Review*, **3**: 15–17.

—— (1947d), 'Film Music', *Penguin Film Review*, **4**: 17–20.

Irving, Ernest (1946a), 'Film Music', *Tempo* (new series), **1**: 31–2.

—— (1946b), 'Film Music', *Tempo*, **2**: 26–7.

—— (1946c), 'Music From the Films', *Tempo*, **15**: 12–13.

—— (1946d), 'British Film Music Outstrips Hollywood and this is Why', *Kinematograph Weekly*, 19 December: 279.

—— (1947), 'Film Music', *Tempo*, **3**: 26–7.

—— (1975), 'Music and the Film Script', *Film Music Notebook*, Summer: 10–13.
Jacobs, Lea (1981), '*Now, Voyager*: Some Problems of Enunciation and Sexual Difference', *Camera Obscura*, **7**: 89–109.
Kalinak, Kathryn (1982), 'The Fallen Woman and the Virtuous Wife: Musical Stereotypes in *The Informer*, *Gone With the Wind*, and *Laura*', *Film Reader*, **5**: 76–82.
—— (1992), *Settling the Score: Music and the Classical Hollywood Film*, Madison: University of Wisconsin Press.
Kozloff, Sarah (1988), *Invisible Storytellers: Voice-Over in American Fiction Film*, Berkeley, Los Angeles and London: University of California Press.
Krutnik, Frank (1991), *In a Lonely Street: Film Noir, Genre, Masculinity*, London and New York: Routledge.
Landy, Marcia (1991), *British Genres: Cinema and Society, 1930–1960*, Princeton and Oxford: Princeton University Press.
Langer, Susanne K. (1953), *Feeling and Form: A Theory of Art Developed from Philosophy in a New Key*, London: Routledge and Kegan Paul Limited.
Lant, Antonia (1991), *Blackout: Reinventing Women for British Wartime Cinema*, Princeton: Princeton University Press.
LaPlace, Maria (1987), 'Producing and Consuming the Woman's Film: Discursive Struggle in *Now, Voyager*', in Christine Gledhill (ed.), *Home Is Where the Heart Is: Studies in Melodrama and the Woman's Film*, London: BFI, pp. 138–66.
Lawrence, Amy (1991), *Echo and Narcissus: Women's Voices in Classical Hollywood Cinema*, Berkeley, Los Angeles and Oxford: University of California Press.
Levy, Louis (1948), *Music for the Movies*, London: Sampson Low, Marston & Co. Ltd.
Lewis, Reina (1996), *Gendering Orientalism: Race, Femininity and Representation*, London: Routledge.
Loesser, Arthur (1955), *Men, Women and Pianos: A Social History*, New York: Simon and Schuster.
London, Kurt (1936), *Film Music*, London: Faber and Faber.
McClary, Susan (1991), *Feminine Endings: Music, Gender and Sexuality*, Minneapolis and London: University of Minnesota Press.
Manvell, Richard, and John Huntley (1957), *The Technique of Film Music*, London and New York: Focal Press.
Mathieson, Muir (1944), 'Aspects of Film Music', *Tempo*, **9**: 7–9.
—— (1947), 'Developments in Film Music', *Penguin Film Review*, **4**: 41–6.
—— (1948a), 'The Film and Musical Taste', *Look and Listen*, **2**(5): 93.
—— (1948b), 'The Time Factor in Film Music', *Film Industry*, May: 6–7.
Modleski, Tania (1987), 'Time and Desire in the Woman's Film', in Christine Gledhill (ed.), *Home Is Where the Heart Is: Studies in Melodrama and the Woman's Film*, London: BFI, pp. 326–38.
Mulvey, Laura (1985), 'Visual Pleasure and Narrative Cinema', in Gerald Mast and Marshall Cohen (eds), *Film Theory and Criticism: Introductory Readings*, third edition, New York and Oxford: Oxford University Press, pp. 803–16.
Murphy, Robert (1989), *Realism and Tinsel: Cinema and Society in Britain 1939–1948*, London and New York, Routledge.

Neale, Steve (1986), 'Melodrama and Tears', *Screen*, **27**(6): 6–22.

Perkins, V.F. (1982), '*Letter From an Unknown Woman*', *Movie*, **29/30** (Summer): 61–72.

—— (unpublished typescript), 'Ophuls Contra Wagner and Others'.

Place, Janey (1998), 'Women in Film Noir', in E. Ann Kaplan (ed.), *Women in Film Noir*, new edition, London: BFI, pp. 47–68.

Poirier, Richard (1992), *The Performing Self: Compositions and Decompositions in the Language of Everyday Life*, New Brunswick, NJ: Rutgers University Press.

Prendergast, Roy M. (1992), *Film Music: A Neglected Art*, New York and London: Norton.

Richards, Jeffrey (1988), 'National Identity in British Wartime Cinema', in Philip M. Taylor (ed.), *Britain and the Cinema in the Second World War*, London: Macmillan Press, pp. 42–61.

Rubin, Martin (1985), 'The Voice of Silence: Sound Style in John Stahl's *Back Street*', in Elisabeth Weis and John Belton (eds), *Film Sound: Theory and Practice*, New York and Chichester, West Sussex: Columbia University Press, pp. 277–85.

Said, Edward W. (1991), *Musical Elaborations*, New York: Columbia University Press.

Sarris, Andrew (1986), 'Max Ophuls', in Virginia Wright Wexman (ed., with Karen Hollinger), *Letter from an Unknown Woman*, New Brunswick, NJ: Rutgers University Press, pp. 217–19.

Segal, Charles (1994), 'The Gorgon and the Nightingale: The Voice of Female Lament and Pindar's twelfth *Pythian Ode*', in Leslie C. Dunn and Nancy A. Jones (eds), *Embodied Voices: Representing Female Vocality in Western Culture*, Cambridge: Cambridge University Press, pp. 17–34.

Shepherd, John (1987), 'Music and Male Hegemony', in Richard Leppert and Susan McClary (eds), *Music and Society: The Politics of Composition, Performance and Reception*, Cambridge, New York and Melbourne: Cambridge University Press, pp. 151–72.

Silverman, Kaja (1988), *The Acoustic Mirror: The Female Voice in Psychoanalysis and Cinema*, Bloomington and Indianapolis: Indiana University Press.

Steiner, Max (1938), 'Scoring the Film', in Nancy Naumburg (ed.), *We Make the Movies*, New York: W. W. Norton and Co, pp. 216–38.

Street, Sarah (1997), *British National Cinema*, London and New York: Routledge.

Studlar, Gaylyn (1994), 'Masochistic Performance and Female Subjectivity in *Letter from an Unknown Woman*', *Cinema Journal*, **33**(3): 35–57.

Tompkins, Jane (1992), *West of Everything: The Inner Life of Westerns*, New York and Oxford: Oxford University Press.

Treitler, Leo (1993), 'Gender and Other Dualities of Music History', in Ruth A. Solie (ed.), *Musicology and Difference: Gender and Sexuality in Music Scholarship*, Berkeley and London: California University Press, pp. 23–45.

Turim, Maureen (1989), *Flashbacks in Film: Memory and History*, New York and London: Routledge.

Viviani, Christian (1987), 'Who Is Without Sin? The Maternal Melodrama in American Film, 1930–39', trans. D. Burdick, in Christine Gledhill (ed.), *Home Is*

Where the Heart Is: Studies in Melodrama and the Woman's Film, London: BFI, pp. 83–99.

Walker, Janet (1987), 'Hollywood, Freud and the Representation of Women: Regulation and Contradiction, 1945–early 60s', in Christine Gledhill (ed.), *Home Is Where the Heart Is: Studies in Melodrama and the Woman's Film*, London: BFI, pp. 197–214.

—— (1993), *Couching Resistance: Women, Film and Psychoanalytical Psychiatry*, Minneapolis: University of Minnesota Press.

Weis, Elisabeth (1982), *The Silent Scream: Alfred Hitchcock's Sound Track*, East Brunswick, London and Toronto: Associated University Presses.

Wheelock, Gretchen A. (1993), '*Schwarze Gredel* and the Engendered Minor Mode in Mozart's Operas', in Ruth A. Solie (ed.), *Musicology and Difference: Gender and Sexuality in Music Scholarship*, Berkeley and London: California University Press, pp. 201–21.

Whittall, Arnold (1987), *Romantic Music: A Concise History from Schubert to Sibelius*, London: Thames and Hudson Ltd.

Williams, Linda (1987), '"Something Else Besides a Mother": *Stella Dallas* and the Maternal Melodrama', in Christine Gledhill (ed.), *Home Is Where the Heart Is: Studies in Melodrama and the Woman's Film*, London: BFI, pp. 299–325.

Wilson, George M. (1986), *Narration in Light: Studies in Cinematic Point of View*, Baltimore: Johns Hopkins University Press.

Wood, Robin (1976), *Personal Views: Explorations in Film*, London: Gordon Fraser.

—— (1993), '*Letter from an Unknown* Woman—The Double Narrative', *cineACTION*, **31**: 4–17.

Wright Wexman, Virginia (1986), 'The Transfiguration of History: Ophuls, Vienna, and *Letter from an Unknown Woman*', in (ed., with Karen Hollinger), *Letter from an Unknown Woman*, New Brunswick, NJ: Rutgers University Press, pp. 3–14.

Filmography

This filmography lists only composers of original scores or, if applicable, music directors (except for the slightly fuller listings for the case study films). It does not list composers of any pre-composed music used either diegetically or non-diegetically.

Case Study Films

Now, Voyager (*Untold Want for Songs of Parting*), 1942, US, Irving Rapper. Music: Max Steiner; Music Director: Leo F. Forbstein; Orchestrator: Hugo Friedhofer; Sound: Robert B. Lee.

Letter from an Unknown Woman, 1948, US, Max Ophuls. Music: Daniele Amfitheatrof; Orchestrator: David Tamkin; Sound: Leslie I. Carey, Glen E. Anderson.

Love Story (A Lady Surrenders), 1944, UK, Leslie Arliss. Music: Hubert Bath; Music Director: Louis Levy; Orchestra: National Symphony Orchestra; Conductor: Sidney Beer; Solo Piano: Harriet Cohen; Sound Supervisor: B.C. Sewell.

Dangerous Moonlight (*Suicide Squadron*), 1941, UK, Brian Desmond Hurst. Music: Richard Addinsell; Music Director: Muir Mathieson; Orchestra: London Symphony Orchestra; Solo Piano: Louis Kentner.

Other Films

All About Eve, 1950, US, Joseph L. Mankiewicz. Music: Alfred Newman.

All This and Heaven Too, 1940, US, Anatole Litvak. Music: Max Steiner.

Back Street, 1932, US, John M. Stahl. Music: David Broekman and James Dietrich.

The Best Years of Our Lives, 1946, US, William Wyler. Music: Hugo Friedhofer.

Beyond the Forest, 1949, US, King Vidor. Music: Max Steiner.

The Big Heat, 1953, US, Fritz Lang. Music: Arthur Morton.

The Big Sleep, 1946, US, Howard Hawks. Music: Max Steiner.

A Bill of Divorcement, 1932, US, George Cukor. Music Director: Max Steiner.

The Blue Dahlia, 1946, US, George Marshall. Music Director: Victor Young.

Brief Encounter, 1945, UK, David Lean. Music Director: Muir Mathieson.

The Cabin in the Cotton, 1932, US, Michael Curtiz. Music: Harry Warren.

A Canterbury Tale, 1944, UK, Michael Powell, Emeric Pressburger. Music: Allan Gray.

The Captive Heart (*Lover's Meeting*), 1946, UK, Basil Dearden. Music: Alan Rawsthorne.

Casablanca, 1942, US, Michael Curtiz. Music: Max Steiner.

Caught, 1948, US, Max Ophuls. Music: Frederick Hollander.

The Cobweb, 1955, US, Vincente Minnelli. Music: Leonard Rosenman.

Dark Victory, 1939, US, Edmund Goulding. Music: Max Steiner.

Dead Reckoning, 1947, US, John Cromwell. Music: Marlin Skiles.
Deception, 1947, US, Irving Rapper. Music: Erich Wolfgang Korngold.
The Demi-Paradise (*Adventure for Two*), 1943, UK, Anthony Asquith. Music: Nicholas Brodszky.
Diary for Timothy, 1945, UK, Humphrey Jennings. Music: Richard Addinsell.
East of Eden, 1955, US, Elia Kazan. Music: Leonard Rosenman.
Gaslight (*Angel Street*; *A Strange Case of Murder*), 1940, UK, Thorold Dickinson. Music: Richard Addinsell.
Gilda, 1946, US, Charles Vidor. Music: Hugo Friedhofer.
The Glass Key, 1942, US, Stuart Heisler. Music: Victor Young.
Gone With the Wind, 1939, US, Victor Fleming (and George Cukor, Sam Wood). Music: Max Steiner.
The Great Lie, 1941, US, Edmund Goulding. Music: Max Steiner.
Hangover Square, 1945, US, John Brahm. Music: Bernard Herrmann.
Home from the Hill, 1960, US, Vincente Minnelli. Music: Bronislau Kaper.
Humoresque, 1946, US, Jean Negulesco. Music Director: Franz Waxman.
I'll Be Your Sweetheart, 1945, UK, Val Guest. Music Director: Louis Levy.
Imitation of Life, 1934, US, John Stahl. Music: Heinz Roemheld.
The Informer, 1935, US, John Ford. Music: Max Steiner.
Interlude, 1957, US, Douglas Sirk. Music: Frank Skinner.
Intermezzo (*Intermezzo: A Love Story*; *Escape to Happiness*), 1939, US, Gregory Ratoff. Music: Lou Forbes.
In Which We Serve, 1942, UK, Noël Coward, David Lean. Music: Noël Coward.
Jezebel, 1938, US, William Wyler. Music: Max Steiner.
Johnny Belinda, 1948, US, Jean Negulesco. Music: Max Steiner.
Jungle Mariners, released 1946, UK, Ralph Elton. Music: Elisabeth Lutyens.
The Killers, 1946, US, Robert Siodmak, Music: Miklós Rózsa.
The Lady from Shanghai, 1947, US, Orson Welles. Music: Heinz Roemheld.
Lady in the Dark, 1944, US, Mitchell Leisen. Music: Kurt Weill; Lyrics: Ira Gershwin.
The Lamp Still Burns, 1943, UK, Maurice Elvey. Music: John Greenwood.
Laura, 1944, US, Otto Preminger. Music: David Raksin.
The Letter, 1940, US, William Wyler. Music: Max Steiner.
Listen to Britain, 1941, UK, Humphrey Jennings. Featured Artists: Myra Hess; RAF Orchestra; Flanagan and Allen.
The Little Foxes, 1941, US, William Wyler. Music: Meredith Willson.
The Locket, 1946, US, John Brahm. Music: Roy Webb.
The Lost Weekend, 1945, US, Billy Wilder. Music: Miklós Rózsa.
Madame X, 1937, US, Sam Wood. Music: David Snell.
Madonna of the Seven Moons, 1944, UK, Arthur Crabtree. Music: Hans May.
The Magic Bow, 1946, UK, Bernard Knowles. Music: Henry Geehl.
The Man in Grey, 1943, UK, Leslie Arliss. Music: Cedric Mallabey.
The Men, 1950, US, Fred Zinnemann. Music: Dimitri Tiomkin.
Mildred Pierce, 1945, US, Michael Curtiz. Music: Max Steiner.
Millions Like Us, 1943, UK, Frank Launder, Sidney Gilliat. Music Director: Louis Levy.

Mine Own Executioner, 1947, UK, Anthony Kimmins. Music: Benjamin Frankel.
Mr Skeffington, 1944, US, Vincent Sherman. Music: Franz Waxman.
Myra Hess, 1945, UK, John Trumper (using spare footage from Jennings's *Diary for Timothy*).
Night Song (*Memory of Love*), 1947, US, John Cromwell. Music: Leith Stevens.
Old Acquaintance, 1943, US, Vincent Sherman. Music: Franz Waxman.
The Old Maid, 1939, US, Edmund Goulding. Music: Max Steiner.
Out of the Past (*Build My Gallows High*), 1947, US, Jacques Tourneur. Music: Roy Webb.
Peeping Tom, 1959, UK, Michael Powell. Music: Brian Easdale; Percussion number: Wally Stott.
Penny Serenade, 1941, US, George Stevens. Music: W. Franke Harling.
Possessed, 1947, US, Curtis Bernhardt. Music: Franz Waxman.
The Private Lives of Elizabeth and Essex, 1939, US, Michael Curtiz. Music: Erich Wolfgang Korngold.
Psycho, 1960, US, Alfred Hitchcock. Music: Bernard Herrmann.
Rebel Without a Cause, 1955, US, Nicholas Ray. Music: Leonard Rosenman.
Red River, 1948, US, Howard Hawks. Music: Dimitri Tiomkin.
Scarlet Street, 1945, US, Fritz Lang. Music: Hans J. Salter.
The Sea Hawk, 1940, US, Michael Curtiz. Music: Erich Wolfgang Korngold.
The Searchers, 1956, US, John Ford. Music: Max Steiner.
Secret Beyond the Door, 1948, US, Fritz Lang. Music: Miklós Rózsa.
The Seventh Veil, 1945, UK, Compton Bennett. Music: Benjamin Frankel.
The Small Back Room, 1949, UK, Michael Powell, Emeric Pressburger. Music: Brian Easdale.
The Snake Pit, 1948, US, Anatole Litvak. Music: Alfred Newman.
A Song to Remember (*The Song That Lived Forever*; *The Love of Madame Sand*), 1944, US, Charles Vidor. Music Directors: Miklós Rózsa, Morris Stoloff.
Spellbound (*The House of Doctor Edwardes*), 1945, US, Alfred Hitchcock. Music: Miklós Rózsa.
The Spiral Staircase, 1945, US, Robert Siodmak. Music: Roy Webb.
Stella Dallas, 1937, US, King Vidor. Music: Alfred Newman.
Strangers on a Train, 1951, US, Alfred Hitchcock. Music: Dimitri Tiomkin.
Tawny Pipit, 1944, UK, Bernard Miles. Music: Noel Mewton-Wood.
Tea and Sympathy, 1956, US, Vincente Minnelli. Music: Adolph Deutsch.
This Above All, 1942, US, Anatole Litvak. Music: Alfred Newman.
This England (*Our Heritage*), 1941, UK, David MacDonald.
The Two Mrs Carrolls, 1945 (released 1947), US, Peter Godfrey. Music: Franz Waxman.
Vertigo, 1958, US, Alfred Hitchcock. Music: Bernard Herrmann.
Waterloo Bridge, 1940, US, Mervyn LeRoy. Music: Herbert Stothart.
The Way Ahead, 1944, UK, Carol Reed. Music: William Alwyn.
The Way to the Stars (*Johnny in the Clouds*; *Rendezvous*), 1945, UK, Anthony Asquith. Music: Nicholas Brodszky.
While I Live (*The Dream of Olwen*), 1947, UK, John Harlow. Music: Charles Williams.

The Wicked Lady, 1945, UK, Leslie Arliss. Music: Hans May.
The Young Mr Lincoln, 1939, US, John Ford. Music: Alfred Newman.
The Young Stranger, 1957, US, John Frankenheimer. Music: Leonard Rosenman.

Index